Finding My Way Home

My journey to a universal spirituality.

David G. Persons

BALBOA.
PRESS
A DIVISION OF HAY HOUSE

Scripture quotations marked KJV are from the Holy Bible, King James Version (Authorized Version). First published in 1611. Quoted from the KJV Classic Reference Bible, Copyright © 1983 by The Zondervan Corporation.

Balboa Press books may be ordered through booksellers or by contacting:

Balboa Press
A Division of Hay House
1663 Liberty Drive
Bloomington, IN 47403
www.balboapress.com
1 (877) 407-4847

Because of the dynamic nature of the Internet, any web addresses or links contained in this book may have changed since publication and may no longer be valid. The views expressed in this work are solely those of the author and do not necessarily reflect the views of the publisher, and the publisher hereby disclaims any responsibility for them.

The author of this book does not dispense medical advice or prescribe the use of any technique as a form of treatment for physical, emotional, or medical problems without the advice of a physician, either directly or indirectly. The intent of the author is only to offer information of a general nature to help you in your quest for emotional and spiritual well-being. In the event you use any of the information in this book for yourself, which is your constitutional right, the author and the publisher assume no responsibility for your actions.

Any people depicted in stock imagery provided by Thinkstock are models, and such images are being used for illustrative purposes only. Certain stock imagery © Thinkstock.

Print information available on the last page.

ISBN: 978-1-5043-6750-9 (sc)
ISBN: 978-1-5043-6751-6 (hc)
ISBN: 978-1-5043-6778-3 (e)

Library of Congress Control Number: 2016916686

Balboa Press rev. date: 10/21/2016

With Thanksgiving for...

My wife Naomi and family, whose patience and encouragement helped enrich my life's journey beyond words.

Teachers who helped formulate my thinking, conclusions and practices including:

Chas Griffin for his support and introducing me to Ken Wapnick and *A Course in Miracles.*

Roman Catholic Priests and Sisters who introduced me to the Roman Catholic Tradition and their willingness to accept me as a colleague.

The late Anthony de Mello who turned my life toward Home with suggestions for India.

The Wayside Presbyterian Congregation whose patience, adaptability and forgiveness were indispensable, allowing me to grow and follow my spiritual path.

The Presbyterian Church, U.S. A, and the Presbytery of Western New York for their guidance, support, abundant opportunities, and wonderful friendships, despite my questions, ambivalences, and personal changes.

Friend Malcolm Muir who introduced me to the Theosophical Society and challenged, questioned, and shared more opportunities to grow.

Contents

Preface

"The man is dangerous! He has publicly attacked our basic beliefs in publishing a recent article in the *Buffalo News*. He has betrayed his colleagues in this Presbytery. His beliefs lie far beyond the basic tenets of our faith." Without mentioning my name, my clergy colleague continued, "I urge immediate investigation into this man's teachings with recommendation he no longer be permitted to speak or teach in any capacity within the Presbyterian Church!" His strident voice then fell silent. He then walked to the clerk's desk and handed her his written remarks before turning around and walking unapologetically to his seat. The Moderator quietly dismissed the body of clergy and lay leaders for lunch, without comment.

Frozen in shock near the back of the old rounded, wooden, theater-style sanctuary, emotions exploded through my mind as if a bomb had detonated. The meeting in North Tonawanda was one of the periodic gatherings of Presbyterians from Western New York. For most of the morning, delegates from around 50 churches debated whether or not clergy could officiate a gay or lesbian wedding. Tempers often rose and impassioned speeches were given. The body, including myself, then voted to approve such marriages. It passed. Now a different kind of energy seemed dominant. A retired gray-haired colleague sat next me. Known for his outspoken views on social issues, he leaned over, and with pointed finger whispered, "You know, he means you!" Other heads swung around toward me as if to say, "Hey Dave, we warned you!"

The morning session concluding, members began queuing up toward lunch tables, to eat and enjoy conversation before returning for the afternoon session. I stiffly rose and pushed my way toward the large exit doors. I needed fresh air. No one spoke to me. Retired for nearly two years, I had come to the meeting naively expecting friendly and stimulating conversation with colleagues during lunch. Shocked, I walked in a daze down the sidewalk. Like a scolded dog, I needed to get away…to go home. Glancing across the street, I surprisingly spotted my accuser striding toward his car. 40 years ago, we were friends in seminary. I highly respected him. Retired as myself, I always appreciated his clarity and boldness when speaking about issues affecting the church. I wondered if I should shout over, "Hey! Can we talk?" I didn't. I kept walking.

I slipped stiffly into my old maroon Toyota, feeling comfort with its familiar smells. I started the faithful engine and began driving slowly home, 20 miles south to Hamburg. I kept asking myself, "What will I say to my wife and family? Will I lose my pension which I had worked nearly 40 years to earn? What will my friends think?" I knew I had walked a narrow line in orthodoxy for many years. Somehow I had always succeeded. I justified my moves by our constitutional words, *Ecclesia reformata, semper reformanda secundum verbum Dei*; "The church reformed, always to be reformed according to the Word of God." I assumed I could once again defend and explain my ideas, that in conversations we could all grow. Until now. "Am I finished with the Presbyterians? Can I ever return? It would never be the same." A lump felt stuck in my throat.

How had I come to this place? Why had my life been an endless trail of searching: through fundamentalism, mainstream Protestantism, Eastern religions and channeled writings? Why was the idea of Jesus being a myth so dangerous? And why did I keep finding new levels of freedom, only to ask more questions, like a restless teenager who wants to befriend someone his parents don't like? Tears flowed down my face.

Years ago, Charlie, one of our older church members, asked me, "Dave, do you know the most popular sport in America?" Not sure, I shrugged.

"Baseball!" he shouted. "Baseball is the most admired sport in America. Ya' wanna know why?"

"Sure Charlie, why?" I asked.

"Because everybody wants to go home! It's all about getting safely home!" as he burst into one of his deep guffaws. Later I found out it was a quote from Yogi Berra.

As a clergyman, I often mentioned the word "home." When people died I might say, "They went home, home to God." For over 50 years I called the church my home, most of them as Presbyterian. I felt proud to be a Presbyterian. Presbyterians provided me a home of safety and peace. I enjoyed acceptance, support and success. I explored ideas and questions with little opposition. Then in my second year of retirement, it all collapsed. I no longer felt safe or welcomed. What happened? Some might ask, "Is there ever a safe and permanent home? Where, and how can we know?" This story tries to give my answer.

Chapter 1

Home On The Farm

> *"Ours is simply the journey back to God who is our home."*
>
> *-A Course in Miracles* by Helen Schucman

On a hot July 20th in 1943, I was born to hardworking parents in Western New York. My home was in a rural township of thriving dairy farms surrounding a prosperous little village of about 1000 people named Sherman. I grew up on one of these farms. Established in 1824, after removal of Native Americans, Sherman enjoyed four distinct seasons with winter snows averaging over 200 inches. My rural farm roots became foundations for my life's development.

I came home to a large white house, set atop a hill at the end of a long gravel driveway. With breathtaking views of the valleys and meadows below, it was a wonderful and quiet place to relax and dream. To my post-depression family, financial freedom was important. During World War II, Dad failed his draft induction physical but maintained his dairy farm by day while working nights in a nearby aircraft factory. He made enough money that when the war ended, he purchased another farm across the road. Now with nearly 300 acres, nearly half being woods of maple, birch, pine and locust trees, we moved off the hill into our new house. The one on the hill became the residence for Dad's hired families. Sensing growing abundance and financial success, I often told myself what a lucky person I was to be in such a beautiful place and family.

Besides my two older siblings, three more were added over the years, another sister, and two younger brothers. As I grew, I respected my older siblings, my sister with her reddish hair and a sharp mind, and my handsome year older brother, blessed with dark hair and matching eyebrows. I had fair white skin, reddish brown hair and before long, lots of freckles to accent my blue eyes. I grew up drinking lots of raw milk and eating fresh meat from home raised chickens and cattle. Each autumn Dad normally added a few weeks of fresh deer meat. Mom supervised our large vegetable garden with us kids helping to "pod peas" before canning. Mom also cooked and canned hundreds of jars of pears and peaches to be enjoyed over the long winter months.

Education, reading and new ideas were important to both my parents who turned their visions into creative actions and accomplishments. When not working the farm and his side businesses of hauling lime, feed and coal, Dad often sat at his old wooden desk in the backroom. There he drew up measurements for other additions and improvements: a new barn and granary, an equipment storage shed, a larger garage, and whatever other ideas came each year. Other times he laid on the couch in our large living room reading magazines to find new ideas to employ his energy and fatten his bank accounts.

Dad sported a thick crop of wavy brown hair, meticulously combed and sealed with sprinkles of Vitalis hair oil. He walked with his head high, displaying his almost unstoppable confidence to succeed. His narrow Swedish nose no doubt enhanced his constant sinus issues. Endless cigarette and cigar smoking didn't help. Around 1953, when he began wheezing, his doctor explained how black tar had thickened over his lungs. Dad immediately quit. I never saw him smoke again, and I was no longer able to steal cigars out of his box under the truck seat!

Dad also loved speed. Many times he risked his own life and others with an almost addictive love of driving fast. I often thought he should have been a race car driver. My mother married him, one of her cousin's told me, since she was the only girl brave enough to ride with him! I still shudder remembering high speed rides and times he raced other cars on narrow two lane roads. Some called him a driving "maniac." We frequently attended races, loving the exciting noise and screams of roaring engines. When I was 6 years old, he took me to the Indy 500 Race in Indianapolis. All I remember is hearing roaring engines and loud "awes" when accidents occurred. One winter we drove to the Daytona Beach races where cars raced along the Atlantic Ocean shoreline. Dad parked carefully on the sand infield, close to tow trucks who waited to extract sand trapped drivers with outrageous fees! We watched cars roar past into the sand-banked curve, often scooting between race cars to get a view from the ocean. It took years to break my own speed addiction.

My parents loved Florida vacations during our long winters. Some years, they took us kids for a couple months near the small rural village of Nokomis. One year, Dad towed a house trailer while others years we rented cottages. Us kids, then five of us, either homeschooled ourselves or attended a small country school. In 1957, all seven of us (one yet to be born!) traveled to Florida in Dad's bright, new red Ford station wagon. We stayed in a little white cottage near Nokomis where we watched for Water Moccasins who might crawl up the back steps for scraps of fish remains.

Returning home to Sherman, Dad became drowsy driving through sparsely populated Georgia on a two-lane paved road through swamps and cotton fields. Dad's usual method to "wake up" was to roll down his window and stomp the gas pedal to the floor! Asleep in the rear third seat bench, which faced backwards, I awakened to see pavement flowing out behind like a wild river. To make room for us, Dad had tied our luggage to the roof. Suddenly, ropes and cords began breaking loose as luggage cases, like cows let out to pasture after a long winter, flew up, sideways and off into the blue! I shouted warnings as gyrating cases crashed and exploded on pavement like small bombs. Debris scattered along the road and into reddish clay ditches like waves. Dad muttered "Oh shit!" and screeched to a stop. Cursing, he circled around and for the next hour, some with silently suppressed grins, we gathered up suitcase parts, underwear, souvenirs and swimsuits. We finished the ride home with laps full and feet resting on fishing poles.

Mom, quieter than Dad, maintained our huge garden, washed loads of laundry, and cooked what I considered the best meals of mashed potatoes, roasts, pies and cakes. With Dad hiring seasonal help during harvest season months, Mom always made enough for all to have extra helpings. Second in her graduating class, Mom read constantly, modeling for her children our own future habits. She also, along with Dad, loved playing evening games, especially before the advent of television. Cards and checkers were among those I remember. When not playing games, we often listened to radio, comedies such as "Amos and Andy" and mysteries such as "Fat Man!"

I remember large family reunions with many aunts, uncles, and cousins. Living close to each other, most then still farmers, I remember reunions with piles of good food, including more than enough pies and cakes to leave us feeling stuffed. Horseshoe pitching and softball were favorite games, softball bases placed on recently harvested hay fields. One summer picnic took place at our relatives near Westfield, a few miles south of Lake Erie. Word spread that new swimsuits were out for women called "bikinis." My uncles decided to take a closer look and I even got to ride along with them. Sure enough, on a bright, warm July Sunday afternoon, we spotted women at the Barcelona beach in those skimpy, two piece suits. One uncle asked another what he thought and he replied, "Wow! I like them!"

One summer reunion took place at a relative's farm along the back road to Westfield. It may have been the 4th of July, one of the many holidays we gathered together. Dad had purchased a new, green, 1952 Oldsmobile 88, one of the fastest family cars of the time. We finally left for home, all of us packed into the four-door sedan. I sat behind Dad in the back seat next to the window which was rolled down. As Dad left the gravel driveway onto the narrow paved road, he suddenly stomped the gas pedal to the floor as many relatives looked aghast, still waiting on the front lawn. Gravel stones banged off the car fenders with flying dust billowing behind into the ditch and road. When we hit the pavement, rear tires suddenly began to screech and smoke rolled up around the back of the car into my window! Mom uttered something like, "Damn fool!" as relatives stood on the lawn laughing and cheering, some with thumbs up for the "great display."

Mom had relatives located all across the country. In the summer of 1955, Dad bought a new two toned sandy brown Chevy Station wagon to go see some of them. With one of Chevy's early V8 engines, he hitched a large green "house trailer" behind and during August, we traveled across the country to see relatives and friends in Iowa, Denver, Oregon and Nebraska. In Yellowstone Park, we drove down to see the Lower Falls after watching "Old Faithful" shoot up on the hour. It was a hot day and the road down to the Falls was steep. Coming back up, the motor whined and labored to pull us up the hilly park road. Dad told us kids to be ready to jump out and help push if the car groaned to a near stop under the load. We didn't need to!

Later, climbing a long mountain pass returning east near California, the car overheated on a record hot day. Dad made it into a mountain side parking lot with several other cars waiting to cool down engines. After resting awhile, Mom went back into the trailer to make sure dishes and chairs were still in place but when she opened the door, an awful, pungent smell puckered up her nostrils. She opened up the onboard bathroom and raised the toilet lid and discovered one of us had left moved bowels in the base, unflushed! In anger, Mom stepped on the flush pedal and walked out, jumped into the car, and ordered Dad, "get going!" He started the now cooled engine and slamming the doors shut, we slowly pulled away as a long trail of raw sewage slowly rolled down the mountain, trickling around and beneath still parked tourists with hot engines.

Our home seemed run like a small enterprise. Beside the cattle business, late winters brought on the annual maple syrup business, tapping hundreds of trees and boiling thousands of gallons of fresh sap into thick sweet syrup. Dad also bought trucks for hauling loads of lime from Conneaut, Ohio, fertilizer and feed from busy Buffalo mills, cattle to Buffalo slaughterhouses, coal from Pennsylvania mines, and corn picked from ripened Ohio fields. I often rode to Buffalo in one of Dad's trucks to haul back feed or fertilizer. Driving up South Park Avenue, I remember feeling pity for people who had to live there, jammed in close like cows in a barn, but without open fields and woods to roam. I often took walks across our fields and through woods alone or with friends, sometimes carrying my 22 hunting rifle looking for woodchucks, or to just pretend I was Daniel Boone. I would say to myself, "I am so lucky to have been born and raised in this wonderful place!

Chapter 2

Grandpa's Death

> "*A man's death is more the survivor's affair than his own.*"
>
> *–Thomas Mann*

By March 13, 1953, bright yellow daffodils and crocuses were beginning to sprout from the recently frozen earth. On a late winter day, I was playing "cowboys and Indians" on the front yard with my brother. Inspired by recent movies at the Sherman Theater, we "shot" each other with life-sized cap gun pistols purchased from Voigt's 5 & 10 cent store. Suddenly, someone hollered, "Grandpa Dean was just killed!" The shootout ended. I stood frozen in disbelief as gentle spring wind whispered through the surrounding maple trees. Was this real or one of my dreams? "It was a tractor accident!" the voice explained.

Driving his small grey Ferguson tractor up a steep hill pulling a full load of cow manure, Grandpa apparently shifted into a lower gear. Releasing the clutch to move ahead, the tractor flipped over backwards, crushing him into the spreader.

I walked numbly into the house. It felt like a dream. Mom, days short of her 33rd birthday, sat at the kitchen table weeping; "My Daddy, oh my Daddy! I can't believe it! I can't believe he's gone."

A couple days later, we rode quietly to the Funeral Home in Sherman. With curious anxiety, I enter the flower-decorated room. With strong fragrances hanging thick in the air, I wondered what Grandpa would look like, crushed under his tractor. Relieved, Grandpa lay dressed up in his best dark suit, stretched out in a beautiful, red maple casket. Looking asleep, his face appeared whitish but his thick black hair was perfectly combed with hands folded neatly over his stomach.

Grandma Dean stood at the end of the casket, thanking each person for visiting. People moved slowly past, stopping to express their shock, murmuring words of disbelief and sorrow with little praises of his being a "good man." Instead of quickly leaving in silence after seeing Grandpa, many stayed and began chatting with each other about farms, families and weather. Laughter even erupted at times, making it seem like the tragedy never happened, or was just normal, not that big of a deal. I worried about Mom, however, who still was in deep sorrow and often cried. I felt sad realizing I would never again enjoy rides and day trips with Grandpa in his big red truck. The sense of being in a dream kept returning.

At the funeral service in the Baptist Church, the open casket lay in the narrow entrance for each guest to pass by and take a final look. Then, with all seated on uncomfortable wooded benches called pews, the service began.

We had never attended church very much. I remember attending one of their summer "Vacation Bible Schools" where I got candy and heard stories about a man named Jesus, the name Dad often used when he got mad. I knew Grandpa and Grandma Dean were quite active in the Baptist Church but I didn't understand much about what they believed or why people thought going was even important.

The service began with a few songs sung, accompanied by the piano. Then the preacher began his sermon. Standing behind a large wooden stand called a pulpit, and wearing a dark suit, he claimed Grandpa was ready to die. He assured everyone Grandpa now resided in heaven, a much better place than here on earth. Such words amazed me. I wondered how the preacher knew this and could say such things. He said it was all in the Bible. I wondered where heaven was and what part of it Grandpa lived in since all I knew of him lay in the casket. It seemed comforting, however, to hear Grandpa was still living somewhere.

The preacher explained Grandpa trusted Jesus to save him from his sins. I didn't realize Grandpa even sinned, or what sin even was. I knew Dad often disagreed with Grandpa, even his removal of some safety bars from the new tractor. Maybe that was the sin. The safety bars, I heard, could have helped prevent the accident. The preacher said, however, that we all sin, which meant doing and even thinking about things that offended God. Jesus, however, died so God would no longer be angry with us, *if* we believed Jesus did this for us. Grandpa believed, the preacher continued, and so God loved and welcomed him into heaven. The preacher also explained if we wanted to see Grandpa again in heaven, we would need to make the same decision. If we didn't, he continued, we would never see Grandpa but spend forever in an awful place called hell. The ideas comforted my mind as far as Grandpa's fate but puzzled me about my own. The service ended with another song accompanied by the piano.

We rode slowly behind a long line following the large black vehicle with Grandpa's body to the Sherman Cemetery. Moving past hundreds of stone markers in all sorts of sizes through large maple trees, we stopped where a large hole had been dug. Some big relatives, including Mom's brother, slowly carried the large case with Grandpa inside to the grave. The casket was set on metal bars atop the deep hole. There I stood in loneliness and fear, my body shaking in the spring chill, as the Preacher said a few more words. After the last prayer, we silently moved back to our cars before Grandpa was lowered into the grave. Someone said Grandpa's body would be sealed in a concrete vault before it was covered with dirt. We were assured if Grandpa got dug up in 25 years, he was guaranteed to look the same.

Grandpa's death made a major impact on my family. I began hearing more about the man who officiated Grandpa's funeral, Preacher Smith. He often came for visits to talk and pray with us. Good-looking and even younger than my parents, he always wore a nice suit. A tall, fairly effeminate looking man, he spoke with a soft high-pitched voice, almost heavenly compared to Dad's loud and often demanding pitch. He had a hearty laugh, however, and seemed quite friendly. Soon, Mom began taking us kids to the church. Grandma Dean seemed pleased but Dad usually stayed home.

I soon heard more about "getting saved" and needing to "make a decision for Jesus Christ as my Lord and Savior." At first, Dad seemed to ignore it but I felt worried. Mom, however, kept going to church. She bought books on the Bible, reading them daily in what I learned were devotions. She then asked us kids to attend services with her. When I went, I learned, along with my siblings, that much of the entertainment we had enjoyed as a family were actually sins. They made God sad and put our own lives in jeopardy. I had never suspected they were sins.

Our family had enjoyed roller-skating as a frequent pastime. I loved the Hammond organ's mellow music, the delicious smells of popcorn and candy, the laughter and quiet buzz of wheels spinning over hardwood floors. Now it was wrong and God didn't want us to do it.

Once Dad took us kids a few times but without Mom, it didn't feel right. One night I watched Dad skate with another woman, a friend of the family married to a nearby farmer. It didn't seem right. I feared Mom and Dad might break up or worse, get a divorce. I heard such things happened to some families. How would I tell my friends? I felt embarrassed and became more afraid. Our proud family worked hard and people thought of us as stable and close, like a small enterprise grinding out success.

One cold winter night, Dad took us kids, in protest and again without Mom, to a movie in Westfield. The feature was an "I Love Lucy" movie called "The Long, Long Trailer." We laughed hard watching Lucy and Desi's calamity-filled vacation trip across America, pulling a long trailer behind their car. When we left, we discovered sleet covered our car like shiny wax. After scraping and chipping it off windows, we rode in nervous tension as the car spun, slipped and crawled up Oxbow Hill. Dad told us kids to be ready to jump out and help push if we needed a little shove. I wondered if it might be God's judgment for the night of laughter.

We stopped attending movies but soon purchased our first television. Somehow, watching movies on a little snowy black and white screen was okay. Nobody called it a sin, although later I heard the Preacher call it "Hellivision." At least, at home, we could sit together to watch "I Remember Mama" and enjoy weekly laughs of "I Love Lucy" in peace.

Mom surprised me when she said we shouldn't even play baseball games or go swimming on Sundays. Sunday was a holy day of rest to be set aside for the Lord. We could do chores, attend church, eat a big dinner, and rest. Dad didn't seem to mind the extra rest. On one of these boring Sunday afternoons, I got my fishing pole and dug up a few worms out back of the barn. I walked to the large pond Dad had dug out for water to be pumped to the barn. I was shocked when Mom came and scolded me. I became more troubled and confused. I loved movies, I loved skating, I loved fishing and I loved doing them with my family. Now they were things we sneaked off to do alone, or with Dad in protest.

Relief arrived in June 1955 when a new preacher arrived named Victor C. Stouffer. Unlike Preacher Smith, Preacher Stouffer was a farmer's kind of pastor. He stood about 6 feet tall with thick dark hair, a deep clear voice and loud laugh. He loved to get out with farmers and help haul hay, drive tractors, and make maple syrup. He occasionally drove one of Dad's big trucks to help get corn or hay. Preacher Stouffer also loved hunting, which Dad did too. Soon, Dad began going on hunting trips with the new Preacher. Preacher Stouffer also planted and cultivated gardens. Dad said, "This Preacher ain't afraid of work!" Indeed, Preacher not only worked on various member farms but jumped right in building and repairing the church. He could do carpentry and roof work. Once, while upgrading the church, Dad excitedly described Preacher walking right along the edge of the steep, 30-foot high roof.

Dad began attending church services. He even attended some of the Sunday evening services, signs that better times were returning to my home. Mom's prayers seemed to be answered. I even felt a little better about giving up roller-skating, movies and Sunday activities.

Sunday evening services, however, were the most difficult. "Why can't we just have one Sunday morning service like the Community Church or the Catholics?" I asked. I loved watching Walt Disney and Ed Sullivan TV shows, popular on Sunday evenings. One by one, however, my older siblings seemed to give in and get "saved." I began attending more services.

On Sunday evenings, Preacher Stouffer pulled out a huge "Map of the Ages" which stretched across the front of the church sanctuary. He preached using it to demonstrate how, according to the Bible, we were very close to the end of the world. It amazed and scared me! "How could he know that?" I asked, sitting with a tense stomach. I heard Preacher studied the Bible in a special school and knew it to be true. He often even told us what the Bible said in its original Greek language. At the end of each service, he invited us "unsaved" people to come forward to repent and accept Jesus. As the song "Just As I Am" began to be sung, I stood clinging to the next wooden pew seat. It seemed to go on endlessly accompanied by the new electronic organ as my head and body swirled with emotion. Always somewhat shy, I would not step out of my seat and make an embarrassing scene walking down front to declare my sinfulness and get saved. What would my friends think? My mind struggled with so many questions and fears. I never heard such scary predictions from a book declared to be "God's Word."

Even though Dad liked Preacher Stouffer, he didn't accept all his teachings and often commented with surprising words. Once, while returning home from church, Mom and Grandma Dean were discussing another sermon about the imminent end of the world. Suddenly, as we neared our farm, Dad slapped his right hand on the new car's padded dash and shouted, "*None* of this stuff is literal, *no one* knows for sure about any of it! It's all spiritual, it's just *ideas!*" Shocked and even frightened, silence filled the car. His words, however, planted seeds in my mind I would not forget.

One week a traveling evangelist and his wife came to Sherman for special revival meetings. Handsome and beautiful, their music was phenomenal! Each night, the evangelist and his wife played music like I heard on the new Lawrence Welk's TV show. With accordion and trumpet, I was overwhelmed.

Some of my resistance and fears began to melt. Each night, the evangelist also preached another eloquent but even scarier sermon about the coming of the End, the Return of Jesus. Apparently, he also studied the Bible at one of those special schools. When invitations for the "lost" were given to come forward, everyone stood and sang "Just As I Am." I remained locked in emotional torture, feeling like I was standing on a cliff, clinging tightly to the next seat with my immoveable legs. Resisting, I would not step out and make an emotional scene like others did, with people weeping and some saying, "Amen! Praise the Lord!" I thought, "What if my friends found out? What would I say if they knew I became a true Christian and gave up pleasures like movies, playing ball or fishing on Sundays?" It was a lonely feeling.

One night, after another of the evangelist's frightening sermons, I came up with a plan. The preacher repeatedly said it was a decision just between God and me. All I had to do was open my heart, whatever than meant, confess my sins, and invite Jesus in. Jesus seemed to be a spirit person, somehow standing all around us. I decided to put this tortuous decision behind me. When we got home, I went quickly to my upstairs bedroom before my brother Jim came, got down on my knees and made my prayer of confession. I said I was a sinner who often offended God with worldly pleasures and thinking (nearly 13 years old, sex *was* becoming a lot more on my mind!) and would accept the blood of Jesus to atone for my sins to hold off God's wrath. I still wasn't sure any of it was real. Maybe it all was just a big lie or a false story. But just in case this really was God's Word, it seemed I had nothing to lose. It was like fire insurance. The idea of burning in hell forever seemed pretty grim. Escaping the awful flames of eternal torture, I would also stand a better chance of seeing Grandpa again.

Chapter 3

Dating and Jesus

*"There are no chance encounters. Each of them has the
potential for becoming a teaching-learning situation."*
A Course in Miracles by Helen Schuman

I finally reached my 16th birthday in July, 1959. Reaching 16
meant freedom and independence. And getting a car. Thankfully,
Jesus had not yet returned. For my birthday Dad drove me to
the Department of Motor Vehicles' office in Mayville to get
my driver's permit. I drove Dad's two-toned green '59 four-door
Ford sedan back home. Cruising along through the rolling hills
to Sherman I felt like a young bird with wings who could finally
fly. After a birthday lunch Mom prepared, featuring my favorite
mashed potatoes, fresh green beans, roast beef, cake and ice
cream, with plenty of fresh cow's milk, I drove Dad to a few auto
dealers to look for a car.

A week later, I drove to Dunkirk, with Dad accompanying
me, for my Driver's test. Driving through the side streets with
the officer, I felt confident negotiating intersections, making
appropriate signals, a 180-degree U-turn, and parking parallel to
the curb. I blissfully drove home with a junior license, permitting
me to drive during daylight and evening hours for school functions.

After trying out several cars, in September I purchased a one-year-old white Ford on a tip from the local Ford dealer. The 1958 Ford was plain with few extras. A two-door coup, it came with standard shift, a "must-have" V8 engine, and black walled tires with small plain hubcaps. Its plain grey exterior was accented with a padded dash but no seatbelts, which then were not required. The engine hood opened from the back near the windshield, which seemed to make high speed driving safer. My younger sister took one look and commented, "It's you!" With giddy disbelief I washed, waxed and cherished my own car! It became like my own mobile room. Mom once called it "Saint Ford" as church services became increasingly skipped to polish, pamper and cruise.

Like Dad modeled, I loved speed and drove too fast. One day after school Dad caught me drag racing a classmate who had his father's new car. On the count of three, we screeched off side by side on a country road which recently had been newly paved. Suddenly I saw Dad coming in the opposite direction toward us! I braked and pulled into the right lane. That night, dreading supper, Dad scolded me, not for drag racing but doing it in a place without a longer stretch of level road.

Being 16 and having a car before the world ended also emboldened me to find a girlfriend. As school resumed my junior year, a cute new girl entered our class named Paulette. She had dark brown hair with equally dark and beautiful eyes. Coming to live as a foster child with a family in Sherman, a friend told me she was a devoted Roman Catholic, even interested one day in becoming a Roman Catholic nun. Immediately I felt attracted!

Our first date was a "double date" as we rode with my drag racing buddy and his girlfriend to a movie in Jamestown. By now I had backslid far enough to feel little or no guilt about going to a movie. A few years before, following my bedroom prayer, I had been baptized and joined the Baptist Church. One of the pledges I made was not to attend movies, drink alcoholic beverages or "break the Sabbath." The pleasures of having a car and beautiful lady next to me were too much temptation. It was heavenly to sit again in a theater with a big screen, clear booming speakers and surrounded by smells of fresh popcorn. The exhilaration of being close to a young lady, inhaling arousing perfume, bumping shoulders, and holding hands immediately became intoxicating. I couldn't resist. Paulette and I quickly became categorized as "going steady." My life changed dramatically. I had reached sixteen, owned my car and enjoyed a beautiful girlfriend. Life seemed very good!

When Grandma Dean heard about my dating, she was not happy. She called and asked me to stop by for a talk in her Sherman apartment. Suspecting the car and girlfriend might cause slippage in my studies, I expected a pep talk about upcoming report cards. Living in an upstairs apartment across from the Sherman School, I walked slowly up the back hall stairs to her door. Sitting across from me with a serious face, she surprisingly scolded me for dating a Roman Catholic girl! There were no questions about my studies. She said, "David, you are a good boy and there are many girls who would be suitable for a friend, many who are not Catholic!"

Shocked and speechless, I left in disappointment. When I got home, Mom said nothing but soon I realized she also was disappointed and worried: first the car and now a Roman Catholic girlfriend.

Defiant but not sharing my scolding with Paulette, we continued to see each other for several weeks. Sometimes I came home late and heard Mom sobbing. Before long, however, the issue of religion came up. One night I asked Paulette questions about her previous family and if she really wanted to become a Catholic nun, and why.

"Yes," Paulette replied, "I have thought of it often."

"Really?" I said in amazement. "Why would you want to become a nun?"

"Because the idea brings me a sense of deep peace."

Religion soon became a frequent part of our conversations. I began reading my baptismal and church membership Bible. I had read the Bible very little, mostly only when I carried it to the Sunday services at the Baptist Church. It seemed most everyone there had the same King James Version.

I called Preacher Stouffer and asked to talk with him. He welcomed me to his beautiful newly pine paneled study. Sitting across from his desk, I asked him about Catholics, what they believed and did which was so wrong and offensive. He slid his wheeled desk chair over near me and opening his Bible, showed and read passages that warned about those who prohibit marriage and observe special feasts and seasons. He said Catholic priests were not allowed to marry and they made big deals out of Christmas, Easter and other seasons of the year, enforcing extra rules about what or what not to eat. He read to me some Bible verses I had never seen or heard before.

> "Now the Spirit speaketh expressly, that in the latter times some shall depart from the faith, giving heed to seducing spirits, and doctrines of devils: speaking lies in hypocrisy; having their conscience seared with a hot iron; forbidding to marry, and commanding to abstain from meats, which God hath created to be received with thanksgiving of them which believe and know the truth." (1 Timothy 4:1-3 KJV)

He showed me a verse where we were told not to call any man "Father" since we only have one in heaven. "...call no man your father upon earth: for one is your Father, which is in heaven." (Matthew 23:9)

"Dave," he said, "Roman Catholicism is a religion of the devil. They are lost in their sins!"

On our next date, I could hardly wait to read the passages to Paulette! Surprisingly, she said she never read the Bible. Instead, she described learning the Baltimore Catechism as part of her confirmation. In a few days I drove to Jamestown and found a bookstore where I bought her a Bible, even a Roman Catholic version recommended by the Preacher. She began reading it.

Her foster father, hearing of our discussions, suggested we visit their priest with our religious questions. Feeling an emotional attraction to such issues, as it also seemed for Paulette, I called the Sherman Catholic Church and made an appointment for the next Saturday evening. As part of a date, we went first to see her priest. I also wanted to see inside their chapel, eager to gaze upon burning candles, Preacher told me about, with incense surrounding their many idol statutes bowed before and prayed to.

I discovered the Sherman Roman Catholic Church was named after a man called Saint Isaac Jogues, someone not even in the Bible. It was a small solid looking stone building with a nice cross on the front roof peak with ornate religious looking doors at the front. It contrasted sharply to the large wooden framed Baptist Church with plain doors.

When we arrived at the Catholic Church, the priest met us on the front sidewalk. Instead of taking us through the sanctuary, he led us around an outside path to a small room in the rear. Sitting in a bare, cement floor room, which looked slightly used, I asked our Bible questions. Both Paulette and I quickly noticed the priest didn't seem to directly answer them. He was nice but actually seemed quite Biblically illiterate, especially when compared to the Baptist Preacher, who seemed to know the whole Bible! We also didn't think the priest showed much respect for the Baptists. When we quoted Preacher Stouffer, the priest just seemed to roll his eyes in kind of a disregarding amazement.

I left with more questions and although Paulette seemed interested, she said to doubt her faith was a serious offense, a "mortal sin." However, I urged us, in fairness, to ask similar questions to Preacher Stouffer at the Baptist Church. Agreeing, on our next date we secretly met him in his wood-paneled study after walking through the brightly lit and very plain sanctuary. True to my expectations, Preacher Stouffer seemed to know the Bible by heart! He quoted verses for every question we asked. I felt like he "blew away" the priest.

Meeting for our next date, Paulette's foster father demanded that although we could have dates, we were no longer to discuss religion. We did continue to see each other but didn't talk as much about the subject, turning our attention elsewhere, which was not too difficult.

Meanwhile, I began reading my King James Bible with increasing interest, trying to make sense of its words and sentences. As car ownership thrills began to wear off, I found myself being drawn further toward religious questions and interests. "How could Preacher Smith know so certainly where Grandpa Dean went after he died? How could it be that simple?" I also felt more drawn toward the Fundamentalist viewpoints since they seemed to know the Bible much better. They even encouraged folks to read it.

Weeks passed and one night I received a phone call from Paulette. She bubbled with excitement.

"Dave! I just got saved!"

"What?" I asked in shock and disbelief. "What happened?"

Paulette explained while babysitting she once noticed a family Bible. Opening it she found the owner's name and date on which he "personally accepted the Lord Jesus Christ as his savior!" She said, "I never did that!" She also confessed secretly calling my mother, whom she trusted, who gave her more verses to read and ponder. Finally, while supposedly at a school play rehearsal, she called Preacher Stouffer and walked the short distance to see him in the Baptist Church. There in his study, she continued, "I accepted Jesus Christ!" So now she was saved!

"O my God!" I thought. "What will happen now?" I couldn't believe it. Why hadn't Mom told me about her conversations with Paulette? Was Mom afraid I might actually marry a Roman Catholic? My head began to swirl. It felt like a very big event had happened but I wasn't sure what to think or do. Would Paulette begin going to the Baptist Church? Would people now expect us to marry some day?

Quickly her foster father ordered Paulette and me to have no more contact with each other. I felt surprised but actually somewhat relieved. Things were getting a little wild over religion and I needed more space to think things through. Religion was gaining more importance for me than even my car. I needed to back off. What could I do?

I had become somewhat of a star on the Sherman Wildcat Basketball team. In my Junior year I was a starter and leading scorer, on track to reach over 1000 points in my high school years. One night, our team traveled to nearby Forestville for a game. After we won, a cute cheerleader from Forestville's team gave her name and phone number to a teammate, asking me to call her. My heart beating with emotion, I saw it as a way out. It seemed time to let Paulette go, and perhaps religion too. "Maybe I better just keep life light," I thought. I could still enjoy girls, cars, and sports, but get more serious about school.

I called the cheerleader and in a couple days drove one evening to meet her. Her home was located on beautiful acreage surrounded by grape vineyards. Lake Erie glistened below in the distance. Eileen met me at the door. She was dark and beautiful, her parents and family having emigrated from Italy. Immediately I felt lost in her dark brown eyes. With my snow-white Northern European skin, I was quickly attracted, my eyes darting over her sparkling necklace which dropped onto her tempting chest. Her nose and flowing black hair seemed perfectly accentuated by her ivory white teeth and luscious lips covered with inviting reddish lipstick.

Her parents left us alone in a private parlor where we began to nervously talk. After a few compliments about my basketball abilities, she suddenly mentioned her deep devotion to the Roman Catholic faith along with her whole family!

"Oh shit!" I thought, "Not again."

I soon wrapped up the conversation, left, wrote her a letter of thanks and ended the relationship.

The next spring, during Easter break, I drove Grandma Dean to Conyers, Georgia to visit her son, my uncle Gordon. The first day, Aunt Janet introduced me to a beautiful tall girl named Pat. With her dark hair, light smooth skin and sharp blue eyes, I again felt in love! I enjoyed a wonderful week with her as my guide, visiting her school friends and attending baseball games. Grandma loved watching us and seemed relieved. Pam was also active in the Conyers' Methodist Church. When I reached home, we began writing letters and exchanging pictures. My grades improved.

Chapter 4

College Decision

"Life is change. Growth is optional. Choose wisely."
– William Somerset Maugham

During high school, I anticipated college. Grandma Dean no doubt influenced me along with older siblings, likely even expecting it. I quietly thought about attending a place like Cornell University to study agriculture.

Near the end of my Junior Year, Sherman's new cattle inseminator, Harry Ottaway, who by now had displaced most bulls, took me and two other farm boy classmates to Ithaca, New York. Ithaca was not only the home to Cornell but where Harry purchased his sperm. A handsome looking man with dark hair and movie-star features of personality and wit, Harry took us to see where cows, called "teasers," were placed in front of large virile donors. The bulls were lead into a room thinking they were mounting eager cows but suddenly found their front legs caught in slippery rails while employees shoved artificial cow vaginas over their two-foot long penises. It was an interesting and memorable process, but I wasn't interested!

Afterwards, Harry took us on a walk through Cornell's adjacent campus. It was beautiful, as spring leaves and flowers bloomed everywhere along lush manicured green lawns. We walked across a deep gorge on a wooden bridge, where I was told a few distraught students had jumped to their deaths. Shocked, I pushed the thought out of mind as I admired the well-kept brick class buildings and dormitories. Students walked past us carrying books, laughing and chatting as they headed, I supposed, to private rooms or classes. I imagined how wonderful it would be to attend there: free of farm chores, free to study new ideas and of course, free to meet more young women.

Beginning my senior year, I took the new interest and aptitude tests that Sherman's new guidance counselor offered. A plump, bald headed man, nicknamed "Chrome Dome" by classmates, my parents did not seem to like or trust him. When my turn to visit came, he stunned me. Leaning back in a leather padded office chair he said, "I've looked over your test results and David, this town is definitely *not* for you! You need to get out of here. There is *nothing* here for you. Your talent is in your head and not in your hands or back." According to my scores, he said I should be studying literature and the arts, not farming and its related concerns.

I left stunned but also with some disgust. True, I loved reading adventure books, one of my favorite being "Two Years Before the Mast" by Richard H. Dana. I dreamed of going to new places, meeting new people, and reading more great books. However, all my life I assumed, as Dad seemed to infer, I would be a farmer, just one with a college education. It was like he put a hook into my brain and emotions. I did love the farm: its open fields and thick woods, the machine variety, the trucks and even the excitement of our four seasons. No, I did not like milking cows but how could I ever become a person of "letters?" The farm was my home.

When I shared with my parents the counselor's conclusions, they assured me he was crazy and had no business giving such advice to students. Dad became angry that the school counselor had the nerve to come into Sherman, where farmers paid a large share of his salary, and tell students there was nothing here left for them! "Show me one teacher," he demanded, "who makes more money than I do?"

Days passed and the counselor's advice continued to churn in my head. I began thinking about other careers he suggested. Since Paulette's conversion, I thought often about religious and philosophical possibilities. It would be wonderful just to know more about the Bible, if indeed it really did teach such things as I had heard Preachers say.

A few months before, I had joined the High School boy's class at the Baptist Church. The Preacher's wife, Mamie, taught it. The same age as Mom, she spoke with an authoritative, know-for-sure attitude in her perfectly set hair and immaculately neat dresses. One of about 10 young men, she often said she felt God would call one of us to become a Preacher. Surprisingly, I felt she might be speaking about me! Maybe I could learn the Bible as much as her husband and attend one of those special schools. Amazed, but feeling relief and excitement, I began seeing myself more interested in my own ideas and questions rather than in machines, crops, and milk prices.

Shortly after the school counselor interview, our English teacher, Mr. Bickel, asked each senior to write and share what he or she wanted to move toward as a career. Mr. Bickel, a large man with a deep voice, reminded me of an authority I could not fool. I felt trapped. What should I say? Should I mention farming? Maybe trucking? Dad had several trucks I often drove. Maybe I could become involved in a trucking business. It certainly seemed cleaner than milking cows or cleaning gutters. Waiting my turn and still thinking, I decided to go with trucking.

As students stood and shared their intentions, I suddenly sensed a voice saying, "A teacher, pastor, or even a preacher." I hated it! This could not be happening to me! What would Dad say, or my friends? My turn finally came. I nervously stood. Pausing a few seconds before 20 classmates who knew me well,

25

the room fell silent. Starring at me, each seemed eager for my answer. I then blurted out, almost as if words were forced into my mouth, "I want to be a pastor or minister!" The room remained silent with disbelief: Dave Persons, a pastor? I sat down feeling my face flush red with embarrassment. Someone jokingly said, "Dave would never make it!" Another exclaimed, "Dave likes to have way too much fun to be one of those!" I sat in disbelief. I had actually said it! Strangely, I also felt relieved. Maybe I could be a minister or pastor, and even have lots of fun.

On October 15, 1960, Grandma Dean suddenly died. She had gone into the Corry Pennsylvania Hospital after school one Friday to have a blood transfusion. She had received them previously for what I heard was an anemic condition. The wrong blood type was given and she died quite suddenly when her veins collapsed. We all were shocked by the sudden death, but no one considered suing the doctor or the hospital. They said they were sorry for our loss.

My older brother had surprised me a few weeks earlier by going to Bob Jones University in Greenville, South Carolina. He came home for the funeral and we stayed at our neighbor's home due to many guests coming for Grandma's funeral. Jim shared with me his enthusiasm for Bob Jones University. It was a strict fundamentalist Christian University and he shared stories which peaked my interest. After Grandma's funeral, he returned to Greenville.

My growing religious interests seemed to irritate Dad. He kept asking more questions about my future. He suggested again the farms would be available if I wanted them. I sought to sooth him, saying I would probably attend an agriculture school like Cornell, but knew I wouldn't. Instead, I quietly wrote nearly 20 Christian colleges from a list Preacher Stouffer gave me. The first response came from Bob Jones University. I didn't know how I would explain my actions to Dad but I knew Mom would be delighted. Besides, I now had a substantial bank account, owned my car, and sensed a new freedom that would not be stopped.

During the Christmas/New Year's break that winter, I drove my older brother back to Bob Jones University. Along the way, we stopped so I could look at a few other Christian colleges including ones in Cedarville, Ohio, Dayton, Tennessee, and Columbia, South Carolina. We also stopped in Athens, Georgia, where "Georgia Pat" now attended college at the University of Georgia. She looked more beautiful than ever and stirred anew, we enjoyed an evening together.

Finally, we reached Bob Jones University in Greenville. Excitement and emotions rose high as I stood inside the huge chapel, visited class rooms, and spent a night in the dorm. Truly this seemed to be the "first among Christian colleges!" When I arrived home, a letter from "Georgia Pat" waited for me. Our correspondence began anew but after a few weeks, she cut herself off from me, the growing religious "nut."

In mid-January I quietly sent an application to Bob Jones and in a few weeks my acceptance arrived in the mail. Excited, I sensed this was the right decision. A few days later the school guidance counselor invited me back in to check over my plans. When I told him about Bob Jones, he reacted in shock and disgust. "A complete waste of time, money and brain energy!" But my decision was made. He now appeared to be the devil's advocate as I moved deeper into fundamentalism, which would dominate my life the next few years. Like a converted disciple, I joined the Baptist Church choir, began teaching a Sunday school class and even attended the Wednesday evening prayer meetings. Mom was delighted. Her prayers were being answered but Dad seemed distant and suspicious.

In January, I also signed up for college preparatory classes at the nearby Jamestown Community College. Sign-up sheets invited drivers to check if we could take passengers. Only a few signed up, myself with the only car. One of the passengers was named Naomi, Preacher Stouffer's tall and beautiful daughter. Since I now attended church regularly, the Stouffers did not mind if their daughter rode with me. The first night the car was filled with students who bustled with laughter and chatter. By the second week everyone had quit but Naomi.

The third week Naomi got into my car and said she and her boyfriend had broken up. We continued the classes together. Surprisingly, our conversation seemed natural, easier for myself than with any girl I knew. The twenty-five-mile trip went by quickly as I drove slower each week. We often began saying the same word simultaneously and laughed, never dreaming anything would become romantic. I felt comfortable with Naomi but she seemed more like a good friend, the well-trained daughter of parents I held in very high esteem. She looked solid and neat, loving her role as a homemaker with great cooking abilities. Some evenings when she got in the car, I could smell delicious supper odors: mashed potatoes, roasted chicken and gravy. Her mom was well known for her cooking abilities. Naomi seemed homey, stable, and secure.

Near the end of the college prep classes, Naomi got into the car obviously dejected and close to tears. Her application to nursing school in Binghamton had been rejected. "All my life I planned to be a nurse, and now it's over!" she said. I wondered why she couldn't simply apply to another nursing school. The next week she surprised me by saying her father had called Bob Jones University for an application. Two weeks later she accepted their invitation and now, she too became a Bob Jones student.

Naomi and I continued our friendship the summer after graduation. She got a job at the Baptist Church camp along Lake Chautauqua where I drove a few times to see her. Hearing the musical "South Pacific" was coming to the Institution, I invited her to go. She accepted and it was a most pleasant evening. Her sharp blue eyes reflected like gems enhancing her regal manner.

I felt romantic flickers growing but knew there would plenty of nice ladies at college. I assumed she felt the same way about its resources of available men.

High School Graduation, 1961

Bob Jones University

> *"Education is what remains after one has forgotten what one has learned in school."*
>
> *–Albert Einstein*

On Labor Day, 1961, I left for Greenville, South Carolina and Bob Jones University. Packing my clothing, Bible and typewriter into my white Ford, my brother assisted driving the nearly 700 miles over mostly two-lane highways, arriving in 16 hours. Still in a daze, I joined 4,000 students and faculty living on a campus about the size of one of our farms. Sounds of laughter, dropped boxes, and backslapping reunions filled the air. Other new freshmen, like myself, moved about with a kind of new planet wonder. My room, about the size of my farm bedroom, contained two bunk beds pressed against opposite walls, two small open closet spaces, one sink and mirror for four students. I immediately became subjected to rigorous regulation in close proximity to hundreds of others surrounded by constant noise.

I began eating strange new foods like grits and cornbread, pulled pork and rarebit, the latter a creamy cheese sauce poured over corn muffins. I walked miles over cement sidewalks linking campus buildings, sprinkled with little signs warning: "Stay Off The Grass!"

Excitement filled my early days with new faces, roommates, rules and major lifestyle changes. People, bells and chatter were ubiquitous. I walked out of my yellow brick dorm which stood among four or five more. Men's dormitories were on one end of the campus, women's on the other. A large auditorium, named Rodeheaver after a famous revivalist songwriter, towered over mid campus near the Student Center. Class buildings and a large library were nearby surrounded by manicured lawns. Stone and fence walls along its borders made me feel enclosed into a small city. Open pastures with rolling hills, fields of grain and thick distant woods, were now gone.

I did not miss farm chores but quickly longed for more solitude, quiet and open space. The only quiet area readily accessible was a single dorm room reserved for "daily devotions." In the second week, like many new students, I became homesick and confused. It was like Dad buying a new car or tractor and suddenly disliking it. I began asking why I had not looked at more colleges, especially non-Christian options like Cornell. I wondered if the baldheaded counselor was right.

Monday through Friday, except Wednesday, all gathered for an 11:00 a.m. chapel service in Rodeheaver. We repeated the university's creedal statement and the fundamentals of the faith, which later I discovered to be similar to the Apostles Creed. The elderly founder, Bob Jones Sr., now in his early 80's, preached frequently but less so as his health had declined and he often repeated himself. His son, Bob Jones Jr., spoke more often along with many guest speakers. Early sermons often included references to homesick students, joking about missing our mom's cooking and "frizz haired girlfriends." Several spoke in anger and judgment against the liberal political drift of the country under President Kennedy, while others railed against creeping communism. I missed hearing about autumn corn picking.

I joined the "Preacher Boy" group. Most Preacher Boys usually made weekly mission or extension trips. Having a car,

I soon volunteered to drive as we fanned out into surrounding communities to "win souls for Christ." At first, feeling a bit odd, it at least gave me opportunities to easily get off campus into the "real world," a world now seen mostly lost in its sins. Dressed somewhat like Mormons or Jehovah Witnesses, with our white shirts and ties, we spoke in small churches, prisons and storefront missions. We conducted children's evangelism programs on front lawns and walked door-to-door inviting people to Jesus. We did "Street Work" by confronting people on city streets to talk about Jesus and eternal life. After quick greetings to hopefully stop a willing listener, we'd ask, "Have you ever made a decision for Jesus? Are you saved?"

A few people actually "got saved" right on the street! Some likely decided out of fear as we showed them "God's Plan for Salvation" including eternal hellfire and torture for the undecided and lost. Others likely accepted Jesus just to get away from us. I once stopped a man and asked, "Have you ever been saved?"

"Yes!" he responded with relief in his voice.

"Praise God!" I replied, "When did you make this important decision?"

"Back there just around the corner," he pointed, "it was the only way I could get away from your friend!"

Everything became opposite to my previous life. However, it could feel very important; after all, we were "saving people" from eternities in hell. Yet, doubts lingered in my mind. Was this truly what the Bible taught? Were other religions, even among the many "Southern Baptists," lost because they didn't believe the Bible as we did? How could I know? I looked forward to more Bible classes.

The most frustrating courses were the large required Bible Survey classes. All freshman students were to read through the Bible and learn names and places. I wanted to learn how we *got* the Bible and how it ever came to be known as "God's Word." In the survey classes, Jeopardy like tests included such questions,

"Now in the eighteenth year of Jeroboam son of Nebat, Abijam began to rule over Judah. What was Abijam's mother's name?" (1Kings 15:1-2, NRSV) Such trivia distracted and frustrated me from what I wanted to learn.

I received some encouragement when I took a theology class taught by Dr. Clemens. I heard Dr. Clemens had been a Presbyterian who once attended Princeton, probably the seminary, until he apparently got saved. A small man with kind of a cynical sounding voice, he held my attention with stimulating ideas and questions. He seemed to say things I felt might put him at risk teaching at Bob Jones. After giving me an "A" on an essay test, he called me into his bookshelf-lined office and asked how I studied. With growing questions and doubts about my surroundings and activities, I said I simply wrote my honest answers to my questions. He responded, "David, you have a 'thinking mind.'" I left encouraged.

Dating at Bob Jones was carefully restricted with absolutely no physical touching. Of course, several of us sneaked in moving hands, knees and legs during dark vesper moments or in fine art productions called "Artist Series." Such touching often became the event's highlight.

Even talking with a date was highly regulated. Most dating took place in an upstairs "Dating Parlor" over the Student Center. Couples arranged times when both could meet in the large area, which reminded me of a furniture show room. We could sit together for about an hour. No touching or handholding were permitted. Women monitors circulated around us like love guards, making sure daylight showed between bodies. Any slouching would quickly draw a chaperone's poke and warning to "sit up!" No dating was permitted into the surrounding community. Obviously, it was quite hard for a couple to sneak away and climb in bed. Senior couples could date off campus but only if one of the older guardians escorted them. An older friend told me he once took his girlfriend off campus on a date. A large chaperone sat between them on his car's "bench front seat" eating snacks before eating another huge meal with them!

Never expecting to become romantically attached, Naomi and I began to meet often in the dating parlor. I expected both of us would date others but it never happened. I saw girls I admired but never asked to date. Choices for activities were limited with no dances, co-ed parties or inter collegiate sporting events. Naomi's neat, proper and stately appearance with her many practical down-to-earth skills continually appealed to me. I felt more balanced around her, a woman raised in a proper Christian home. I couldn't imagine her parents ever having quarrels such as mine occasionally did. However, Naomi also vowed she would never marry a preacher.

Bob Jones allowed men and women to write notes to each other. Each day they were delivered across campus if dropped in a "mail box" by 8:00 p.m. Naomi and I began writing notes and over our years exchanged hundreds. Our feelings of love deepened through the notes along with the awareness her parents approved of our relationship. I still held her parents in high esteem and trusted their opinions and guidance suggestions. With Naomi, I felt my wild mind and emotions could be better kept under control.

Both our parents married before age 20 and I did not want to wait another three years burning with desires while living in a small box cell dorm room with no privacy. Premarital sex, or "living together, was out of the question. Early in our second semester, as our dating parlor meetings resumed, I told Naomi I wanted to one day marry her. I asked her to think about it but with no rush. I said if she wasn't as attracted to me as I was to her, tell me directly. That evening in a campus dormitory note, she wrote she was thrilled! I was a bit overwhelmed at her quick reply, especially to me, a potential "Preacher," a person she vowed to never marry.

Naomi's parents drove from Sherman to Bob Jones in early March. On their way to Florida, they surprisingly arrived in a new Mercedes Benz. Meeting together in their small motel room, I asked their opinion of our becoming married, perhaps even next summer. Naomi's older sister had already dropped out of college and now planned to marry. Her parents were supportive of our marriage but questioned our timing and finances. They encouraged us to wait longer. Respecting them, I agreed, realizing it would no doubt be simpler and more financially practical. However, that evening, I received a note from Naomi expressing disappointment in the way I allowed her father to change my mind! Soon after her parents left, things turned cold between us. I could not understand why but by early April sensed the relationship might soon end.

In mid-May, shortly before the first school year ended, I walked Naomi slowly back to her dorm after supper. Things seemed awkward and unnatural amid the very warm temperatures surrounded by landscape bursting with flowers. Along the narrow cement sidewalk, she suddenly said, "I am thinking about quitting Bob Jones and enrolling in a beauty school!" I thought our relationship stress might be affecting her thinking. She did well in studies and was attractive to many--why would she want to quit?

My brother and I returned to Sherman the summer of 1962 and worked on the farm. Dad paid us a dollar an hour, which averaged 300 hours a month. Naomi returned to her family's parsonage home and worked as a maid for a well-known family at the nearby Chautauqua Institution. Amid our long working hours, we began seeing each other again and our relationship seemed to improve. I avoided any discussion of marriage.

On Sundays, I taught church school classes and preached a few sermons in the Sherman Baptist Church. My brother and I seemed like local "spiritual heroes." We continued doing the required Preacher Boy evangelism as we walked sidewalks and streets of nearby villages, winning more souls to Christ. I sent back my weekly numbers to Bob Jones. I tried to avoid such activities in Sherman. I was feeling increasingly awkward, becoming aware that even Naomi's father, as the Preacher, never did such activities.

Some of my "evangelizing" began to annoy Naomi. One night I took her for supper at one of the many restaurants, which flourished during summer months around Chautauqua Lake. Sitting opposite in a booth, I shared my recent efforts to "win people to Jesus on the streets." Starring at me with her large blue eyes and perfectly combed hair she said, "David, you must learn how to live in *this* world!" I nearly choked on my hotdog, shocked to hear such from the Preacher's daughter. But it carried authority. I sensed permission, if not an order, to stop. I never again walked the streets looking for lost souls!

Shortly after returning to Bob Jones, we received news Naomi's parents had resigned from the Sherman Baptist Church. They were moving to Wabash, Indiana. Naomi, surprised as myself, again became more distant and upset. I assumed again this might be the time to permanently break up. Maybe she decided I was not the one--too crazy with my religious fanaticism, too short, or too whatever!

We spent Christmas in separate places, she in Wabash and I in Sherman. In Wabash, Naomi's father told her she must quit college. Her savings were gone. He had used them to help with the move to Wabash. Naomi stubbornly resisted and courageously returned to Greenville. She secured student loans and worked thirty-cents-per-hour rates for the university, a tribute to her own determination and independence.

I remained unaware of Naomi's family's financial issues but her attitude toward me changed. Seeing her, she asked how I was doing, and soon we resumed walks down cement sidewalks to her dorm after evening meals. We began meeting again in the upstairs dating parlor. I felt more comfortable with her and soon we began talking again about marriage. I felt more content. Naomi always seemed like an anchor in my life, although we were opposite in so many ways. She was super organized and conservative about change and new ideas. I was always drifting away into another space, questioning, journaling my ideas and progress. I tended to do things without waiting. Naomi represented stability and a sense of being grounded. She gave me a sense of homey-ness and stability with her independence and skills at cooking, sewing, making clothes, perfect penmanship and spotless cleanliness. She seemed like the ballast to my oft storm troubled mind when drifting into deeper waters.

In a few weeks, I decided again to ask her about marriage. Yes, there were many nice ladies around campus. I never saw or talked with many without feeling I could fall in love! But I didn't want to lose Naomi. She seemed unique. My mother even said once, "She is the one for you!" So one night in the parlor, surrounded by the usual unmarried patrol guards, I brought up the subject of marriage again. She immediately accepted! I wanted to grab and pull her down into the large sofa, kissing her all over and shouting to the guards, "Hey! I love this woman and we are going to get married!" I could hardly believe it. I doubted the longer waiting period, knowing I would be impatient. Yet I felt more settled. Just the idea of one day having a marriage and home with Naomi deeply appealed to me, like seeing the lighthouse appear after crossing a turbulent ocean.

More settled, my interest in studies surged. So did my questions and doubts. Fascinated with studies of the ancient Greek language, I discovered there were several manuscripts from early Christian writings. It became an important "aha!" moment. There *was* no original Bible or New Testament. The New Testament contained around 5000 complete or partial Greek manuscripts, 10,000 Latin manuscripts and over 9000 more in various languages. Most were written years after the time of Jesus. I learned Jesus neither spoke nor read the Greek language. On each page of my Greek New Testament, footnotes revealed various ways a word or phrase could be translated from various manuscripts. The Bible was a compilation of various texts gathered over many years. There was no early "Apostles Creed." It was written in the fourth century under Emperor Constantine's orders to make "one holy Catholic Church." I learned the Bible we use became canonized as the only rule of faith and practice 300 years *after* the time of Jesus. With this awareness, my mind began to spin anew with emotion, excitement, and risk.

Returning to Bob Jones for my junior year, my Literary Society, Alpha Omega, elected me as their chaplain. Bob Jones did not allow normal college fraternities and sororities. They created "Literary Societies" with Greek names signifying something Christian or Biblical. Mine was called "Alpha Omega." Naomi's was called "Sigma Lama Delta." My brother had served my "society" the year before as Chaplain. Preparing the weekly sermons became much harder than expected with my growing questions, often leaving me feeling empty with little to say. I continued to grow steadily unsure of everything. I believed in God, but so did other people who called themselves "Christian." Maybe they had ideas I could learn and use. Maybe the continuous guilt and worry about the "unsaved" wasn't needed.

Adding more confusion came from a student friend who startled me with comments on the racism that often was vocal at Bob Jones. The student seemed sort of a loner, but to me, very bright and brave. Tall and overweight with coal black hair and large black-rimmed glasses, Howard drove a large Buick his grandmother had given him. Stunned at his remarks, I never questioned the frequent racially biased remarks, nor ever considered my own racial prejudices. I realized the college excluded African American and nonwhite students, even though many worked as janitors and cooks. Growing up, I often heard disparaging comments about African Americans from some relatives, frequently with the "N" word. It became more prevalent to me at Bob Jones and the surrounding community. Senator Strom Thurmond of South Carolina, who spoke almost yearly during the chapel services, was a strong segregationist. Once the elderly founder, Bob Jones Sr., referred in a sermon to the African Americans as recipients of the curse of Canaan, who was Noah's grandson, a curse to become our servants. He also quoted a verse stating God established divine boundaries to keep the races separate. I didn't know how to respond. This was a whole new arena for me, one I had never faced. I became thankful for Howard's comments, as troubling as they were.

On November 22, 1963, all were shocked to hear of President Kennedy's assassination in Dallas, Texas. The news came just after lunch as Naomi and I walked together to a classroom building. Classes were not cancelled, and my Old Testament Bible teacher, never mentioned the tragedy! In the dormitory evening prayer meeting, a California student said, almost with relief, "The President is now burning in hell!" I asked myself, "How can he know?" The next day an almost celebrative atmosphere seemed to permeate the campus and chapel service. In the Preacher Boys' class, the faculty leader declared Jackie Kennedy a great actress in her show of sorrow. The college even refused to lower the American flag as a sign of national mourning. I never heard a prayer offered for the Kennedy family, or country. It seemed wrong to me and I wanted to talk about it with my friends, but "griping" was a harsh crime. Students could be "shipped" for griping, and for not reporting another.

With growing concern about my finances and a desire to spend more time off campus, I began working part time at one of the new McDonald's fast food restaurants on weekends. It felt refreshing to be among "normal" people again. The large supervisor, Russ, liked my attitude and quickly put me in charge of one of the order windows, waiting on people standing outside in line. I quietly gave up doing weekend "Preacher Boy" trips. Being on campus, I attended the Sunday Chapel services and found them increasingly uninspiring. They seemed more aimed toward impressing visitors and attracting donors than discussing ideas. My doubts grew deeper about the validity of the school being the number one Christian place on earth, the "Vatican of Fundamentalism." More questions arose over my career track, my finances and future marriage. I began experiencing loneliness and confusion, writing in my journal, "Why doesn't God give me more energy and peace? Why did I ever come here?" "Loneliness," I wrote, "seems to be part of following God."

My brother graduated in May and no longer returned to the farm. I returned to Sherman to work with Dad, happy the school year had ended. Disillusioned with some of the spiritual teachings, I turned my mind toward politics. The "Good News" became Barry Goldwater leading the race for the Republican nomination. I put a Goldwater sticker on my Ford.

Again, I enjoyed working on the farm. Driving equipment, hauling lime and helping with the busy hay season gave relief from my religious and life questions. The old familiar fields and woods gave me peace with a sense of stability. On weekends I still spoke at area church services, taught Sunday school classes and spoke at youth meetings. Most of my talks and sermons now became more laced with right wing political ideas than religion. It seemed like a relief from trying to "save people."

In late July, I drove 375 miles west to Wabash, Indiana to be with Naomi. Her parents were pleased with our marriage decision. Her father's new church seemed to be going well and people were getting "saved." He also sensed my doubts and questions about Bob Jones University and suggested I visit the campus of Grand Rapids Baptist Seminary. He said the fine staff, many whom he knew, could better answer my questions. He suggested I needed a Baptist school without the confusion of multiple denominations. They were too "ecumenical."

So Naomi and I drove north a few hours to Grand Rapids where the Seminary boasted a new campus on the eastern edge of the city. With new buildings scattered over formerly flat farmland, its smaller size appealed to me. It struck me again, however, that if I attended this or any seminary, I would be preparing for one career: a form of religious teaching, speaking and perhaps a pastoral ministry. Business partnership ideas with Dad would surely end along with its sense of financial security.

I returned to Bob Jones for my senior year with a more positive attitude. The college buzzed with hopes of Barry Goldwater becoming President. To help deflect more of my religious doubts and questions, I volunteered to help conduct area political surveys and campaign meetings. I drove some friends to see Barry Goldwater when he came to Greenville. I trained to become a poll watcher for the upcoming elections, even receiving instructions on how to help people vote twice. I remembered an Uncle's comments about politics—it's a dirty business.

In contrast to Kennedy's assassination, Bob Jones promised a day of no classes if Goldwater won. A few days later, I drove some fellow classmates to shop in Greenville. While stopped at a red light, one of my fellow "Preacher Boy" friends shouted to the car driver next to me, "Hey, some nigger put a sticker on your car bumper!" It urged voting for Lyndon Johnson. Of course, we were excited and hopeful but devastated when Johnson won by a landslide! Goldwater only carried two states--South Carolina was one. A somber spirit swept over campus like the bereavement of a hero, perhaps as others felt when JFK was killed. We wondered if our country may have lost its last chance to remain Christian and not drift further into communism. I felt the darkness.

Returning to campus after Christmas, I surprisingly spotted one of my former Sherman neighbors walking across campus. Ted Williams, whose parents converted from the Spiritualist Church in Lily Dale to become Baptists in Sherman, lived down the road from us. Ted often drove his dark Hudson Hornet past our farms, a blurry hiss at wide-open speeds. I remembered the night he lost control of his Hudson on the curve coming out of Sherman, hit a telephone pole and suffered a serious head concussion. Now married with two beautiful children, he and his lovely Greek wife lived off campus in an apartment. At the time, Ted was big into health foods. Always a risk taker, Ted had several serious accidents, his most recent falling several floors while washing skyscraper windows in New York City. He now walked with a noticeable limp. He had long wavy hair with pits left on his face from earlier acne and accident scars. When he talked, his eyes were always shifting back and forth, unable to make direct eye contact for more than a second or two. He claimed his new eating awareness and habits were making him stronger.

Ted talked rapidly and endlessly about several subjects, always planning to make "quick and big dollars." In some ways he reminded me of Dad, only Dad actually made more of the "big dollars." Ted also rambled on about the many corruptions of the world and ways he could make some "big" money. I listened with interest but became more astonished, even shocked, by his continual irreverence and criticism of Bob Jones. I realized if I ever reported him, he would be immediately shipped. If I didn't, I would!

Below Ted's apartment was a vacant one. Ted urged me to move there and get off campus, get back some of my freedom. I liked the idea. I decided to make a visit to Dean of the Men.

The Dean of Men, a short wiry man with a high pitched, preachy kind of voice, once saw my parents visiting campus, walking alongside my brother and me. He came up to my parents and putting his hands on our shoulders said, "As parents I want you to know you have two wonderful sons. Real gems!" Thus I used my stellar reputation for being an honest, devoted Preacher Boy with Spiritual Room Captain, Dorm Hall Monitor and Alpha Omega's Chaplain credentials and good grades, to persuade the Dean of Men to grant me permission to live my final semester off campus in an apartment. I only needed six hours to graduate and in anticipation of marriage, I argued the need for more money working longer hours at McDonald's. Permission was granted with congratulations!

Shortly afterwards, Dad called and wanted to know my plans after graduation. He urged me to return home and offered to help purchase a new car, saying to drive one with over 80,000 miles, which mine had, was risky. He also assured me there was much money to be made if I came home. He even offered to loan me money, hinting it might be a gift, if I returned to the farms.

Knowing now I would not return to the farm, I went car shopping. I drove to a small town called Travel's Rest, a place I once passed while preaching in Ashville Prisons during my Freshman year. I discovered the Ford dealer had two brand new black police cars. They were refused by the police and were to be sold. One was standard shift with an overdrive option. I just *had* to have it!

I made the deal and called Dad for the extra money needed after selling my old Ford. Again, Dad asked about my plans. I told him I planned to marry Naomi and enter seminary. After a long pause, Dad said, "You know Dave, I'm sorry, but this really isn't a good time for me to be loaning money!" Stunned and angered, I called the man who loaned Dad money to purchased his first farm in 1940, an older retired Jewish man who lived in Sherman. Proud of my family, he immediately sent me a check!

I got the car. It deeply disappointed Naomi. She had wanted an automatic. I never seriously considered her feelings. After all, Dad *never* consulted with Mom about such things! I then quit McDonald's to sell Tom's latest "get rich quick" scheme with juice extractors. Making $100 dollars on each sale, I could soon pay off the car loan. After gaining deposits for 12 of the appliances, I discovered Tom didn't have any juicers in stock! He then asked me to call my father for money to order a couple dozens of them! In anger and disgust I quit and began working nights at a Texaco gas station.

The short experience at the gas station furthered sealed the direction in my life. Working the night shift, a red headed man often stopped for gas who seemed well educated by my standards. He loved to talk religious issues and discovering my Bob Jones status, one night we talked for a couple hours without interruption. I could be as open as I wanted with questions and opinions. He spoke freely of the limitations of a fundamentalist education and ideology, of how it tends to cut off thousands of people from conversation. He chided Bob Jones for criticizing and castigating similar fundamentalist groups as the Southern Baptists, doubts I often entertained, even though I heard they had dances! The conversation stuck in my mind. I began to think of the tremendous possibilities for thought and growth if I could begin dialogue with other groups. Still remaining deeply suspicious of those considered liberal, excitement and possibility filled my mind. One day I would be brave enough to at least meet and talk with them.

Following the night's conversation with the stranger, I became increasingly frustrated with my past studies and experiences at Bob Jones. Much seemed to have been a waste of time. My floating and wandering mind struggled to concentrate on particulars. The last semester I took my one and only philosophy class, reading Descartes and Kant, brilliant philosophers whom I wanted to understand. Finding them difficult and expecting help, the teacher told me he never could understand them either!

As I neared the final weeks of my years at Bob Jones, things began to unravel. I questioned the school policies and attitudes more than ever. Suddenly, the Dean of Men called me back into his office. Someone had reported me, or "turned me in" for negative attitudes. Chills ran up my spine as I climbed the stairs to his office. I knew I had been walking on thin ice. I wondered if my time had come to be "shipped." Sitting across from his desk, the Dean sternly chastised me for attitudes he heard were turning me away from the university. He questioned my move off campus because of the need for more money and then purchasing a new car. I felt very uncomfortable. I said little. He warned me I could never be close enough to graduation not to be shipped! I wondered, "Should I just immediately end my association with the college?"

I left the Dean's office wondering what to do. The degree seemed nearly worthless, especially being a "Preacher Boy" with a major in Bible. I sensed I may have wasted nearly four years of my life. Yet, I had studied religion and earned a Bachelor's degree with a Bible major. The deep desire to know more about religious issues remained strong: about God, Jesus, the Bible and other groups. I did not want to return to the farms. Naomi was about to graduate, our families would soon arrive, and our wedding was scheduled. I stayed but remained quiet, keeping thoughts to myself.

Chapter 6

Marriage

In the best of relationships, you have two people who
cannot think of anything that was not part of the deal.
— Robert Brault

After graduation and a short visit to Sherman, my brother and I drove my new Ford to Wabash, Indiana. My brother stayed with Naomi's parents in their new ranch style home on the edge of the city while I stayed with a family in the country who were active members in her father's new church.

Having already experienced a split in the older city Baptist Church, Naomi's father invited my brother and me to help grow the new church, using our Bob Jones "evangelism skills." While a new church was being built, the new group met in a rented fairground building and featured a young country singer named Brenda Webb, soon to be known as Crystal Gail. My brother and I sang a few songs but kept our names.

Quickly finding jobs in a General Tire factory, I soon missed the farm work in open fields with fresh air. I couldn't imagine such a job for life. My routine consisted of operating four hot rubber presses, throwing chunks of rubber into hot iron molds and pushing the door shut until the time buzzer sounded. I did this for eight hours in temperatures over 100 degrees. Overhead fans did nothing, it seemed, to alleviate the heat but their buzz along with steam relief values blasting throughout the night, left my ears numb with tinnitus. After three weeks, however, the plant shut down due to a union strike. I was relieved.

I quickly applied for a job cutting trees for a new power dam. Asked to show up at 6:00 a.m. in the next morning, I met a large, muscle bound foreman standing near the tall trees.

"Do you know how to use a chain saw?" he asked scanning my thin wiry body.

"Yes," I replied.

"What do you normally do?"

"Well, I just graduated from college and plan to begin seminary in September."

He stood in silence before spitting out a large wad of juicy chewing tobacco.

"Well, we really don't have any wood for you to cut!"

I returned to Wabash and invited people to church.

Two weeks before our wedding, I worked a few more days in General Tire's "oven room" before returning to Sherman. With few savings, I grew anxious. All my life, I never worried much about money. Now I had little and planned to be married in a few days. With no help from her family, Naomi alone assumed costs of the wedding, which were less than $500 including dress, accessories and reception. I hoped faith would sustain us.

On July 30 at 8:00 p.m., farmer's wedding time, our service began. The small Baptist church sweltered in 90-degree heat. Naomi's father, dressed in his best suit, walked her down the familiar aisle amid smiling friends and happy relatives. Meeting her in my rented suit, he gave her away before taking over the ceremony. As we joined hands and exchanged vows, I worried about dropping her ring into the large furnace grate beneath us. A singer from Wabash then sang "Always" before the benediction. Following the brief ceremony, we moved downstairs to the cooler social room to share the wedding dinner: ice cream, cake and punch. Before eating, we stood in a reception line. Naomi's father then turned to me and quietly said, with a large grin on his face, "Dave, you are now responsible for all of Naomi's debts!" Her parents had once told her, "You marry a Persons, and you'll never worry about money!"

A few days later, we gathered up our wedding gifts and headed to Grand Rapids. We stopped in Wabash to collect our last paychecks totaling $510.00. I wondered where it all came from. I wrote, "Praise the Lord!"

Chapter 7

Baptist Seminary

> *"When we live in a system, we absorb a system and think in a system."*
>
> *-James W. Douglas*

A week after our wedding, we arrived in Grand Rapids, Michigan, a bustling and growing Midwestern city. Pulling a small U-Haul trailer full of wedding presents and apartment furnishings, we found a motel for the night. The next morning, I called the Baptist seminary to confirm our new apartment's availability. My jaw dropped as I listened to the apologetic secretary. Due to heavy rains, apartment openings would be delayed another week or so. Naomi and I looked at each other in disbelief.

Discouraged but hopeful, we drove around the city and found a large old tourist home. Shaded by tall maple trees, it seemed more settled and less expensive. We unhooked the U-Haul trailer and stayed overnight. In the morning, we drove to north Grand Rapids. We found the beautiful new elementary school where Naomi would teach in a few weeks. A one level, brick structure with large windows, it looked beautiful, giving a needed boost to our young marriage.

A short distance from the school we noticed a large Baptist Church named "Northland." Recently built, it coincided with the new suburb sprawling over former farmlands. We parked and walked inside, noticing lighted offices with busy personnel. A short, stocky man came out of an inner office and walked briskly to greet us. Within minutes, Pastor Chuck Wood had our names, why we were in town, and our situation with seminary apartments. Welcoming us into his office, he immediately began giving options. He seemed like a divine intervention to our first marriage disappointment. The next day we attended the church's Sunday service. After a lively hour with inspiring music and preaching, Pastor Wood asked us to meet him the next morning in his office.

When we met the Pastor, he gave immediate options. He had already called the seminary and discovered the new apartments would not be ready until September 1. A church member would store our U-Haul contents in an empty garage. He then offered complimentary use of a mobile home owned by church members away for the summer. Close to Naomi's school we could use it until the seminary apartments opened in September. It seemed like a miracle!

On September first, the day before expecting to move into our new apartment, the seminary reported that due to more unexpected rains, the apartments could not be ready until a much later date! Shocked and frustrated, we drove to a realtor. Again, as if led by special guidance, a friendly salesman showed us a little house on Fuller Avenue, located midway between the Seminary and Naomi's school. With a small front and rear yard with an $80.00 monthly rent, we signed and moved in with our few items. We purchased our first new furniture on credit with Naomi's expected teaching salary and bought a little parti-colored Cocker Spaniel dog we named "Frosty." Seminary classes began, Naomi taught her 1st grade class, and we felt happily settled in marriage.

The Baptist Seminary contrasted sharply from Bob Jones. The one story class and administration building, brick-covered with clean tile flooring, looked more like a large motel rather than a divinity school. No chapel or steeple with bells dominated the site. A family-like atmosphere permeated the campus with only 40 or 50 seminary students. Adjacent to the seminary building, a new Baptist College covered many acres recently filled with grazing cows. With small seminary classes, students and faculty became quickly known as new friendships were made. I immediately enjoyed the classes and the sense of staying with a religious vocation.

On October 3rd during a Sunday morning service, Naomi and I went forward at Pastor Wood's invitation and became members of Northland Baptist Church. The mostly young congregation with many professionals was friendly and treated us with love and acceptance. The following week Pastor Wood asked me to lead a Junior High youth group. The church had purchased a new full sized school bus with the church name printed on each side. With my truck driving experience and license, I drove for a few events including a day's canoe trip.

In October, I found a part time machine shop job at a company called Keeler Brass. Many seminarians also worked there and it added to the sense of family. Busy with a full life and boundless energy, we loved our new status, feeling independent and free.

The small machine shop became an important community to my development. I worked two nine-hour shifts each week from 5:00 p.m. to 2:30 a.m. Many other students were from nearby Calvin Seminary and another school called "Grand Rapids School of the Bible." During 30-minute meal breaks, lively discussions often broke out over politics and religion.

Several older men in my department were refugees from Latvia, Lithuania, Poland and Hungary. My foreman was a wiry small man from Latvia with a mostly bald head and named "Arvis." He and his Latvian assistant, "Frank," became my friends and we shared frequent opinions. Arvis admired my work and since I was paid for an allotted number of pieces each night, I often finished two hours before the shift ended. He then allowed me to spend extra time in the bathroom reading, always alert for warning when the plant supervisor came by. "The Old Man is coming!" was the alert code, reminding me of sermons heard on the "Return of Jesus."

One of my favorite co-workers was a short, plump Lithuanian refugee named "Adrvis." Adrvis drove a little grey Volkswagen "beetle" which he claimed was safe since he could quickly veer away from threatening traffic. He had served as a school principal before being driven out of his country. Adrvis was also an excellent painter and during the day painted blue-ribboned pictures, which he sold to augment his income. Adrvis never said much, but in one conversation, he bluntly told me, "You don't belong here! You should be teaching and working with ideas."

Another coworker I deeply enjoyed was named "Orie." Orie was half Native American and loved to hunt and eat turtles. "Nothing beats fresh turtle soup!" he often declared. He also loved to hunt and resell old bottles he found among early settled areas and old area garbage dumps. From his "digs" he brought several of his treasures to work and bragged about their history and how much he could make selling them.

Some of my other co-workers often came to me with personal or religious questions. One tall, red-headed man about my age, confided about his young marriage. A faithful member to the Christian Reformed church, he told me that before marriage, his wife had given him many sexual liberties while dating. She coaxed him into more intimacy than he had ever expected, but thoroughly enjoyed. After marriage, she had become cold and much less seductive! "What could I do?" he implored me. I honestly didn't know, but suggested he talk with her or his pastor, surprised someone would share with me such personal issues.

Another co-worker, Bill, a quiet, introvert who studied at the Grand Rapids Bible College, asked me often about his religious questions. His wife cut his hair and some nights he walked in looking like a poorly clipped dog. One weekend he came to hear me preach in a nearby church. Afterwards he commented, "Dave, someday you will have a large congregation in an important church!"

As the second semester began, exciting new ideas began swirling through my mind. In an ethics class, the older, plump instructor suggested the ideas of evolution and that of a "social gospel" were reasonable options. He also told us there were no such things as "bare facts." Such ideas would seem to be outright abomination at Bob Jones. My mind spun as I found myself questioning the idea of creationism, the teaching that God created the whole universe in just six days, 6000 years ago. Always finding such ideas amazing, I began to question the literalness of the story from the first Bible book, Genesis. The ethics teacher then introduced me to Charles Darwin's theories of evolution, which I discovered were respected by Baptist writers who earlier taught in Rochester, New York: Augustus Strong and Walter Rauschenbusch. I discovered the term, "Theistic Evolution," the idea of an evolutionary life development guided by God. My thinking exploded into these exciting new areas and interests. I had little idea or fear where they might lead.

Near the end of the semester, Naomi was elected the "Seminary Wives' President." Proud of her, I sensed a wonderful future for us as pastor and spouse. Although finances remained tight, life became more settled. Naomi's father and mother beamed with pride. My Mom was delighted but Dad still seemed to wish I'd stayed on the farm.

In June 1966, after classes ended, the annual conference of the General Association of Regular Baptist Churches met in Grand Rapids. Interested, I wanted to see if this group might be a fit for me. Both Naomi's father and the seminary were members. Naomi's parents drove up from Indiana to attend and invited me to go with them. Seated together in the large downtown Civic Auditorium, energy and joy were everywhere as the large crowd belted out its favorite hymns and gospel songs. Then came the sermon. It stunned me as the speaker raged over the necessity of the Genesis Bible creation story being a literal, seven-day event, 6000 years ago! I sat in disappointment and confusion, wondering about my future as a Baptist.

After a summer working full time at Keeler Brass, Naomi and I returned to our respective teaching and studies. I placed my name on a "Preaching List" from which area churches called the seminary for speakers. Immediately I received invitations. When I spoke, people gave me positive feedback. Preparing sermons was difficult but as soon as I began, I became more confident. It was exhilarating standing before people speaking "divine inspiration!" Listening and watching sermons given by Pastor Wood, I yearned to be as good. I could see myself two years later as a full time pastor in a Baptist Church with Naomi as my beautiful and organized companion.

In mid-September, we moved to a small farm just east of Grand Rapids. Referred by a teacher friend of Naomi's, it lay off a narrow rural gravel road with a 100-yard long gravel driveway. We left the busy and noisy city streets and moved into a sequestered, pine-paneled, cape-cod farmhouse. Set on 75 acres, surrounded by trees and a small yard, it included a small useable barn and narrow bubbling trout stream. It was paradisiacal, a place to become quiet and think, plant a garden, mow some lawn, sit or work out in the barn, get another dog, and grow in our early marriage. We felt deeply happy and increasingly at home. So much seemed to be going our way. Yet, mental conflicts and questions lingered.

I began studying the Hebrew language, enjoying the serious Hebrew professor, Dr. Leon Wood. He pointed out the Hebrew word for prayer, *palal,* basically meant "self-reflection." I always thought of prayer as getting something for others or myself, a supplication for God to intervene and change things. Now I began to see prayer as more self-reflection and self-observation, a watching over my own mind and actions rather than judging others. The idea went deeper into my routines to stop, ponder, and allow my mind to wander in "wasteful dreaming." It opened more doors of permission and freedom to question myself and choose alternative actions.

Another important teacher was named Dr. Victor Matthews. To help us understand our surrounding culture, he assigned readings from various philosophers who represented views other than the usual Christian ones. My last semester at Bob Jones neither the teacher nor I understood such writings. I could not understand why we needed these people, obviously not Christians. Naomi's father had once referred to such readings as "Foolosophy." Now I couldn't get enough!

The German philosopher Frederick Nietzsche became a favorite. His words in "Thus Spake Zarathustra" and "The Will to Power" describing the "superman," the person of realized potential, thrilled me. I reflected about how I felt lost among life's sheep. I, like superman, also wanted to find my truer self and live my life to the fullest!

Dr. Matthews also introduced me to Soren Kierkegaard and existentialism. I began reading his "Works of Love" and "Purity of Heart is to Will One Thing." They fascinated me. His "existentialism" gave me permission to move further in reading non-familiar teachings and beliefs. The goal of life was to stay connected to the thinker and living rather than in just ethereal or dogmatic ideas of others. How do the teachings and ideas connect with me and affect my daily existence? He wrote, "Don't forget to love yourself!" Such new ideas helped liberate and lift me into more bewilderment and anticipation. They also would open more doors to conflict. Yet, like a wide-eyed child with new toys at Christmas, I craved to learn more, not assuming I had to be right or absolute about issues, but more honest.

No doubt the growing sense of freedom in the later 1960's also influenced me along with other seminarians. The Viet Nam war began expanding amid growing protests. Young people were leaving traditional homes and universities to become "hippies." A spirit of open questioning and doubting "experts" filled the air. Bolstered by comments from colleagues and teachers, I began facing my own racist attitudes, followed passively since childhood but deepened during my Bob Jones years.

As a sign of rebellion, a tall seminarian from Texas named Robert, began growing a beard. Some days he quickly shaved it off through insistence of his young wife and would come to class with little cuts and specks of dried blood on his face. One day, he stood up and shockingly declared to a bewildered class, "Martin Luther King, Jr. must be seen as one of the true heroes of our time! We ought to be praying for and supporting him."

Dr. Martin Luther King Jr., vilified by many in our families and among Bob Jones colleagues, began to be seen by some of us as a hero, an extremely courageous Christian leader. I felt shame for my own racist attitudes and words. I wanted to move beyond the unrecognized prejudices of my youth, the disgust I often heard toward interracial marriages, and keeping people of color in subjection. I began seeing our country as more of a white male creation--one still needing to move beyond many of its earlier prejudices. My life was turning upside down.

One of my closest seminary friends had been Matthew Getz. Matthew also graduated from Bob Jones University in my class. Shorter than I, with light blond hair, Matthew was a bright and diligent student, earning straight A's in all of his classes. As we met for lunch one day, he quietly mentioned to me, in his low-keyed thoughtful voice, what a waste of time so much learning at Bob Jones had been. A native of a small town just north of Grand Rapids, he had decided to attend the Baptist Seminary, but his growing interest and true love was becoming computers. He had read about them and predicted one day we'd all have them sitting on our desks opening up vast areas of information and communication. With Matthew, I found I could freely share my growing doubts about fundamentalism without fear. He kept urging me on.

In early November, we drove a few miles south to Plainwell to meet Naomi's mother Mamie and younger brother, Steve, whom Victor brought up from Wabash. Uncertain what to say with my growing doubts, Victor surprised us by saying Mamie might be close to a nervous breakdown. Both approaching 50 years in age, Mamie was going through kind of a life crisis. He thought staying with us a few days might help her.

Mamie came home with us. Soon she wanted to have long discussions with me about what was happening to my thinking at the seminary. She urged Naomi to help "un-confuse me." When Mamie returned home, she suffered a nervous breakdown and became hospitalized.

At Thanksgiving, we drove to Wabash to be with Naomi's parents and seven-year-old Steve. We returned home further discouraged. Her parents, now both concerned about my drifting into new areas of thought, said we were neglecting them.

In early December, I received a shocking letter from Mom suggesting she might leave Dad! I knew they often had arguments, but separation and divorce in these years did seem more socially acceptable. A few days later Naomi's mother called and said she *was* leaving Victor! What was happening? Were there any homes remaining stable? Everything seemed to becoming untethered. Nothing seemed certain.

Chapter 8

My Baptist Home Ends

"People wish to be settled. Only as far as they are
unsettled is there any hope for them."
—*Ralph Waldo Emerson*

In early March of 1967, Naomi told me she was pregnant. Proud and excited, the news pushed me to press on with studies, still expecting employment after graduation as a Baptist minister. In early May, my chance came. After leading a Baptist service in nearby Spring Lake, the church board asked me to meet with them. The chair asked if I would consider becoming their pastor. Though flattered, I sensed I was not ready. So many doubts and questions lingered but confident of more opportunities, and answers, I refused the offer.

Word soon began spreading around Seminary I had become a "doubter of the faith." In June, we attended a morning service at Northland Baptist where Pastor Wood refused to greet us in his normal cheerful way. Remarks in his sermon seemed directed toward me. He spoke of a seminary student who once questioned his faith but refusing his counsel, later fell into deep regret. After the service, he turned away from me as if I were an infectious leper. Such coldness continued the next week, yet I never received a call or explanation. We decided, with sadness, to no longer attend.

My older brother drove out to stay with us that summer and find work in Grand Rapids, an area with many available jobs. Maybe he could give me counsel. He had finished his first year at Princeton Seminary, a place I considered "liberal." I thought he seemed happy and free, and he quickly found a job sanding wood drivers for Wilson golf clubs, but soon got in with me at the better paying Keeler Brass Company. Before long, it became obvious we had drifted apart in our journeys. He seemed surprised when I revealed I doubted the literalness of many Bible stories, especially the creation ones.

In July, my brother, Naomi and I attended a Bob Jones regional banquet reunion in Grand Rapids. Standing among the alumni and student recruiters, the men dressed in the usual blue sport coat and dark tie Bob Jones' look, I felt like an outsider. I realized how far I had moved away from my earlier thinking. When we returned to our house, I felt deep loneliness. I walked the short distance to sit alone in the barn. Hunched over on my workout bench, I began to cry as I wondered where I was headed.

Grand Rapids was a city of mostly Christian Reformed people, and on Sunday mornings, cars jammed the roads taking people to church services. With a new sense of freedom and determination, I decided to learn more about their beliefs. Christian Reformed people seemed more organized, traditional, and grounded with a certainty I did not share. Their local seminary helped formulate my favorite teachers like Drs. Wood and Matthews. They also did not have prohibitions against movies, smoking or even drinking alcoholic beverages.

Unlike the Baptists, I also discovered Christian Reformers did not teach or warn of an imminent or literal return of Jesus. The Christian Reformed Church also baptized infants and did not give public invitations to "accept Christ."

Much better trained and schooled in classical languages and history, I grew to respect answers I received from various Christian Reformed seminary students who worked with me at Keeler Brass. When I asked one about the "Return of Jesus," he exhaled some sweet smelling smoke from his pipe and answered, "Dave, he's already returned! He's in our hearts!" Rather than debate, defend, or feel distant from them, I asked more questions as my admiration deepened. By late August, I thought seriously of transferring to Calvin Seminary, the Christian Reformed Seminary a short distance south from the seminary where I already attended.

The last night of my brother's summer stay, we worked until the shift ended at 2:30 a.m. Driving home, as if to wash away all the questions and thinking in my mind, I suddenly jumped into another road race with two other cars, screaming wide open through what were called the "S curves" with my 330 horse-powered police car. After arriving home, disgust and shame poured over me, realizing how close again we had come to disastrous injuries or deaths. The model Dad had given me seemed increasingly dangerous and thoughtless. Feeling I had to "grow up" I confessed to Naomi in the morning the incident and vowed if I ever road-raced again, I would sell the car. The next morning, my brother left for Princeton spinning and sliding sideways out of the driveway. In the evening, Naomi and I went to drag races.

The next Sunday, we attended the Fountain Street Church. Some students at the Baptist Seminary described the church as liberal, un-Christian and apostate. In the late 19th century, led by graduates from the University of Chicago Divinity School, the church had moved to embrace the growing liberal ideas of the period. In 1959 they dropped the word "Baptist" from their name under leadership of the present pastor, Rev. Duncan Littlefair whom Baptist seminarians called Rev. "Littlefaith." I *had* to visit.

Naomi, somewhat uncomfortable and concerned, went with me. In the full church, a surprise itself in such a conservative, Reformed city, Rev. Littlefair gave a sermon titled "A Patch of Blue." Based on a book by Elizabeth Kata, it had recently become a hit movie starring Sidney Poitier. It told the story of a little girl, blinded by her drunken mother at age five. A few years later the young girl found a friend in the park named Gordon, but being blind, did not realize he was African American, and soon fell in love with him. One day, he described to her the sky as very blue, one of the favorite colors she remembered. Rev. Littlefair talked movingly of how we all need a "patch of blue" in our lives, a vision to draw us away from the narrowness and brutality of life. Such a patch and vision often comes, he suggested, from those most different among us. Fighting to hold back tears, I thought of myself finding new patches of blue from unexpected sources.

The next morning, with strong ambivalence, I registered for classes at the Baptist Seminary. Beginning my last year, I wondered how and why I got there and where I was going. More loneliness and confusion flowed over me. Deeply lost, I felt homeless.

A few days later, still brooding, I decided to meet with another one of my favorite teachers at the Baptist Seminary, Joseph Valestak. A dark skinned man with thick black hair and deep brown eyes from his Slavic roots, Naomi's father had spoken highly of him as a Greek scholar and solid Baptist. Joe had been raised in Western New York near Sherman. Impressed with an advanced course I took from him in Greek, I hoped he might help to answer my questions and offer a few suggestions. Quickly, he stunned me with his frank, sharp, and critical evaluation of the school and our denomination. He summarized clearly my issues, feelings and questions.

I invited Professor Valestak for supper and an evening in our home so that Naomi could meet him. We talked for hours and again I noted his cynical and critical remarks about fundamentalism. The next morning, I realized I did not want and could not continue to be a Baptist. I thought of quitting immediately, calling Dad to see if I might even return to the farm.

Instead, I took another Hebrew and Old Testament class with Dr. Wood, which only added more fuel to my mental flames. Dr. Wood said the Reformers were wrong in teaching the covenant of grace as only between God and a special "elect." Grace and love included the whole world! Suddenly, the liberating idea of a universal God of love in and for all people sprung to mind with emotion and possibilities.

I wrote a paper for Dr. Wood on the history and present state of Israel in which I further questioned the teachings and sermons I had often heard about Israel being God's specially chosen people with a very special land. Handing me back the paper, he told me he loved my thinking and wrote across the top of page one, "I feel you are heading in a good direction. I'm glad your thinking has been stimulated. Great areas of truth are involved. You have made a good start."

I began rereading Frederick Nietzsche and found his writings even more thrilling and easier to understand. Dr. Matthews, who introduced me to Nietzsche, encouraged me to continue. I poured into Sigmund Freud's "Totem and Taboo," hardly able to stop as I pondered his amazing new ideas. I saw myself in a church of "totems and taboos." I had been living by many of them that needlessly frightened people.

I continued to move in a progressive direction from Fundamentalist to Conservative, and now, to Liberal. I went from supporting Republican candidates and the party to registering as a member of the Democratic Party. Naomi, surprisingly, joined me.

In late October I received a letter from Pastor Fred Robb of the Sherman Baptist Church. He asked me to return and answer a list of charges before him and the Deacon board. He wrote out each charge for me to read and return with answers. Charges included my apparent belief in infant baptism and my disbelief in the "imminent return of our Lord Jesus Christ." I shared the letter with Professor Valestak. He laughed broadly with his deep voice and told me to tell them I was simply doing what they always taught, "Following the truth of Jesus the best I can!" Until this time, I had not thought about explaining my recent changes to him, the church or my family. I had planned to be ordained in Sherman as a minister when I finished this year. Someone from the seminary, perhaps Northland Baptist Church, had written or called Pastor Robb to warn him about my drift from the "truth."

At Thanksgiving, we returned to Sherman and I met the Deacons with Pastor Robb. I was excited, if not naively confident, I could defend my thinking--maybe even help them understand my progress. We sat together in the same paneled study, where years before, Paulette and I met with Preacher Stouffer, and probably the same room where later, she "accepted Jesus." The ten or so Deacons sat in a circle around the pastor's desk, many arriving shortly after finishing evening chores. One was my Uncle Everett, with whom I had once enjoyed racing our Fords against each other after Sunday evening services. Not long after the questions began and my answers were given, I realized my idealism was hopeless. They remained adamant in opposing my broadening views. Still, I did not feel overly concerned as relief poured over me. But never again would I be asked to preach or offer a prayer in the Sherman Baptist Church, the church that kick-started my life's journey. My Baptist spiritual home closed.

It became a critical time for our marriage. Naomi, pregnant with our first child, gave her school notification of resignation at semester's end. Financial pressures increased, pressures for so many years, unknown to me. In my last year of Seminary, we once expected I would easily be accepted into a church position by school year's end. Now, I found myself in a major career transition and my wife would soon be giving birth to our first child. I needed to find something soon to give new birth for a career to support us.

In early December, I applied to the nearby Calvin Seminary. Expecting them to be more open and liberal, Naomi and I had begun attending services in a nearby Christian Reformed Church. In a few weeks, I drove through the college and seminary's well-maintained entrance roads lined with mature, well-trimmed trees and shrubbery. It felt anchored and solid. Walking into the administrative department, I was warmly greeted before the Registrar led me into his cozy office, lined with shelves of books and regulation papers. Sitting across from him, he treated me like a lost sheep that had come home. He had read my college and seminary transcripts. Quickly the middle-aged man, dressed in a solid gray suit, read me their requirements. I would need more college courses in language and history before acceptance into seminary. Twenty-six more college hours were required, which included eight hours of a modern language, six in history, six in philosophy and six more in Biblical Greek (I had already taken 12), or another ancient language. I could take the college courses along with seminary classes on the same campus. It would take at least another three years before ordination. Still, I felt relief that all my previous work had not been in vain. Confidently, I saw the challenge as acceptable and exciting, even though finances would remain tight for longer than expected.

A few days later, several Baptist Seminary colleagues, who worked at Keeler Brass, surrounded me at lunch break. Sitting around a makeshift table on work stools, they peppered me with questions, amazed at how "mixed up" I had become. Some charged I had never been truly saved, others accused me of becoming a communist, while others threatened I would be filled with shame and regret upon reaching heaven and the Great Day of Judgment!

On December 22, our daughter Lisa Marie was born, a welcomed and happy distraction. Her birth sparked a wonderful and happy time for us, a break from the whirlwinds of the past months and weeks. Lisa was a beautiful baby and, for a time, my career troubles disappeared. We brought her home Christmas Day from Blodgett Hospital, wrapped in a decorated stocking.

Naomi's parents drove up to see our new baby. Mamie and Steve stayed to help a few days but Victor, who said little to me, returned to Wabash.

The following Sunday, we took Mamie and Steve with us to the Christian Reformed Church. Dad, who suddenly showed up with his truck to get a load of fertilizer, went with us. They were impressed walking into the large, recently built colonial styled church. While Naomi cuddled our angelic looking baby, we watched the baptism of an infant during the service. Mamie seemed to enjoy it, especially the beautiful, majestic colonial-styled church building with its reverent order of worship. Dad, who wore one of my suits, appeared confused about the course of events in my life, and never again asked about my return to the farm.

Chapter 9

Who Am I?

"Clearly, going home is both a powerful urge and a dangerous trek. But it's not something you can even contemplate until you have stepped apart from the clan and stood in your own right."
- David R. Anderson in his memoir,
"Losing Your Faith, Finding Your Soul"

Naomi and I often became discouraged and worried. Tensions between us could rise suddenly, like an unexpected storm. After two and a half years of marriage with our first child, one day after a few hours of silence, Naomi exclaimed, "David, you are not the man I married! What happened to you?" Startled and frightened, my mind swirled into a spiral of guilt and anxiety. Had I become too impulsive? Our seminary friends no longer called to check on us. We no longer attended Northland Baptist Church. Pastor Wood had never called to ask why. With spurts of doubt, I questioned why we moved here, why I ever chose such a profession. Who was I? What did I really want to do?

I finished classes at the Baptist Seminary in mid-January. Strangely, I did not feel bitter, just relieved, with even gratitude for freedom and new ideas. The last day I walked slowly to the offices of my favorite teachers: Drs. Joe Valestak, Victor Matthews, and

Leon Wood. I entered their offices with trepidation and tightness in my stomach. I thanked each one for the stimulation, freedom and excitement given me. I explained my plans to transfer to nearby Calvin Seminary. Each man surprisingly stood and offered a handshake, expressing admiration for my honesty and courage. Dr. Matthews spoke with a smile and directness saying, "Well, good for you!" A bit dazed, I drove home with renewed energy to search and learn.

Classes at Calvin College and Seminary were to begin in a few days. I returned to hand in the necessary papers and documents. Warmly greeted and remembered from my previous inquiry, I talked with the registrar. With my application papers in his hands, he glanced up from his glasses and in a parental tone suggested I might want to take the required college courses at the Grand Rapids Community College. Noting my financial situation with no family help, he said tuition would cost much less. I thanked him and drove straight to the Community College in downtown Grand Rapids, where I found the administrative office. Quickly, a staff member gave me application papers.

On February 1st, upon finishing two full weeks in the machine shop, I thus attended a class at the Community College named, "Modern European History." It felt wonderful to be back in a public school, one without religious belief expectations.

My excitement returned as we discussed and debated many issues, including the present Viet Nam war. Aware of growing controversy over our military involvement, I read the history of Viet Nam's status as a French colony. The teacher, Mr. Bolt, a soft-spoken man with arms and shoulders toned like a weight lifter, soon became a friend, giving me confidence and encouragement. One day, he asked if I had ever thought of becoming a teacher. Surprised, it became another affirmation.

After becoming more settled, Naomi and I discussed purchasing a house. Naomi, once vowing to never marry a "preacher," seemed relieved I might not ever return to seminary.

Baby Lisa added to our joy, a beautiful little girl whom people often claimed looked like the "Gerber Baby." We were happy with new freedom to explore and question without the turmoil of church opposition. Like many of the Christian Reformed men who worked with me at Keeler, I purchased a pipe. With that, Naomi was *not* pleased!

On the evening of April 4th, working in the noisy machine shop with our small radios nearby, we heard a special report; Dr. Martin Luther King, Jr. had been shot and killed in Memphis, Tennessee. Stunned, I began to feel increased numbness as cheers of celebration rose from several workers! More shouts of jubilation rumbled throughout adjacent departments. A few years ago, I too, would have felt the same way. Choking with emotion, I shut off my machine, and quietly walked over the oil stained floorboards, amid jovial workers, to be alone in the rest room. I sat alone in a booth sobbing in shame.

For the college class, I read Karl Marx's Communist Manifesto, along with writings from his friend Frederick Engel. I thought, "How silly, I hated communism so much but never read any of these sources!" I wrote a paper on communism, which Mr. Bolt loved so much he asked me to present a class lecture and discussion on the subject. I did, and it went well. Again, he encouraged me to move toward the direction of speaking and teaching.

On May 7th, again while working the night shift, I listened to another radio program in which a local Methodist pastor, Rev. Donald Strobe, was a guest. He addressed the current debate in religious circles over a book called, "God is Dead!" Shutting off my machine to hear better, I heard Rev. Strobe explain the phrase meaning that many ideas about God *were* erroneous. He said Nietzsche was correct 100 years ago, when he wrote that the idea of a transcendent God was incompatible with current worldviews. If such ideas were erroneous and unscientific, they ought to be discarded. *That* God is dead! The next morning, after little sleep, I called Rev. Strobe's office to schedule an appointment.

I met Rev. Strobe in his comfortable office in the large downtown, First United Methodist Church. A tall, middle-aged man with a clear speaking voice, he seemed pleased his radio discussion brought my response. After discussing the "God is Dead" theme, he asked about me: my life, questions, thinking and desires. I shared a quick summary of my years at Bob Jones, getting married, going to the Baptist Seminary, and now having a small child. When I paused, he looked directly at me and firmly suggested I look at other seminaries and pursue a goal to either teach or become a minister. He claimed I would be a natural for such vocations. He then suggested I meet his good friend, Rev. Donald Lester, pastor of another large downtown church called Westminster Presbyterian. Realizing I had been Baptist, he felt their government might be more appealing. Methodists, he explained, were more hierarchical with a more centralized government. They appointed bishops to watch over districts, enforcing church edicts and rules. Presbyterians were more representative with democratic processes to enact and enforce church laws.

Two days later, after calling for an appointment, I met Pastor Donald Lester in his church office. Nervous but excited with anticipation, I wandered, wide-eyed, into the large, stone steeple building. Meeting the secretary, she pleasantly led me to the pastor's office. Getting up from his chair behind a paper-covered desk, surrounded by shelves of books and a four-door gray file, Pastor Lester heartily greeted me. He and Rev. Strobe had discussed my coming. Pastor Lester, a shorter man than Pastor Strobe, in his early 40's with a receding hairline, exuded energy and confidence and talked quickly with a no nonsense tone. Apparently feeling a sense of urgency, or excited over the prospect, he soon picked up his phone and called McCormick Seminary in Chicago. After chatting with someone he knew, he turned and asked when I could visit! I stammered out a possible date after looking at my small pocket calendar. I also would need to check with my wife. He then phoned Rev. Strobe who agreed to arrange a tour and interview for us at Garrett Seminary on the nearby Northwestern University Campus in Evanston.

More alive and hopeful than in weeks, I could hardly wait to get home and tell Naomi the exiting news! I drove slowly, relishing the positive, almost unbelievable developments. It was like God or Destiny, *had not* forgotten me. I walked proudly inside our little house to share what seemed to be a miracle for new opportunities. Busy with Lisa and house chores, Naomi was justifiably less than enthusiastic. After summarizing my time with Dr. Lester, she looked up from her home work clothes and rolled her eyes as if to say, "Oh my, not again!"

In a few days, however, after more questions and discussions with each other, we wrapped up Lisa and drove to Chicago to visit the two seminaries. Maneuvering through the most congested traffic ever seen, we arrived at McCormick Seminary, located near downtown Chicago. A great site for learning inner-city work, we both felt uncomfortable and boxed in. Before entering a building or even an apartment door, we needed to give identification through an intercom. The old brick apartment housing units were well guarded. With our rural roots and small baby, we were not ready for such a transition.

We stayed overnight in a suburban Howard Johnson motel northwest of the inner city. The next morning, we visited Garrett Seminary at Northwestern University. A beautiful and open suburban campus, we felt more comfortable. The enthusiastic dean promised I could easily transfer with Rev. Strobe's recommendation, holding up a copy he had already received!

"You mean I won't need to take another year or so of undergraduate studies?"

He replied, "No, you already had quite an education at Bob Jones!"

The following week, with Rev. Lester's credit card and more pre-arranged recommendations, we visited Louisville Presbyterian Seminary in Louisville, Kentucky. The new campus, south of the city in an upper class neighborhood, impressed us but the setting seemed too remote. I wanted to be closer if not even within a larger city. I wanted such an experience, always being such a "country boy." After a guided tour by a staff member and talking with a welcoming instructor, we returned to Grand Rapids.

Weary and rushed, I realized September would come quickly. Which seminary should I choose? This could not be another passing fling. Lingering doubts remained. "Do I really want this?" Wanting to slow down, for the sake of Naomi and our five-month old baby, I cancelled seminary plans for September. I would work another year. Paid well, we could save money, visit more churches, take another class and see what might happen. It proved to be a wise decision.

With growing disinterest, I decided to sell the black police car and placed an ad in the newspaper. In one day, a man less than a mile away, came and bought it. Two days later we purchased a slightly used white 1967 Pontiac Catalina two door coup, which came with an automatic transmission and small sluggish V8 engine that could hardly outrun a Volkswagen. But Naomi was happy and I was relieved. A few days later I drove past the house of the man who purchased the Ford police car. He was cutting it up into a racecar!

I continued to work full time. That Autumn we even began talking again with some of our former Baptist Seminary friends. A few came to our "farm" for one of Naomi's delicious meals. I was surprised to learn others also doubted their "calls" and seemed more open to my new ideas. One guest was my good friend Matthew, who had dropped out of seminary shortly after I did, and began teaching math. Another couple, Frank and his wife, also came for supper. He too had quit seminary and now worked toward a new career. He'd resumed his smoking habit. Classmate and Keeler Brass coworker Sam had finished the Baptist seminary, and came with his wife for an evening. No longer angry or trying to "win me back," we renewed our friendship. One Sunday, we even returned with them to the Northland Baptist Church. Pastor Wood was actually kind to me, perhaps relieved I was no longer a Baptist.

In October, with the seminary itch still scratching, I sent for an application from Pittsburgh Seminary. I had always admired Pittsburgh. In the 1950's, before interstate roads proliferated, my family had driven through Pittsburgh on winding and mountainous Route 19 while traveling to Florida. One of my first big cities, I loved its sweeping views of buildings, poking themselves up from surrounding hills as we came into the valley. Busy factories with puffing smoke stacks hugged shorelines along the Allegany and Ohio rivers. We puckered our noses from sulfuric odors as we crossed the bridges to continue south. Some of my relatives, Ernie and Caroline Bold, with their two boys, lived nearby in Allison Park. Wanting to be in a larger city, but not as large as Chicago, maybe this would be the place, I pondered. The application arrived and I put it into my desk drawer. I kept thinking.

A few days later, Dr. Lester called. He had another friend for us to meet, one who also graduated from Bob Jones University before I attended. Surprised, we soon were on Interstate 96 to Ann Arbor, on our way to meet another Presbyterian minister named Rev. Ernest Campbell. Rev. Campbell graduated from Bob Jones University in 1945, and went on to Princeton Seminary and later became ordained a Presbyterian minister. In a few days, he would leave for New York City to become pastor of the prestigious Riverside Church.

In the large, grey stoned University Presbyterian Church, Naomi and I sat in his office amid books packed in boxes for shipment. Rev. Campbell, tall, thin and a seasoned-looking minister, stood and greeted us with his white shirtsleeves, rolled up from packing books. Given a summary from Dr. Lester, Rev.

Campbell began asking questions about our journey. "Where did you grow up? Why do you want to return to a seminary?" Impressed with his willingness to meet us while preparing to move, we talked for around 30 minutes. I expressed my lingering sense of inferiority--a weak background in education with a lack of serious college studies at Bob Jones University, a school I now considered racist with very conservative politics. Rev. Campbell responded with a tone I could almost hear resonating from a pulpit:

"David, your Bob Jones experience ought never to be considered a failure or something for which you offer apologies. Your experiences there gave you valuable insights and gifts that others did not learn. Never apologize for the events of your past, but see them as important steps up the ladder toward maturity."

He then encouraged me to consider returning to seminary. I drove home dreaming of being in a church denomination broad enough where I could question and seek answers in freedom with openness of thought.

We began to regularly attend the large downtown Grand Rapids Westminster Presbyterian Church. With wonderful nursery care overseen by a registered nurse, we enjoyed the more formal Sunday services. I help conduct a few "Children Worship" times suggested by Dr. Lester. He asked me to lead in a few congregational prayers. The strongest impact came from the adult discussion group. Made up of mostly professionals—a lawyer, dentist and business owners with their spouses, we sat in a circle discussing various books. On our first visit, they continued a discussion of Keith Miller's current bestseller, "Taste of New Wine." I found myself quickly jumping in. They suggested I might be part of this "new wine." By the second week, the attorney turned to me and asked, "Dave, have you ever thought about attending a Seminary?" By then, I had become the go-to person if they had Bible questions, especially location of verses. They considered my Biblical knowledge rare among themselves!

A few weeks later, Dr. Lester called and invited me back to his office. We chatted and went out for lunch. He asked again about my desires for seminary. I shared comments from the adult class and told him I was thinking of Pittsburgh.

He replied, "I wouldn't recommend Pittsburgh Seminary for you. It's located near the very conservative Presbyterian Lay Committee which creates a strong reactive presence in the Church."

"Maybe my background might help," I thought.

My continual hunger for more "spiritual" discussions and knowledge of religions continued. I could not stop dreaming of finishing a seminary experience. I wanted to be in a place where new ideas and questions could be openly discussed, debated, and studied without charges of "heresy" or "abandonment of the faith." I hoped to find it among Presbyterians. I yearned to learn more answers from the question, "Who am I?"

Becoming Presbyterian in Pittsburgh

"I will not allow schooling to kill my education."
- Mark Twain

In early spring 1969, I sent my application to Pittsburgh Seminary. Two weeks later Naomi and I drove to visit the campus and talk with staff members. The registrar, a reddish-looking, athletic older man with sharp wit and a direct manner, reminded me of Dad. Dr. Jackson sat with my papers in hand, and looking up said, "David, you are just the kind of student we like to see!"

"Why?" I asked, already feeling a flush of pleasure.

"Because you are interested in helping others rather than just gaining a place of authority!"

He also added, "Since your previous work was done at Bob Jones and then an unaccredited Baptist Seminary, you will not be eligible for any academic awards."

The seminary boasted new apartments with an attractive Day Care center staffed by trained personnel, perfect for Lisa. Naomi accepted a teaching invitation in a nearby suburban elementary school. Everything seemed to becoming together. Deep relief and confidence filled my whole body and mind as we returned to Grand Rapids. We would be moving to Pittsburgh in late August.

A few weeks passed and surprisingly Naomi told me she was pregnant! Sitting down in a daze, I stared in shock and disbelief. Now what? The school in Pittsburgh that hired Naomi cancelled her contract. Embarrassed we had been so careless, and with a bit of shame, I called Dr. Lester and shared the news. He asked me to come in. When I arrived, I walked dejectedly into his office. Seated across from him I bluntly said, "We can't go to Pittsburgh Seminary, Dr. Lester. Naomi is pregnant. She will have no job there. We don't have that much money saved."

"Dave," he asked, "do you really want to attend seminary again?"

"Yes!" I replied. "But without Naomi working, how could we afford it?"

"Just go!" he answered. "It will never be any easier and as a church, we promise to do all we can to help make it successful."

I returned home upon a rising cloud of hope, again.

In early September 1969, after packing our supplies into a U-Haul truck, we headed east to Pittsburgh Seminary. My parents surprised us by driving out to help with the move, a most appreciated gesture. I hoped for a healing in their disappointments with me. After a long hot day of driving, without air conditioning, we turned into the campus. A few yards in on the driveway, we were forced to stop by protesting students. Finally, we were allowed to pass and found our apartment, Dad and Mom helping us to move in. They stayed the night in the adjourning apartment but silently left the next morning without saying goodbye. Noticing their empty room and missing car, another wave of loneliness washed over me, realizing anew I had failed both their expectations in career and religious beliefs.

Other married couples, some with children, soon arrived. Our living atmosphere quickly changed. No longer in our secluded little country home, inner city noise dominated our space. A half block away, city bus brakes screeched to a stop at the Highland Avenue intersection. Nauseous blasts then arose from roaring engines as they slowly crawled back into the street. Noisy garbage trucks below our bedroom window awakened us mornings as droning hydraulics hoisted refuse and banged them into metal garbage caverns. I parked our white Pontiac along the street curb and someone soon walked past and dug a deep line in the paint. Our former country life had ended as we adjusted to an inner city.

Most students, staff and teachers seemed kind and open as I began classes. Many students, however, spoke with sharp criticism of apparent injustices and wrongs in the seminary, church and society. Early in the semester, protesting students took over the Seminary President's office, urging immediate changes in the Seminary's policies. Slang, swearing and cursing were commonly used in conversations and classes. Students used such words to describe our government and military along with the church and seminary administration. One day, early in the semester, a student urged me to join a Sunday morning anti-war demonstration in "front of one of those big rich churches we are sure to 'piss off!'"

I was shocked. I too disagreed with many government policies, including the Viet Nam war, but I was proud the seminary at least allowed such protest. I was proud the seminary had recruited African American and women students in record numbers that autumn. But the degree of anger and disgust about so much in the church and society I could not share. I had come to the Seminary after months of struggle, after giving up a good income and disappointing family members.

I heard many students say they had no interest in entering a religious profession but had come in order to gain draft deferments. One student, raised in a Presbyterian home, wrote a scathing article published in the seminary paper attacking the "immorality" of building a new chapel. He claimed the golden cock on the steeple signified Judas' betrayal. Drama seemed to be everywhere. "No wonder," I thought, "Dean Jackson said I was the kind of student they wanted!" At times, I felt like one of the few happy and contented ones. The drama certainly made for a lively campus atmosphere. Thus began my walk into a church denomination becoming more involved in social action and justice issues.

Amid several student actions and attitudes, in contrast to the Baptist Seminary, I remained honored and content to be there. I loved roaming among the many good books housed within the large quiet Barbour library. Walking through the large lobby, I often paused in awe before the late, great theologian Karl Barth's desk. His son Marcus then taught New Testament and I had signed up for his seminar on the book of Acts.

I soon discovered I was far ahead of most in knowledge of the Hebrew and Greek languages. Presbyterians only required three semester hours of Greek and no Hebrew. I still longed to learn where the Bible came from, and how. I wanted to learn about "higher literary criticism," a phrase often spoken with disdain at Grand Rapids Baptist and Bob Jones. I was surprised and disappointed when the registrar told me I had studied enough Bible. They wanted me to study further ethical and social issues, giving me opportunities to "catch up," I suppose, on some of the social debates raging within the Presbyterian Church.

I dug in the best I could. A student friend named Chuck claimed he could set his clock as I walked past his apartment each morning to classes or the library. Like a farmer doing daily chores, I began reading books at a faster pace than ever. I felt at home in my small, quiet library study carrel but seldom saw other students around me. Many seemed busy planning weekends protesting war and civil rights unfairness. I wondered when and where they studied? Why were they here?

In the student lounge, I heard one of the faculty teachers, Lynn Hinds, had graduated from a Baptist Seminary. Lynn taught a preaching class while working as a radio and TV announcer at a Pittsburgh station. A handsome man with a deep clear voice, Lynn was energetic, witty and fun to be around. During my second year, he put all his religious and theological books on tables for pick up. He had decided to "leave the ministry," a popular choice in those years.

Before he quit, I took a preaching class from Mr. Hinds who co-taught with a quiet, Episcopalian teacher called Fr. Jack. Mr. Hinds wore leisure clothes with open collars and no tie while the Fr. Jack wore black suits with stiff white clergy collars. I loved the contrast. Centered on the book of Hosea, we were to study, explain and preach it. When my turn came to speak and I nervously finished, both teachers commended me as a model of how to interpret and preach! One of the student leaders commented:

"This is one of the best examples I have ever seen and heard of weaving in and out of a passage, applying it to today's problems."

The comment became another affirmation of my decision to be where I was.

Amazed at the widespread smoking, fresh pipe tobacco smoke often swirled into lazy gray clouds over heads and around class discussions. Dr. Barth smoked an old tooth worn pipe, giving one the distinct feeling of being in a room of deep and reflective thinkers.

In one class on contemporary culture, mellow tobacco smoke became mixed with pungent marijuana. I smelled the unique odor as the "weed" passed around from student to student. It came to me. I took a quick inhale before passing it along, much like being in a Holy Communion service. I felt a bit of pride in doing it, a sort of a rebellion in breaking the law. It added to the excitement of being in such a place where I could inhale and pass along my first, and only marijuana joint! Meanwhile the teacher continued on, undisturbed.

Pittsburgh Seminary also allowed alcoholic beverages. The professor of "Christ in Contemporary Culture," invited a group of us to his suburban home for a picnic where kegs of beer were available for everyone. Oh, the days of revolution and rebellion: throwing Frisbees, smoking pot and drinking beer!

A more serious professor, Dr. Paul Lapp, taught my archeology class. Harvard trained, physically fit and strong, he led several archeological digs in lands around the Eastern Mediterranean Sea. I found his assigned readings boring but loved him as a person and teacher. One day, standing before us with his broad shoulders, he said archeological evidence showed Israel as always part of the ancient Palestinian area. The Israelites had never migrated into the ancient Palestinian area from the East or South as the Bible stories depicted. He said there was no archaeological data to give evidence the Israelites had ever lived in Egypt, or came north through an Exodus. Dr. Lapp also said archeological evidence showed the Israelites as intermarrying with other peoples of the area as well as adopting many of their idolatry and religious forms. The idea never left my mind as I pondered, "If not, then what do the stories mean? Were the Israelites not more special than others around them?"

By late October, as our dwindling financial resources caused more stress, a phone call came from Dr. Lester. Hearing and feeling our concern, a generous check quickly arrived in the mail! I decided to join the seminary Preaching Association, much like the Baptist one, and began speaking nearly every weekend in various churches, receiving helpful stipends. They also gave me an excuse not to attend "protest rallies." Unlike speaking in more fundamentalist Baptist Churches, I enjoyed my new freedom. The resumed speaking seemed to help bring more stability to our lives. Perhaps I wasn't as far off track as we previously wondered. Both Naomi and I seemed more settled about our future, and our love deepened.

Still, with financial pressures mounting, I decided after the semester ended, I would cut back and attend part-time. Naomi was near to having our second child, and Pittsburgh, a steel-producing city, was full of machine shops. I would seek a job and stretch out my seminary requirements for as long as it took. Almost as soon as I made the decision, however, Dr. Harold

Scott, a Seminary administrator and friend of Dr. Lester, called me into his office. His staff helped to provide field experiences for students. Commending me on my studies and positive reports received from weekend speaking, he suggested I visit a small church near suburban McKeesport. On the southeastern side of Pittsburgh, the church was located in an area called Boston. He thought they might accept me as a student pastor until I finished seminary. They might even provide us with a house to live in along with a fairly substantial stipend! I would be responsible for preaching on weekends, visiting the sick and other duties, but no more than ten hours a week. I was stunned, it seemed too good to be true!

With no second thoughts, I knew I would rather do this than return to a machine shop. I rushed back to the apartment and, after sharing the news, Naomi and I dressed Lisa, jumped into the car and drove the 10 or so miles through city traffic to the small suburb of Boston. The United Presbyterian Church set a hundred yards or so from the historic Youghiogheny River, just off the main road. I would offer a trial service and sermon the first Sunday of January.

Without sonograms, Naomi's doctor kept telling her she was carrying a very large baby. Finally, hardly able to drive to the doctor, he took a quick x-ray. We would have twins! We spent the next couple days scrambling to move across the hall into an extra bedroom apartment. We celebrated Lisa's birthday on December 20 and the next morning, drove to the huge West Penn Hospital for the induced delivery. On December 21, 1969, Naomi gave birth to our twins! First came Dorinda and a few minutes later, Dawn. Standing behind a glass window in an adjacent room, I watched their amazing births. Dorinda slipped out quickly, crying and screaming while Dawn, flipped backwards by the umbilical cord, came much slower in breech condition. Feeling paralyzed by anxiety at Dawn's delay, her lifeless body finally appeared. The staff quickly began pumping her ingested lungs. Suddenly I heard her first screams as a nurse caught me wilting to the floor, my head spinning. I faintly heard the doctor declare, "We have two healthy babies but are worried about their father!" As with Lisa two years earlier, we spent a wonderful Christmas in a new hospital maternity ward.

Our kind relatives from nearby Allison Park, Ernie and Caroline Bold, came to care for Lisa and a few days later helped bring Naomi and the twins back to the apartment. It was a bitter, cold, wintry day. We soon became a seminary fascination. My archeology professor, Dr. Lapp, also with twins two years older, gave us clothes and supplies. The Bolds continued their support and Caroline's mother, who lived with them, Mom's Aunt Catherine, gave us paid diaper service.

Though short on money, in graduate school with a family of three children, I felt little, if any disadvantage. The healthy twins, a beautiful daughter Lisa, and now I had an opportunity to work as a student pastor! All things again seemed to be coming together. My heart overflowed with affirmation.

I began work as student pastor, overseen and mentored by a neighboring pastor and the seminary field education office. The church provided an efficient secretary who did weekly bulletin preparations. In spring, the congregation invited us to move into their parsonage. Accepting the offer and giving paint advice, carpet colors and other suggestions, they prepared for our move that summer. We would miss the companionship of the seminary but the new home gave us a more settled place. We quickly made new friends, some with whom we remain in contact today.

The experience at the Boston United Presbyterian Church set a definite direction for our lives and my form of ministry. The church not only gave us financial security, but also a bridge to choose the parish for my life's work. The people as a whole were supportive and kind. Naomi was immediately welcomed and loved for her practical gifts and friendly personality. People told me, "She makes me feel like we've been friends for a long time." Our daughters became featured attractions as the church became a new, supportive family for us all. A board member's wife gave me a new clerical shirt to wear. "We just love you!" she said, handing it to me while I stood in shock.

Boston introduced me to sharing common problems of many people: crumpling marriages, young people with terminal illnesses, alcoholism, sudden tragic accidents and death. I began visiting hospitals and officiating funerals.

The last year in Seminary sped by quickly. I received valuable support, wisdom and advice from teachers. Some came to speak in Boston and helped with special services.

My classes, however, continued to deal mostly with social issues. Discussion of ancient teachings seemed unimportant. One older student felt a lack in spirituality so he invited some of us to join together for Bible reading, discussion and prayer. I quickly lost interest and my past studies of Greek and Hebrew languages went unused. I wanted to take a class on the Resurrection, as I heard the teacher helped students question whether or not the event was actually literal. I inquired and was told, "You don't need it!"

True to my style, I continued reading many unassigned magazines and books from the library. I studied Presbyterian Church polity and learned how to use Books of Order and Confession to guide church boards in planning and decision-making. I took the newly required Ordination Exams, four tests in various areas of ministerial leadership, and was one of the few who passed the first time.

I also began receiving more invitations for pastoral positions while some lifetime Presbyterian students were turned down. Some churches said they felt drawn to me after reading I graduated from Bob Jones University. Puzzled, I became more thankful for my varied and sundry diversions along the path toward ordination. Maybe Rev. Ernest Campbell was right, as he had told me, "Never apologize for your past."

At Pittsburgh Seminary, however, I was thankful to learn Biblical passages, which aimed directly at social issues of the day: racism, war, and poverty. However, I naively assumed the social positions of Pittsburgh Seminary would be more common in the churches. The Presbyterians became our home. I felt comfortable and proud to be among them. They seemed to offer a broad range in beliefs. I felt free to question things as they were as I grew to understand more.

Our commencement featured Rev. Dr. William Sloan Coffin as speaker, a recognized leader in the anti-war movement who then was chaplain at Yale. The service was conducted in the huge East Liberty Presbyterian Church a few blocks south of the Seminary. The church towered over the city area as a majestic gothic cathedral, atypical of most Presbyterian Churches. Nearly overcome by the architecture, I soon became mesmerized by Coffin's speaking style and content. He gave one of his powerful denunciations against the country's war machine, sapping resources from public schools and infrastructure.

My mother surprisingly drove down for the event and joined Naomi's father, who sat next to Naomi a few rows behind me. They embarrassed Naomi with a few outbursts of disbelief during Coffin's forceful anti-war address!

On June 5, 1971, I was ordained to the ministry in Grand Rapids, Michigan at the Westminster Presbyterian Church. Pastor Lester gave the sermon and asked me the questions for ordination. As a gift, the church gave me a black pulpit robe. I had never worn such vestments. I remembered Joe Valestak at the Baptist seminary saying he liked pastors who wore robes. It gave them a sense they were speaking on behalf of God and not just themselves.

Pastor Lester and the Westminster Church had remained our supportive and gracious friends throughout our two years in Pittsburgh. They had sent hundreds of dollars to a family most members hardly knew. Our new Boston friends from the small church, Ron and Karen Howell, drove to Grand Rapids to be part of the ordination. None of my family came as around 20 people sat in the front of the several hundred-seat sanctuary. A deep sense of relief overwhelmed me. My formal education had ended as I entered full time employment as an ordained minister. I could now moderate church boards, administer the sacraments, and conduct weddings and funerals. And, hopefully, do more thinking about who I was and the one we referred to as God.

With increased attendances, I began working full time at the Boston United Presbyterian Church. A kind Methodist neighbor pastor, Rev. Hollenbeck, became a mentor to me. An experienced pastor with a full head of beautiful, silver hair, he helped me prepare pre-wedding meetings for couples and gave practical advice in conducting funerals. Our two congregations, half a mile apart, near the banks of Youghiogheny River, shared in Lenten and Advent services. We met often for exchange and prayer in each one's office. Once after we concluded our time of coffee and conversation in his old church study, he told me he had never felt such closeness with a fellow minister. I was humbly overwhelmed with confidence and peace in my new life. At times, however, I deeply missed the open country without the constant smell from steel-making coke ovens.

The pastoral role, however, continued to remain mostly an enigma to me. My mantra became what Dr. Matthews once told me in the Baptist Seminary: "Just love the people for it will help cover a multitude of 'sins!'" My vision was to keep reading and studying, preparing talks and papers to share.

My ordination titled me a "Teacher Elder." My pastor's office had an engraved plaque on the door calling it "Pastor's Study," and that's what I expected to do. I envisioned myself teaching people spiritual and life truths through public worship, conducting funerals and weddings, and taking time to meet them privately in homes and my office. The people, through elected members ordained to be "ruling elders," were to govern the church, looking after practical matters of upkeep and fundraising. However, I still remained unsure about what I ought to teach!

I still had more questions than answers. I discovered an immediate disdain for much of the needed administrative work and fundraising, passing off as much as possible to the "Ruling Elders." My foremost desire remained to learn and live the role of "spiritual leadership."

Thanksgiving arrived and our guests were Naomi's father and mother with her 11-year-old brother Steve. We recorded movies on an old Kodak camera Dad had given us, movies of the twins and Lisa with them, one showing Naomi's father proudly holding the twins. A few days later, early in the morning, our phone rang on the nightstand. It was Naomi's mother Mamie. Victor had died suddenly a few hours earlier of a massive heart attack. He was 51. In shock and grief, I sat in disbelief on the edge of the bed feeling helpless and useless as Naomi cried in deep sorrow.

December, once a month of birthday celebrations, became a month of mourning. After a few days, we traveled north to Olean, New York for the funeral. Victor looked so young in the casket. The funeral was conducted in the small country church he pastored before moving to Sherman, and burial in the adjacent cemetery where graves had been given as farewell gifts.

We celebrated Christmas with an aura of sadness and loss lingering around us. Shortly after the New Year, I received a call from a man named Mike Campsey. Mike chaired the church's pastoral search committee from a Presbyterian church in Claysville, Pennsylvania. The Claysville church was located in a small rural town nestled in the country. Mike said I was on his "short list" of prospects, coming highly recommended as a candidate from one of my student friends at Pittsburgh Seminary. He and the pulpit committee wanted to hear and watch me lead a worship service.

Chapter 11

Back Home to the Country

The ache for home lives in all of us, the safe place
where we can go as we are and not be questioned.
- Maya Angelou

On February 28, 1972, we moved to our new home in Claysville, Pennsylvania. I became the first pastor of two congregations after merged by Washington Presbytery into one, Claysville United Presbyterian Church. Set within the Appalachian foothills, the rural village was half way between Washington, Pennsylvania and Wheeling, West Virginia. The 20-year-old manse was built on the lawn 25 feet below the church. Both were half way up a steep hill with several homes on each side of the narrow village road. About a quarter mile south of the village of 1500 people, meandered the busy and noisy Interstate 70 through the valley. With a financial package nearly one third more, I felt relief from our financial stress.

Unable to meet the part time secretary before arriving, the second morning I climbed the cement steps and through the old wooden church side door to meet her in a makeshift office. Having a very efficient secretary in Boston, this one seemed overwhelmed. A few months earlier her 36-year-old husband had suddenly died from a heart attack. Left distraught, with two teenage daughters, the former pastor hired her for a couple hours a week to print Sunday bulletins.

Founded in 1820, the present building was erected in 1912. Covered with red brick, it was well maintained with manicured lawns, priceless stained glass windows and a theater shaped, rounded sanctuary. Speakers could easily feel connected with everyone. Next to the speaker's chair, as if to serve as reminder, a magnificent 25-foot high tiffany stained glass window portrayed Jesus holding a lamb in one arm and a staff in the other.

During my first weeks I did not always wear my black pulpit robe. After a couple months, Jo, one of the Pulpit Committee members, asked me why I didn't always wear a robe, speaking on behalf of a few who wished I would. Jo, a beautiful and trim older woman, married to the village doctor and mayor, offered to purchase me a lighter color robe if I would wear it. I said I would think about it. A few days later a new white robe hung on my office door.

My office once served as the "Lady's Missionary Parlor" located atop a round tower reached by climbing winding dark oak stairs. Large and comfortable with a small gas stove, several smaller stained glass windows circled the room displaying the church's 200-year history. At first, it felt very comfortable and impressive as a quiet place where I could read, study and pray. I imagined hours I would spend, as did my predecessors, studying theology and philosophy, writing and preparing sermons. That vision lasted only a few days.

Quickly I became distracted by many parish expectations of visitations and administration. I flung myself into the role the best I could, trying to balance study and action, the latter immediately tipping the scales downward. Within weeks, I began doubting my choice. Was this really my place, my home, even my calling? I began reconsidering requirements to teach school.

On invitation, I spent an evening with an older, single member who lived three houses up the hill from us. A retired schoolteacher, she was a life-long church member and spinster. A short, gray-haired lady, she spoke in a low pitched, gruff tone, one I suspected easily could intimidate students. Her home could have passed for an enlarged dollhouse. Entering through a freshly painted porch door, I found myself in her perfectly adorned living room. Several old antique cups, saucers and dolls sat in a wood framed curio hutch along the wall, while the spotless furniture rested in perfect places. After greetings, I sat in a padded antique chair across from her on a floral patterned sofa. After sharing greetings, tea and small talk about my family, she stunned me saying, "Rev. Persons, if you and Naomi are not Republican Party members, you will have a difficult time here!" Despair and confusion swept through me. At Pittsburgh Seminary, the few Republicans seemed out of place. I didn't argue or criticize her but a sense of "what have I done?" swept over me. I walked home, chilly with loneliness.

The roads around Claysville were very narrow, meandering through valleys, along ridges and over Appalachian Mountain foothills. Picturesque valleys boasted several historic covered bridges, and small family farms still remained active, with barns and fields making the area look quite pastoral. One older member and his retired teacher wife owned a sheep farm to which we took our children a few times to see newborn lambs. I loved the area's beauty and charm, but my heart was not finding the home I had expected.

One strong sign of hope was the pulpit committee chair member named Mike. Both he and his wife Judy were smart and progressive thinkers, and both quickly became trusted friends. Mike stopped in often to check on how things were going. A couple inches shorter than I, with black hair and dark skin, he often invited us with our children to their beautiful home, set in a sweeping valley surrounded by sheep and riding horses. They had a beautiful black Doberman Pincher, which was well trained and performed numerous tricks. With two small children, they became a family of refuge and release.

Expectations of many members included daily visits or "calls" to hospitalized members. I limited most to one a week, unless critical, as hospitals were located in Washington, Wheeling, and often in Pittsburgh. I soon subscribed to a theological tape service called "Thesis," and after installing a plug-in player, listened to lectures as I traveled miles and hours for short hospital visits.

A few months later, I began taking a day each week to study at the historic Washington and Jefferson College library in nearby Washington. There, I could study without interruptions amid welcomed racks of books. Once, I was admitted to the old archives room where I read 18th century documents, some hand written by George Washington who demanded squatters be removed from area lands he owned.

My friend Mike had graduated from Bethany College in Bethany, West Virginia. Located about 12 miles west over backcountry roads, I added it to my study sanctuaries. There, I enjoyed being alone to read, write, and look up books.

Still, I continued to ask myself what my pastoral role included and how to manage it. How could I teach, as my ordained title stated? Why did it include administrator, visitation leader, and community representative? What exactly was I supposed to teach? Was it the Church constitutions called the Book of Order and the Confessions of the Church? Or should I spend more time trying to teach the Bible? As far as the Bible, I still had more questions than answers.

As I conducted more funerals, I realized I did not even know what to say or believe in regard to death, so I just followed the Presbyterian "Worship Book" which proclaimed:

> "Our help is in the name of the Lord, who made heaven earth. God is our refuge and strength, a very present help in trouble. Therefore, we will not fear."

The words seemed to contain comfort and a sense of hope, but how could one know?

I shared my doubts with a fellow Presbyterian pastor in nearby West Alexander named David Campbell. Only four or five miles west along Interstate 70, David was a tall, older man. With thinning gray hair, he had served many years as a Presbyterian pastor. We soon became good friends. He responded to my question saying, "When I conduct a funeral and graveside service, I honestly tell myself I do not know what happens." I appreciated his refreshing honesty but it still left me wondering. The Baptists always seemed to know, or at least said they did. Wasn't I supposed to know? Was I lying? I began to more seriously question the Biblical miracles. Missing such discussions in both seminaries, I wondered how to interpret these stories.

My first year, I conducted a funeral for the proverbial "town drunkard." Shunned by most in the community, the funeral director, a member of our church, asked if I would speak a few words of comfort to his family. He told me the man had quite the irresponsible reputation as drunkard and womanizer. I accepted and found myself speaking of a possible universal salvation for all people, saying I appreciated the idea from the Unitarian Universalists. It felt right and I enjoyed sharing the ideas, which seemed to bring comfort to the worried family members. I shared my thoughts that evening with Naomi who expressed her disagreement and worry about where I might be heading, again. The retired teacher up the street who warned me about not being Republican, heard about my talk and agreed.

The first summer in 1972, we drove to visit Naomi's mother and brother Steve in Gaithersburg, Maryland. There, they continued to struggle adjusting to Victor's death. Mamie was restless and wanted to move and find a job. I took Steve sailing on a nice blue lake that was part of their apartment compound.

We returned to Claysville pulling a U-Haul trailer load of Mamie's furniture she wanted to give us. A hot, humid summer day, we sweated profusely in our non-air-conditioned car. The Pontiac overheated climbing a long mountain toward the Pennsylvania Turnpike. Just as we began its descent, the engine started smoking and then seized and stalled from extreme heat. Wondering what to do, we luckily coasted down a few miles and veered off a ramp into a service station. A grease covered mechanic from the garage walked out to check the car engine. "Yep, your engine is frozen" he said in his country boy accent. "Let it to cool for about an hour and we'll see if we can start it." An hour later, all five of us weary and tired, the girls complaining, scrapping and worried, the mechanic returned. He climbed up inside the hood like he'd done it many times, and began pulling and pushing on the fan to loosen the frozen crankshaft. Every few seconds he hollered to me, "Now try it!" In about a minute, the engine began smoking and coughing as it sparked back alive and we were soon off. Arriving home late and anxious for bed, I suddenly received a call. A young man from the church lay seriously ill in a Pittsburgh Hospital. Would I please come to pray!

Arriving at the hospital, weary and dazed from the adventurous trip home, I walked in through a sheet surrounded ICU room to see the son of a church family dying in a bed. In his 20's and newly married, he had been diagnosed just days earlier with acute leukemia. I stumbled out a few words with a short prayer after reading a verse about God's comforting presence. Opening my eyes, I looked down and saw him gasping for life and beginning dying convulsions. Overwhelmed by the sight, I became nauseated by the shocking scene, feeling dizzy and unstable. A nurse caught me as I began to go down and helped guide me back into the waiting area. Deeply embarrassed and in sorrow for the family and myself, I felt helpless, lonely and completely unqualified for such a job.

As a nurse waited with me, the crying family soon appeared saying their son had died. After more weeping by all, the father surprisingly broke the silence and said,

"Well, some help you were, Pastor! We call for you to bring us comfort and here we are comforting you!"

After a long, awkward pause, he and the family began to laugh with more tears mixed into the sad and surreal scene. Later, the family became our most loyal and supportive friends. Their surviving son, a Viet Nam veteran named Jerry, began calling me his "new brother."

A few weeks later a similar situation occurred in the Washington Hospital ICU unit. A 35-year man lay dying from a heart attack. His family asked me to stop in and pray, as if I might be their one last remaining hope. As I prayed over what I assumed were his last hours, again I became sweaty and dizzy. I turned and walked out making it to the nearest restroom where I splashed my face with cold water and began to cry in embarrassment. Discouraged, I shared the incidents with an older medical doctor in the congregation, Doc Hutchison. In his early 80's, he told me many young doctors experience similar reactions early in their careers. "It's a sign," he said, "of having a heart of kindness and compassion." I felt a little better.

In early January, an older retired farmer told us about a nice place to stay for two or three weeks in Clearwater Beach, Florida. Located along the beach, it would cost only $50.00 a week for a small efficiency apartment. Naomi and I decided to go as the January cold deepened.

Before leaving, Naomi went for blood tests and returned with news we both suspected; she was again pregnant. Money wasn't the issue now but Naomi expressed feeling already confined to the home with three young daughters. I had promised to use protection. I contritely vowed to get a housemaid after the baby arrived so she could at least teach as a substitute. I also vowed to get a vasectomy, a growing choice during those years.

With memories of my 1950's family trips, we drove to Florida in early February. When we crossed the state line we stopped for fresh orange juice as my family had two decades earlier. The girls woke up and we exclaimed, "We are here, this is Florida!" Two-year-old Dorinda, looking sleepy-eyed, squinted through the blinding sun to see the surrounding palm trees and asked, "Where? Where is it?"

We stayed on Clearwater Beach along the sandy shore in a wonderful little stone and cement walled hotel called, "The Castle." However, a record cold front moved in making it too frigid to swim or even walk along the ocean. Then Naomi's leg veins became sore and red. We found a doctor who diagnosed phlebitis. He suggested she do as little as possible and keep her leg raised. He recommended she also fly back to Pittsburgh rather than ride in the car.

Despite Florida's record cold weather and Naomi's diagnosis, I began feeling refreshed in body and mind. I recorded new ideas about classes I might teach and actions to take. I also read John Steinbeck's "Grapes of Wrath," amazed at the powerful way he made people think about social issues. Such relaxed reading habits would typify most of my vacations, often to Naomi's disappointment.

One Sunday, we attended a large interdenominational church, a short walk from the hotel. Naomi and I attended an adult discussion group while the girls went to a children's Sunday School. A woman in our class said, "When I hear someone tell me they have been born again, it just turns me off, it makes me sick!" It seemed so refreshingly honest, but again I asked, "What does it mean? If it doesn't mean instant access to a heavenly room over yonder, or a sudden decision to attend church and give tithes, rejecting various pleasures and supporting conservative politicians, what then does it mean?"

Naomi showed improvement over the three week stay and so we all rode home together. When we arrived back in Claysville, the girls seemed more excited than in reaching Florida. Naomi's veins, however, worsened and, feeling sick from the pregnancy, she spent hours each day with her feet raised.

On Wednesday, September 5th, after a record breaking hot August with no air-conditioning in our poorly ventilated home, our handsome son Eric was born. Words failed to express my delight! I was filled with pride and joy. Eric was a tall, beautiful baby, well formed, with bright blue eyes. From the hospital in Washington, I called Claysville to a church lady to report his birth. When I later returned home, a couple people stood along Main Street waiting with thumbs up! The next day, I called and scheduled a vasectomy.

The summer glow culminating with Eric's birth soon faded with the autumn church schedule. Another member sent a scolding letter attacking me for not making more home visits. I received such criticism almost weekly, even though I tried to budget "home visitations" eight to ten hours each week. In disgust, I stubbornly took a whole day off and drove back to the Bethany College Library to read. I went swimming in their beautiful pool and returned home refreshed and relaxed. I decided, if needed, I would begin the process to switch into another profession.

One of the older, middle-aged members, stopped by one day to check on my attitude and well-being. He knew I was criticized by a few but told me I was just what the church needed. Harry was a successful insurance salesman and looking at me with a wry smile asked, "So are you keeping up calling on all those older members?" Perhaps sensing some of my frustration, he then said, "Dave, if you ever want to become a salesman, I can get you in. I promise you will double your income in less than a year!" Surprised, I kept his option in mind.

In late February of 1974, I assisted in a funeral for a member's older relative. Afterward the member asked, "Would you like a new 10-speed bicycle?" It had come with their recent purchase of new furniture. "Why yes!" I replied and took it, still boxed, to assemble and ride up a valley road! Soon I rode regularly with encouragement from my friend, Mike. I pedaled it to make home calls and once along the beautiful, narrow tree and river lined road to Bethany.

Shortly after getting the bicycle, our aged organist suddenly died. Following her funeral, we hired a young organist to replace her. Jay, also a Viet Nam veteran, was an avid bicyclist. We took a few rides and became friends. We decided to take a trip. That summer, I purchased a used, but upgraded blue Kabuki bicycle and said to Jay, "Let's ride to my parents in New York!" In a few weeks we strapped some items on our bikes and took a three-day trip to my parents in Sherman. Even with poorly packed bikes, steep hills and disrespectful trucks and cars, I became hooked. Thus launched 20 years of bicycling, much of it spent with youth on weeklong journeys.

In autumn, I experienced a vivid dream in which I lived and worked in a church located in an area I would really want to live. The church was located near a large body of water, either a lake or ocean. Such dreams were rare, but this one remained and echoed in my mind. "Could such ever be possible?" I asked.

My confidence and satisfaction in the pastoral/community role grew stronger. Following the overflowing 1974 Christmas Eve service, a quiet but admired member said to me, "Dave, I hope you never leave Claysville, that you will stay until retirement!" On Christmas Day, Naomi reminded me it was our first Christmas in nine years of marriage when we remained home. We exchanged more gifts than ever as the girls' excitement with young Eric bubbled over amidst Naomi's beautifully decorated home.

In February 1975, the denomination flew me to Indiana University in Bloomington for a "Young Pastor's Conference." With temperatures falling to bitterly cold levels, I roomed with a former colleague from Pittsburgh Seminary, the one who had once commented how skillfully I wove together scriptures and life. A tall man, about six feet, five inches tall, he continued to give me encouragement. He suggested I had been too honest in questioning and irritating a professor we once shared. I could have received a higher grade, he maintained, if I was less questioning, especially the teacher's evangelical leanings. I doubted it.

One of the conference projects asked us to write an obituary to be published at the end of our lives. The obituary should list everything we wanted to accomplish before death. We were to "think big!" I sat alone in our room that evening and wrote my obituary at the desk. I saw seeing myself developing into a successful pastor, who in my early 50's, switched to politics and won a vote for a congressional seat in Washington! I served 10 years or so before finishing my career, teaching in a respected Seminary. It felt big and even somewhat possible for me. After reading my "obituary," the group surprisingly urged me to "go for it!" One young pastor said, "You even have a nice catchy name for politics!" After the remarks, the leader urged me to return and begin steps to move into a larger area with a more supportive congregation in order to live out my dreams. The group concurred saying, "Dave, go for it!" I sat in disbelief, yet delightfully hopeful.

I returned home charged and soaring with confidence. Pushed by the conference leader, I updated my dossier to see what might happen. A feeling of freedom came over me as I decided to give up more responsibilities and goals for Claysville's leadership to concentrate on my future. I asked Naomi to go with me for a week at the "Career Evaluation Center for Clergy" in Princeton, New Jersey. Spouses were welcomed to work together evaluating and planning their futures.

Naomi responded saying some believed I was discouraged, which surprised me. I realized frequent frustrations invaded my plans, but sensed a growing confidence about my future. The Indiana conference had emboldened me. I continued to question remaining in a place so rural and conservative. I anticipated the work at Princeton in July might clarify issues and further aid us in deciding whether or not to move. Naomi, however, was disappointed and frustrated I would move again so soon. I urged her to wait after the July week at Princeton, then we would decide whether or not to remain indefinitely or move. She agreed and joined me in filling out the inventories, willing to remain open and to consider all options offered.

In mid-July, we drove to Andrews Air Force Base to leave our children with Naomi's sister and family. Her husband, also from the Sherman Baptist Church, had joined the Air Force for a career. We both had young families. Naomi and I spent three days at the Princeton Eastern Career Center Counseling Services. In preparation, we sent in over 20 required inventories, answering questions about our likes, dislikes, our history and education. The staff had read and analyzed them before our arrival.

After pitching our family tent in a nearby state park, we found the center not far from the middle of Princeton. Counselors spoke individually with us and together. The lead counselor was a kind, middle aged man who'd apparently helped guide many clergy out of the ministry and into better-suited careers. I expected he might do the same for me.

The psychological tests revealed I had a very intuitive, feeling mind, one that finds it difficult to anchor down anyplace very long. I was only moderately extroverted but liked to get things accomplished. To get things done, I'd often become sloppy with a tendency to disregard minute details. I would not make a good engineer. Naomi, on the hand, was much more introverted. She liked tradition, orderliness, details, and tangible things that endured. We were a good compliment! The affirmations given us were overwhelming and seemed quite amazing, like having our minds read by a psychic.

Rather than suggest I leave ministry, the consultant said I was in a natural profession for my temperament and abilities. I liked to be in groups, groups that would support me yet give room to roam. Tests showed I had a very high intelligence, something I never seriously considered true, and could use it skillfully to dig myself out of difficult circumstances. The tests also pointed out, however, I lived with a constant "fear of failure" which limited my self-acceptance and use of personal gifts. The strong suggestion was; "Move out of Claysville within a year and begin using more of your abilities." Tests suggested I was in a too confined area and needed more diverse people around me to challenge and push me into new areas. Naomi, the counselor pointed out, was a good balance for my somewhat "wild mind," one who could help keep order in my life without allowing it to spin out of control. We picked up our children at Andrews Air Force base and returned to Claysville in a mild state of shock.

On September 20, 1975, I sent my dossier packet to the New York City denominational relocation office. I secretly hoped to move near a larger city, perhaps even the next year. Two weeks later, I received several information forms from possible churches. I read each one and applied to a few for interviews. Most were located further east in the New York City and New Jersey area.

By December, no responses had arrived. Three days before Christmas I received rejection letters from three churches near New York City; they felt I did not have enough experience, even with my assorted religious background. I began resigning myself to remain in Claysville much longer. Maybe this was our answer. Disregarding aspirations to move, we enjoyed another wonderful Christmas season celebrating the twins' and Lisa's birthdays and of course, two-year-old Eric.

After Christmas Day, we drove north in cold and snowy weather to Sherman. Several inches of beautiful new snow blanketed the peaceful countryside, as we gathered with family to celebrate the season. In 1973, Dad had sold his two farms but kept 20 acres on the western edge of the north farm. He had built a new house which included a large fish-stocked pond laying around 30 yards from the front door. Two large, picture windows gave broad views of the glistening pond during sunrises and sunsets. A five-minute walk reached the thick maple woods I had known so well as a boy. Retired, Dad bought a new snowmobile and during the days, I zoomed across familiar fields and forest trails.

My family slid down hills on sleds and toboggans. I cross-country skied over open meadows and through quiet woods. On our last day before returning home to Claysville, I spent the afternoon skiing and snowmobiling one last time, over sun speckled fields. My 15-year-old brother and I raced the snowmobile up and down the recently excavated road, carved through one of our old farms for the proposed Interstate 86. It was a perfect winter day with bright sun, crisp white snow and freezing temperatures. I felt so alive being back on familiar acres.

Near sunset, my young brother Mark climbed with me to the top of a steep snow covered embankment, which was part of the carved out expressway. We planned to retrieve the wooden toboggan left earlier at the top. I noticed the glistening snow surface freezing over with a sheet of small ice crystals under the still brilliant, but now setting sun. Loving the view, we took a deep breath and decided to ride the toboggan down the embankment. My brother sat in front as I climbed in behind him and wrapping in my legs, shoved off. Within seconds I knew the speed was much too fast on the ice crystal snow. The toboggan became uncontrollable. In seconds we slammed hard onto the flat road bottom of the proposed interstate. I felt a hard pop in my ears as my lower back quickly stiffened. I struggled to breathe.

Paralyzed into a fetal position, my back and stomach muscles cramped tightly into spasms as we came sliding to a rest on frozen snow. My brother was okay and getting up frantically, shouted to nearby Naomi, who stood in horror. We needed help. My brother then roared off on the snowmobile while Naomi waited on the packed snow beside me in deep concern. Shortly, the local Sherman Volunteer Firemen First Aid crew arrived, most being our high school classmates. Still only able to take short breaths, they carefully strapped me onto the fateful toboggan and pulled me slowly, with watchful eyes, to the waiting ambulance. Arriving at the WCA Hospital in Jamestown, the staff diagnosed I had suffered a compressed fracture of my 4th lumbar vertebra.

I remained hospitalized for a week, flat in bed, discouraged and unsure of my future. Fortunately, no surgery was required as bone fragments had not penetrated the spinal cord. I would not suffer paralysis, but it would take months for the injury to heal. I would need to lay flat in bed for six weeks.

We returned to Claysville on January 6th. In a body brace, hospital staff placed me in the back of our station wagon. With worried children watching over me, Naomi drove carefully back to Claysville.

When we arrived home, men with whom Naomi had made arrangements, met us with a gurney on which to carry me into the house. Twisting and turning through doors and halls, they lowered me onto the board-hardened bed. Relieved to be home, rejected by churches and uncertain when I could resume work, I gave thanks I was not paralyzed. We would likely remain indefinitely in Claysville. It seemed God had answered clearly, albeit a bit roughly.

The next two months were unexpectedly difficult, another test of my own emotions and Naomi's patience. I became depressed, hating bed confinement, needing to use a bedpan and urine bottle. I often projected anger toward Naomi without realizing my own inner despair. "Was she remembering to dress the kids warmly? Were the bills being paid?" Flashbacks of the accident lingered like a repeating movie. I often awakened in cold and emotional panic. I thought of soldiers returning from combat and tried to let my smaller issues go.

By late January, my temperament began to improve. Visits and support of friends were overwhelming. "My God!" my friend Mike said when seeing me, "You are the last person I expected to see like this!" I reread test conclusions from the previous summer in Princeton, and felt a deeper appreciation for Naomi with her attention to detail and order. Her patience seemed unending.

One member came and left me the book, "Freedom at Midnight," the story of Mahatma Gandhi. I couldn't stop reading, making hours pass by more quickly. I dreamed of one day visiting India. The high hopes of relocating dissipated. I would find contentment here in Claysville.

By mid-February, I was allowed to stand for an hour or two each day. Putting on the brace, steadied by Naomi, I took slow steps around the house.

Suddenly a call came from a church named Wayside Presbyterian in Hamburg, New York. The voice sounded like a professional radio announcer with its baritone resonance. The Pulpit Committee was interested in my dossier and wished to interview me! Surprised, I told the caller of my accident. I would be out of circulation a few more weeks. He asked what happened and after summarizing, he replied in his soothing, pastoral voice,

"Oh, there ought to be no problems! You'll soon be in good shape. A few years ago," he continued, "I suffered several broken vertebrae when a semi-truck ran over me in my stopped Volkswagen. I remained unconscious for three weeks. You should make a full recovery!"

He then said the church had a couple other candidates to interview. If still uncertain, he would call me back in a month or so. He described the church as located along Lake Erie with a view of Buffalo in the distance.

In late February, in my body brace and Naomi watching carefully, I shuffled outside and moved slowly across the lawn sidewalk. Clinging to the oak rail, I stepped with the caution of a Mt. Everest climber, up the old wooden staircase into my warm, cozy study. It felt so good, like I had returned to my place in life.

Still weak, I resumed leading services the first Sunday of March. The treasurer reported decreased offerings as people questioned my abilities to return. Some suggested I quit bicycle riding. As weather improved, I took longer walks, soon able to climb a high hill south of the village. Sitting at the top edge like a bird on a perch, I looked out over the village below and felt a deep peace with renewed perspective. Yes, if I remained here, it would be okay.

On Monday March 29th, after an inspiring Sunday with encouraging responses about my returning strength, the Wayside Presbyterian Church called again. The Chairperson from Wayside asked about my health and then reported the church could not decide on a candidate, but they remained drawn to my resume. Would I be willing to speak or at least be interviewed? I summarized my condition and told him about the body brace and recovery. Could they come hear me in Claysville? They would consider it.

Wayside's Pulpit Committee never visited Claysville but kept contacting me, and discovering I had roots in Sherman, invited me to visit the area and look over their church and community. In the following weeks, Naomi and I made two trips to the area. We met the Presbytery Executive, a middle aged bald man who spoke forcefully with a sense of authority. He described Wayside's congregation as positioned to become one of the strongest churches in the area. However, he advised, the former pastor, who had founded the church, purchased a nearby house and remained in the area. He would be "the problem."

Some pastor friends advised me not to consider moving into such a situation. Curious, I drove again to Hamburg to meet the former pastor in his home. Rev. Dr. Walker Brownlee was a tall man, with a scholarly, erudite aura. I found him bright and friendly, though more politically and theologically conservative than myself. However, I felt he would be no threat if I accepted a call. If he had given 36 years of his life to build this church, he certainly would not want it to collapse due to his interference.

We loved the closeness to Lake Erie and the beautiful traditional looking church. We could look across the water and see downtown Buffalo, 13 miles away. The large manse was located a block away on a somewhat exclusive street adjacent to a beautiful country club. The committee also expressed a desire to help us purchase our own home if we came. The church, built in 1941 and remodeled in 1958, was in good repair and well maintained with a large paved parking lot. Besides the pastor, the church employed four staff members with a second office for an Assistant Pastor. It seemed to fit my earlier dream even though not near New York City. However, we would be near a fairly large city but not right in it, as Naomi preferred.

Naomi and I met with the 12-member "Pulpit Committee" in their beautiful and spacious parlor. I wore one of Naomi's homemade leisure suits with a string of wooden beads around my neck. I wanted to assure them I would be different from their former pastor! I thought the conversation went well amid the diverse group of ages and gender.

On May 4th, the Chairperson, Mr. Allison, called again and asked if I could come as a candidate on May 16. Without ever hearing me speak, he asked me to be a candidate with a congregational vote to be taken afterwards! Things seemed to be moving quickly.

We said nothing to the Claysville people about our possible move, which was normal, but I still felt somewhat ungrateful. They had been so kind to me and loved us as a family. They were extremely patient with my accident and period of convalescence. Yet, I felt peace and Naomi seemed ready to go, hopeful of the chance to purchase our own home, something her family never had enjoyed.

The Western New York Presbytery Minister of Relations Chair, Rev. Tom Stewart, returned a call giving me his opinion of Wayside Presbyterian Church. He said Wayside remained quite divided over theology and church government since created in 1928 as a "Community Chapel." Dr. Brownlee led them into the Presbyterian Church ten years later, but the church still remained "Presbyterian-Light." I was impressed and wrote in my diary, "Wayside and I might get along quite well!"

The church employed a very capable secretary along with a competent Christian Education Director. They employed a choir director with a Manhattan School of Music graduate as organist. There was also an empty office waiting for the next assistant Pastor. The potential seemed great.

Our family traveled to Hamburg the second Friday of May and was accommodated in a beautiful hotel. On Saturday evening, we attended a "meet the candidate" night in the church social room. I answered several questions to a crowded room of people. One man said following six feet plus Dr. Brownlee required very large shoes. I thought of my size twelve.

The next morning, I spoke and led worship in a full church. It seemed fun and the sermon went well. To give a little symbol of my independency, I used the small lectern rather than the large wrap around preaching pulpit. I also did not wear a robe. Afterwards, a man who had recently retired, came to me with a bright gleam in his eyes and asked,

"Is this the way you always preach?"

"I try," I responded.

I received over 95% of the votes with a few voting against me saying it was a "protest against Presbytery!" During their two-year vacancy, many members were hurt and angered when the Presbytery disallowed a candidate the people apparently loved. He wasn't Presbyterian.

We returned to Claysville and received many emotional calls. My former colleague, Dave Campbell from West Alexander said, "Moving is always a traumatic experience." I recalled my troubling early months in Claysville and wondered anew what awaited me at Wayside. Hopefully, my dream for a more perfect home had come true. Maybe, as Naomi often hoped, I would now be happy.

Chapter 12

Unhealed Healer In Hamburg

> *"There have been many healers who did not heal themselves."*
>
> *-- A Course in Miracles, Helen Schucman*

My first weeks at Wayside passed with ease and hope, what some call "The Clergy Honeymoon." With four staff members including a part-time Christian Education Director and competent, seasoned secretary, help surrounded me. Most of Wayside's 600 members lived along the lakeshore area but many had become inactive during the two-year vacancy. Lake Erie, with its bright blue waters, a plethora of birds, and bobbling boats, provided a relaxing and quieting effect. The nearby public beach made the area feel comparable to a resort. We soon adopted a mixed Labrador Retriever puppy from the Humane Society and named her "Deacon."

In contrast to Claysville, I now worked among a team of supportive staff. Like Claysville, I made many visits riding my bicycle to hospitals and homes. With the flat lakeshore landscape, I could cover miles quickly. And like Claysville, a few firemen urged me to join the nearby Volunteer Lake Shore Fire Department as chaplain.

With Pittsburgh Seminary Chapel services in mind, I tried to bring more relevance to worship by accompanying songs with my guitar. In Claysville, after taking a few lessons, I added guitar playing to my repertoire. After the first Christmas Eve services, my secretary exclaimed, "You even made them cry!" The long wait for Dr. Brownlee's replacement had arrived.

Soon, however, stress and conflict poured over the community like cold water on a fire. In August of 1977, one year after arriving, the nearby Bethlehem Steel plant announced it would cut back production by 40%. The major employer of the Hamburg area, economic shocks crippled the area. The downsizing launched years of worsening financial concerns at Wayside as many wealthier employed families moved away. Others took early retirements. The steel plant had employed over 12,000 people and owned a large nearby country club, where many Wayside members belonged. The country club was sold.

As if this shock wasn't enough, or my bicycling and guitar playing didn't rile enough nerves, in October I attended a "Convocation to Reverse the Nuclear Arms Race," conducted at the Riverside Church in New York City. Rev. Ernest Campbell had recently retired and the new pastor was my fiery commencement speaker, Dr. William Sloan Coffin! Fired up by the conference, I returned charged like a bull with a renewed passion to get involved in social justice.

Never much involved in "social justice work" at Pittsburgh Seminary, I now jumped in with both feet. I invited a couple from the congregation, including our Christian Education director, to join me for a return trip in early December. Another pastor friend named Paul Moore, along with his Christian Education Director, returned with us. Sitting in the large upper Manhattan church, we were amazed at the bombastic lectures, inspiring music by Peter, Paul and Mary, and parades around the sanctuary of huge state-of-the-art puppets demonstrating the imminent threat of nuclear war. We returned home for Christmas bubbling with energy and ready to *stop* the Nuclear Arms Race!

The Presbytery Executive, excited with our new "calling," immediately invited us to share our experience in Presbytery. He asked us to get more organized and present a stronger voice for halting the arms race. The Presbytery's General Council, impressed with their new young pastor, asked me to become a member. I turned down the invitation but accepted the bid to Co-Chair the new "Task Force to Reverse the Nuclear Arms Race." We had one year to fulfill our mission.

Conflict soon appeared in Wayside. A few began criticizing my worship style playing guitar and discarding the robe. Other members quit saying I went too far outside familiar traditions. A few complained about my bicycle riding, saying it degraded the church as well as my profession. Still, many claimed Wayside was on the way up while others argued it was quickly sliding back down. However, new folks kept arriving, eager to join the anti-nuclear war movement, and although busy and stressed, I remained confident. Like Dad needing fresh air for more energy, I rolled the window down and pressed the accelerator to the floor!

Encouraged and pushed more by the Presbytery Executive, I became more involved in the anti-nuke leadership. We planned to conduct a "Convocation on the Nuclear Arms Race" with Wayside as its host. I began accepting invitations to give anti-nuclear war talks in area churches and appeared on local radio and TV programs. I accepted offers to conduct classes at Frontier High School from supporting teachers. I gave a video enhanced anti-nuke program to the local Kiwanis group, of which I was now a member. It seemed to be a good example of bringing Christian principles to the community, fulfilling the true meaning of "Onward Christian Soldiers!"

We brought in special speakers for the "Convocation to Reverse the Nuclear Arms Race" including Sidney Lens and a retired military officer from the Pentagon. Far fewer than expected attended and we were left with over $1000 in expenses. I reported the deficit to Executive Donald Brown who immediately bailed us out from one of those "many little extra pockets" he said Presbytery maintained.

Amid growing controversy, we began looking for our own house. I had an odd sense we would be staying much longer. A newer church member, who owned a real estate business, began looking for a home we might purchase to settle our family. A retired Navy Commander, who once served on a White House Military Advisory Board, thoroughly opposed my anti-war and anti-nuke views. We seemed like an odd couple.

The congregation, however, voted to sell the church manse and help us purchase a home. The retired Commander, Tom, then helped us secure a loan in a time when rates were very high along with high down payments. A small group quickly raised a $17,000 gift for down payment and closing costs. The Presbytery Executive Don Brown, who supported me, claimed he'd never heard of such a generous offer.

In October 1979, we moved into our own home, assisted by friends and some of my young bicycling companions. It was an old place, once a farmhouse, built in 1892 as one of the first homes in the area. It obviously would need frequent upgrades and maintenance. Some considered it a "starter home." The grey asbestos sided house was located only a 10-minute walk from the church on an adjacent dead end street which branched off onto a side street called Eastwood. It included a more recently built two car detached garage with an upper room. Ample lawn surrounded the property with wooded areas bordering two sides. Two newly planted trees graced the front lawn.

During the winter of 1979, amidst the still growing turmoil of my worship styles, political views and personal tiredness, I spotted a book in the Hamburg Library that would profoundly shift my future life and ministry. Taking a break from sermon preparation, I wandered through the tall bookrack tunnels, amazed at the number of books people wrote. Suddenly a title jumped out to me like a woodchuck from its burrow. Its title was, "Getting What You Want" by J. H. Brennan. It stunned me as I stood asking myself, "Dave, what is it you *do* really want?"

Through the years from farm boy to college to seminaries, I realized I never knew. In moments, I felt deeply discouraged by the controversy I had caused over my "social action" efforts, even causing some members to leave. I wanted to find truth, but it seemed so elusive. It was always a new idea or a direction which only satisfied a short time. Where would the search end?

The book, authored by an Irish psychiatrist, shifted me toward another direction. It introduced me to the idea and power of meditation, meditation using visualization and mindfulness. I read, and reread the book, and soon began following its guidelines. I wrote down what I thought I wanted, and began spending time each day reading them, visualizing each one in my mind. It seemed related to the words of Jesus, "Ask and it shall be given to you." But what *did* I want? More money? I never seemed to have enough since I left the farm.

I suggested Naomi consider a full time teaching job to help bolster our finances. She accepted occasional teaching substitutions but the pay seemed paltry, with no pension plan. Her response startled me. She said my career made it impossible to do house and family work while parenting full time with four children. I suggested we hire a part time maid but she expressed disappointment and hurt. Giving up, I wondered how my income could manage maintenance and improvements to our old house. It tested my goal setting/affirmations, but the search continued. What did I really want? What would make *me* happy?

Life, meanwhile became more difficult and confusing. Repeating daily affirmations, as Brennan advised, the arms race didn't slow down or even begin to reverse: it increased. Yet I still kept speaking about it like a blind person walking toward a cliff.

The conflict over my social justice themes floated around me like brewing storm clouds.

Key members from the board and congregation began to confront me for speaking too much about politics rather than sticking with religious topics. Many, if not most members, were fairly conservative Republicans and many were veterans of World War II, while a few had sons who served in Viet Nam. An elder and his family suddenly transferred to another church. Another took me aside into my study and said, "Pastor Dave, I don't know which would be worse; another one of your sermons on nuclear bombs or just have one drop!" I was confused, sad and stressed. Criticisms bothered me, but wasn't social justice central to my role? Wasn't this Jesus' model, what he died for? Unlike a shepherd leading the sheep, I often felt more like the lost one.

Ronald Reagan was then elected President! The Arms Race would not be reversed but shifted forward into a higher gear. I continue to meditate and visualize change, but mostly I longed for a lasting and deeper personal peace within myself. If I could just find peace, I could cope with life anywhere.

Tired of the controversy, the secretary resigned and we scrambled to find a new one. Within days, we hired a lady named Betty, who attended the Hamburg Episcopal Church. I discovered she practiced regular prayers and even supported my more liberal political views. Stricken with polio, shortly before the discovery of vaccine in 1952, she lived with some immobility, but nothing limited her kindness or efficiency. A deep tranquility surrounded her even though she struggled with financial limitations due to her husband's recent death. Without at first realizing it, Betty was an answer to my prayers.

In the autumn of 1980, I drove our new little two-toned brown Plymouth Arrow to Princeton Seminary to learn more about "Reformed Liturgy." Enjoying the time gliding along through colorful autumn leaves, I planned to learn more about Presbyterian worship services. I knew they were more formal than Baptist but I wanted to learn about their history--another deficiency from my seminary days.

The workshop surprisingly added another adjustment to my ministry and lifestyle, pleasing and relief to some, but troublesome for others. For the first time, I learned the use of a lectionary, an order for public and private prayers, which followed an annual church calendar. During my years in fundamentalism, preachers usually followed certain books of the Bible, often taking years to complete. The preachers were free to pick and choose whatever they felt "God laid on their hearts." While preaching in seminary, I used favorite topics or repeated sermons written for classes. I once asked a student friend at Pittsburgh Seminary what he used and he said a "Lectionary." It was the first time I ever heard the word.

I returned from the Princeton study feeling soothed with relief. If nothing more, the order would add more variety for the parishioners. Arriving home, I began making the shift. It came as a mixed blessing. Many were relieved to have less politics but others felt alarm at my becoming "too Catholic".

The idea of following a common lectionary began to give me a sense of stability and order. I did not need to think about being "special," but one of many ministers who taught the Bible to people, even still unsure of what that meant.

With my friendship with Roman Catholic priests at nearby St. Mary's, I soon discovered a deeper interest in Roman Catholic Liturgy. I often shared lunches with Fr. LaRusch, the older senior pastor at St. Mary's. When coming to Wayside, I helped continue the yearly ecumenical programs Wayside had shared during Lent and Thanksgiving. Fr. LaRusch, nearly 70 years old, was a short, bald man who loved cigars and black Oldsmobiles. When our kids saw him in the pulpit, he reminded them of "Yoda" from the recently released movie, *Star Wars*.

In February 1982, I suggested we help relocate a Laotian family waiting in a Thailand refugee camp. With support of highly organized Naomi and a few members, we sponsored a young couple named Tiengkham and Bouala Vannaphavong. They arrived one cold February evening from a tropical camp in Thailand with their baby boy, Chittakorn. The project provided a rich education and deep satisfaction for my family. The extra time required, much of it directed or done by Naomi, removed me further from the anti-nuke emphasis.

The Vannaphavongs, short in stature but tall in courage, lived with us for two weeks discovering telephones, television, and strange new foods. Tiengkham spoke fairly good English, having taught school in Laos. He was direct and honest and immediately, I felt a deep respect for him. I wanted to learn more about his Buddhist religious beliefs. We moved them into a nearby apartment, where Naomi helped deliver their second child, a beautiful girl named Linda. Tiengkham finished a two-year college training program and secured a good job. Smart, independent, and hard workers, they purchased their own home in Buffalo, and continue today as friends and inspirations.

During these post anti-nuke years, I also became confronted with my deep ignorance toward the gay and lesbian community. An older member of Wayside, one of the first ordained women elders of the denomination, came to my office one day to discuss the issue. A widow and retired schoolteacher, she wore glasses and spoke with a warm twinkle in her eyes. Trusting me, despite my sheltered past and lack of experience, she told me of a gay member who was writing a memoir about growing up in Wayside. He had married a woman in the congregation and they had a family. Conflicted, he wanted the older widow's respected opinion about his struggles, and now she wanted mine. I read the pages with trembling amazement but shocking enlightenment. The author wrote describing his hope that marriage would cure his orientation. It did not. He also wrote of being physically attacked by a trusted member of our congregation who also was gay and married! Suddenly, the issue I had avoided for so long, yet never was asked to address, sat squarely in my lap.

Shortly afterwards, another young man from the church came to my office and shared his homosexuality, realizing his orientation from around age 10 or 11. Thin and looking unhealthy from years of hiding and stress, he wanted my response to his story. Both parents were also active and respective members in Wayside. Obviously nervous, he asked if I would accompany him to share his lifestyle with them. I nervously accepted his offer.

We drove to his parents' home a few evenings later, wondering what might happen. Both parents were fairly strong, conservative Republicans. After greetings, we sat around a table in their beautifully decorated and maintained home. His parents seemed suspicious of our presence, making nervous glances at both of us, with stiff short sentences. "How are you doing, Dave? How's the family?" The equally nervous but brave son began telling his story. When finished his parents said, "Dear son, we always suspected you were gay! And we will always love you."

I grew into a deeper awareness and appreciation of the issue of sexuality, especially within the gay/lesbian, bi-sexual and transgender community. I began to counsel, listen to, and read what I could on another issue totally ignored and deleted in my education. Soon, I was invited to become a partner of the "Friends of the Gay and Lesbian Community," receiving frequent visits from families in the area who discovered their child had "come out." This, to me, also became "social action."

In the fall of 1982, despite Wayside's board members and my earlier expectations to hire an assistant minister, the talk and process halted. Bethlehem Steel announced it would shut down most of its plant in the next few years. It would create a huge financial loss for the southtowns area of Buffalo, including its churches.

Many new attendees were young families with few discretionary monies. Offerings slipped downward. Some blamed my recent anti-nuclear programs along with the liturgical changes. At times, the stressful attempt to lead the church seemed completely beyond my control. I continued to doubt my profession and often asked, "How did I ever get into this?" My meditations and affirmations at times seemed worthless.

With confusion and doubts, I called Executive Don Brown, always supportive of me, to ask for advice. Still disappointed from our failed "anti-nuke" efforts, he recommended I call a congregational meeting to help clarify where I stood. "Having been at Wayside over five years," he said, "and with your past controversies, perhaps it is time to move on." He suggested my "interim type ministry," following a long-term pastor, had worked. Perhaps it was finished. I grew more anxious. We had recently purchased a house and our children were settled in the same school system for over five years. Moving would be uncomfortable, stressful, and a bit crazy. Again I asked, "Where *is* the place I could happily call home?"

We called a special Congregational Meeting, which occurred the Sunday before Christmas in 1982. The sanctuary seats were filled, like a crowded Christmas Eve service. I expected conclusions would come quickly and clearly. At best, I expected my salary to be significantly cut. During opening minutes, a few expressed anger towards me. One older man scared our children shouting, "Why do we even give this man an auto allowance when he degrades us and himself by riding around on a bicycle?" A few groaned in protest as silence settled back over the crowd. Then, a tall older member, one who had given several thousand dollars to help us purchase our home, stood and faced the congregation. Respected by all, including myself, we waited in stilled silence for his words. Without explaining, he simply recommended the church give me a $2000 raise! The vote was then called for and out of nearly 300 attending, less than 10 were opposed to my remaining pastor and receiving the raise. My worst opponents never returned, but in coming years, most of our friendships were renewed.

Chapter 13

Karen

"Each meeting occurs at the precise moment for which it was meant. Usually, when it will have the greatest impact on our lives."
— Nadia Scrieva, in <u>Fathoms of Forgiveness</u>

In early 1983, more staff changes came to Wayside. After nearly seven years, it seemed people began to surround me with whom I could easily work. In early January, the organist announced her resignation and moved to the larger and wealthier Westminster Presbyterian Church near downtown Buffalo. Tall, single, and reserved in her comments, she had remained patient and forgiving of my guitar and trombone playing amid the social justice and liturgical shocks. She often looked at me with eyes which seemed to say, "I hope someday you find what you are looking for!" Wayside had been her home church since birth and her parents were active and important in the church's success. When she moved to the downtown church, her parents followed.

On February 2nd, we hired a new organist/pianist from the village of Hamburg. A few years older than I, she exuded energy, bubbling smiles, and hope. Short with shiny and often curly hair, Jo Osborne arrived ready to jump in! Bright and loyal, she would become a major part of my tenure at Wayside.

A few weeks after Jo began, a friend told me about a young woman minister named Karen Lipinczyk. Ordained in the United Church of Christ, he described Karen as a talented young minister who had previously worked in a large Presbyterian church with an older pastor. Perhaps Wayside might hire her as an assistant staff member while she awaited another full time job. I remembered sitting behind Karen in a Presbytery meeting, admiring her curly brown hair, striking beauty and outspoken participation.

Since our Christian Education Director had also recently resigned, I called Karen and asked if she might be interested. Within days, she began work. A Buffalo native, Karen graduated from Buffalo State College and the Pacific School of Religion in Berkley, California.

Immediately, it seemed like lightning struck Wayside. With Karen's radiant energy and support from Jo, she greeted everybody with smiles and hugs. Her husband Steve, a tall, handsome, and outstanding athlete, joined our church softball team. Karen attended the games, often becoming vocally clear in her rants over umpire decisions. At one game, while holding a cigarette in two fingers, she loudly challenged the umpire's call. Someone shouted, "Who do you think you are?" Karen answered, "The Assistant Pastor at Wayside!" Some of the Waysider bleacher crowd looked over with raised eyebrows.

At first she seemed the natural answer to my desire for more shared pastoral responsibilities. I felt confident in Karen's abilities despite some of her eccentricity. She reminded me of my own oft-changing values but with even more passion and impulsiveness. The young people loved Karen and before long they were introduced to a lively dose of women's liberation. Karen did express a desire to stay full time as a staff member. I welcomed the idea but it seemed difficult given the church's present financial situation.

That summer I planned to lead another bicycle tour around Lake Erie with ten or so young people. A yearly activity since

1978, Karen wanted the challenge of riding and to prepare, pledged to ride her bicycle nearly 30 miles to Wayside and home on the days she worked.

In early July we began a 10-day trip around Lake Erie, riding west through Canada toward Leamington, Ontario. One of Karen's friends, Betty, joined us. Although recently diagnosed with a nerve disease, Betty was a strong athlete and excellent rider.

On the fourth day, planning to reach Leamington and board a ferry to Sandusky, Ohio, we discovered miles of road under construction. Fresh tar covered with sharp stones caused a few bike tires to explode. One rider ran out of tube patches and with no extra tube, we repaired it with a plastic coke bottle and duct tape. It got him to Leamington, the constant thumping leaving his hands numb.

As temperatures climbed to 90 degrees with high humidity, riders grew discouraged, losing interest and stamina. Karen was one of them. She began swearing, cursing the trip and her joining the venture. Impatient, I rode ahead, leaving her to receive help from others. Her University of Buffalo feminist friend, Betty, pedaled alongside me and called her a "candy ass." The person with most patience to coach her along was a young man named Dennis, a member from our neighboring Roman Catholic Church. Dennis, a strong rider and good mechanic, stayed behind with Karen, patiently listening to her curses about the bicycle, the trip and me.

Due to Karen's lagging behind, we were late reaching the ferry terminal. Reaching the dock, we rode up in time to see the ferry floating away from with passengers waving back. Being a national holiday in Canada, I luckily found a church in which the pastor sat in his office planning a funeral. He graciously allowed us to stay in the large old stone building for the night. There we took "baths" in church sinks, gave back rubs, crawled into our sleeping bags, and slept soundly.

The next day, we boarded the ferry to Sandusky, Ohio where we stayed two nights in a small wood sided church. After rest and a day at the Cedar Point Amusement Park, we began the four-day trek back to Buffalo.

The last night, we stayed in a Presbyterian Church just west of Erie, Pennsylvania, also named "Wayside." Soaked in sweat and hungry, we found a nearby public pool in which to swim and cool down. Having a young rider who was an excellent cook, we gorged ourselves on mashed potatoes, corn on cob, salads and cold drinks.

After cleaning up, Karen conducted a communion service, which she had suggested. Having picked up a bottle of wine and some bread, we gathered on the thick maroon carpeted chancel, around and beneath the large communion table. Karen led most of service telling the youth how much she had learned about herself, deeply appreciating the constant support, patience and love when she wanted to quit. Soon everyone began sharing trip stories, many crying with relief and perhaps even bits of dread it would end.

The next day we completed the 100-mile ride to Hamburg, relieved and happy to have survived the nearly 600-mile trip. Many of the riders, most from Wayside, have stayed in touch with me over the years. A few years later I conducted a wedding for two who met on the trip. I never saw Karen ride a bicycle again.

Although Karen only stayed two years, she spoke often of her studies at the Pacific School of Religion in San Francisco. As part of a network of seminaries connected with the Berkley Graduate Theological Union, Karen suggested I apply for the Doctorate of Ministry program at the San Francisco Presbyterian Seminary. It was one of the five bay area seminaries in the graduate program. She said the experience would be good for me.

After the turmoil of my reverse-the-arms-race years and with new staff, I had found more tranquility in life. The summer bicycle camps actually helped, along with Algonquin canoe trips. Our children were doing well in school and Naomi was an excellent mother and home keeper. Becoming more "liturgical" added needed order, for my sake and the parishioners. Yet I still questioned what I was doing in the ministry. It was such a busy vocation with mediocre pay, but gave moments of deep satisfaction. I loved working with people, my personal freedoms, and my endless energy as I approached 40 years. I could not decide what else could satisfy me as much.

I completed and returned a seminary application and in a few weeks was accepted. I began reading required books and writing papers for a local mentor. Loving the readings, I wondered, "Will this decision begin another major shift in my life?" Karen later accepted a position as pastor in a Buffalo church and over the years, we remained friends.

Chapter 14

Home in San Francisco

*"People wish to be settled. Only as far as they are
unsettled is there any hope for them."*
                                    -Ralph Waldo Emerson

"Are you crazy?" Naomi responded when hearing about San
Francisco. Thinking in her practical mind she continued, "How
would we get there? How could we afford it? How can you take
that much time off?"

Somewhat prepared I defensively replied, "I've accumulated
two years' worth of study leave time along with financial
allowances." To keep costs down, I suggested we purchase a used
van and a few more camping items. She remained quiet, rolling
her blue eyes in a dazed look, normal after sharing one of my new
ideas. In a few days, she asked, "So when do we look for a van? If
we are going to leave in June, we can't wait until the last minute!"
She suggested we get banana boxes from the grocery store. Each
box would be the allotted space for a family member. I loved my
organized wife!

We drove to a Chevy garage in Orchard Park where a used
1977 Chevy van sat on the vehicle lot. With 70,000 miles, a
powerful motor and good tires, we asked to take the blue deluxe
model for a ride. After a 20-minute test drive, we made financial

arrangements and drove it home the next day. The van featured two front bucket seats with a rear-padded bench for two or three. Behind the bench we placed two lawn chairs, now appropriately unlawful and dangerous, but in ignorance and with possible angelic protection, we planned the trip for all six of us.

We left early Monday, June 29, 1984, leaving our dog, Deacon, in a country kennel. Tiengkham would care for the lawn and house. Planning 10 days to reach San Anselmo, we camped the first night in Indiana, faced fierce winds in flat Kansas, and reaching Denver, camped on a relative's lawn for the 4th of July. Leaving Denver, we climbed 8,000 feet for a two-night stay in the Rocky Mountain National Park. Ten-year-old Eric and I hiked the Anastasia Cliff Dwellings in southern Colorado while the ladies stayed safe with the van. We made camp and slept on desert sands in Arizona near the Four Corners, and camped along the south ridge of Grand Canyon. We tried to sleep on 100-degree sand in Las Vegas, after being thrown out of casinos, and at a large campsite in Los Angeles before touring Hollywood and the Universal Studios. The next night, at 2:30 a.m., we scrambled out of ant-infested sleeping bags on sands alongside the Pacific Ocean. The last night, we camped in Petaluma where the kids ran breathlessly back from the pool to report their first sight of recognized lesbians. Welcome to San Francisco!

Reverend Bob Sanford, a San Francisco Seminary graduate and minister friend from Buffalo, welcomed us at the seminary. A kind person and California native, Bob helped us unload and settle into our very small apartment for the next four weeks, the most expensive ever rented.

Nestled close to beautiful Point Reyes National Park with Mount Tamaulipas visible to the south, it was a wonderful setting to study. Huge oak and eucalyptus trees lined the campus creating a park atmosphere among the earthquake-enforced buildings. Lisa, always wanting more money, found a summer nanny job while Eric and I played imaginary baseball games, and the twins watched the little TV we brought along when not taking day trips with Naomi.

The first morning, Presbyterian staff members outlined the summer program and needed steps to earn a Doctorate of Ministry degree. I reminded myself I came mostly for the "counterculture bay experience," show my family the country, have time away from the church, and receive a tax deduction.

Both of my classes, each for two weeks, were relaxing and enjoyable. 10 of us seasoned ministers sat in a relaxed circle of chairs, sharing our stories of ministry, four or five from Australia and New Zealand. Dr. Rambo requested we just call him "Lew" even though the recent movie, "Rambo," had raised the popularity of his name.

I loved the relaxed format hoping he would weed out those of us with unrealistic expectations while giving us little mental health check-ups. The purpose seemed to be helping each one of us discover whether or not we wanted or even needed the doctoral program. Assured the title would add little, if anything thing to our salary packages, we listened to each one's vocational story for about 10 minutes, and then we asked questions.

After our first day's class, walking together down a hilly sidewalk under old oak trees, Lew surprised me saying, "Dave, I envy you. You seem to have so much together in your life!" Really? Surprised, I felt myself blushing before my mind questioned his competence. During our stay, we jogged together several mornings and became friends.

I then took classes, better described as "group sharing times," with a Chinese instructor named Jim Chuck, who also served as a Baptist pastor for a group of Chinese Americans in San Francisco's China Town. He was an open and kind person. One day he took us to see his church in downtown San Francisco where we met members and learned about their arrival in the area. Afterwards, we walked a short distant for a little tour of China Town. Having been at the church nearly 30 years, Jim said he often thought of moving but added, "The opposition always seems to have poor leadership!" He also encouraged me to continue in the program, telling me my writing was "readable and lucid."

I worried about Naomi, however, as she suffered with asthma and upset stomach for much of the trip. Traveling over the high peaks terrified her and she now lived in a strange place teaching more religion, a topic never her major interest. I felt her discomfort and often questioned our relationship with my continual uncertainty of so much, but thankful to be together in this wonderful place. I often wondered if I needed a more "free spirit" as companion, but something about her naturalness at being orderly and attentive to details, attracted and amazed me.

On weekends, we took frequent side trips into San Francisco and the surrounding area. We walked along the festive wharf enjoying the colorful sidewalk entertainers. We rode trolleys up and down the hills, laughing and loving the atmosphere. We took a boat tour to Alcatraz and toured the Japanese Tea Garden on the Presidio. We ate in restaurants discovering Chinese and Mexican foods. We drove through Napa Valley touring wineries and walked the Petrified Forest as well as the nearby magnificent Muir Woods, but by month's end, we all longed for our home in Hamburg and desired to leave our cramped apartment.

As we prepared to leave, a New Zealand pastor came to say good-bye. Giving me a huge California hug, he spoke in his strong accent of appreciating my participations in classes and morning worship services. Then he asked, "Would you consider a pulpit exchange with me?" He wanted to visit and live in the eastern part of the United States and of course, I would love to visit New Zealand. Stunned at his cordiality and invitation, I never seriously pursued it.

The last night in San Anselmo, Eric and I walked to the large porch area in front of the seminary chapel. We became caught up into the brilliant night sky, amazed at falling meteorites and the steady lights of passing satellites. Like two starry-eyed kids, we stood, sat, and watched for an hour. Far away from the responsibilities of the parish, I felt refreshed, renewed, and ready to return. Why couldn't I feel this more often?

On August 11, we headed east, the girls anxious to get home, Lisa with her purse full of extra money. With ten days left, we stopped at more memorable places: Sequoia National Park, where we stood in awe before 3,000-year-old Giant Sequoias, Yosemite Park where we watched dot sized rock climbers scaling El Capitan, and a spectacular sunset and rise while camping on sands of Wendover, Utah.

We reached Salt Lake City and stayed overnight, toured the Mormon center and listened to an organ recital in the Tabernacle, which reminded me of Bob Jones University. We drove north to the Grand Teton National Park for two nights, Eric fascinated by the abundant falling stars. We climbed aboard a large rubber raft and floated down Snake River, the raft maneuvered by a handsome young college man named Earl, whom the girls admired by taking pictures of his "nice ass."

After a couple nights in Yellowstone, with temperatures dropping into the 20's and Old Faithful showing signs of aging, we drove through the Bad Lands and stopped at Mount Rushmore. After a short visit with Naomi's mother and brother in Wisconsin, we arrived home on August 27. Naomi and I were exhausted. Dorinda declared "Never again!" as she and the kids scattered to reconnect with friends. The Oldsmobile started, the lawn looked great, but the kitchen sink leaked with some dirty dishes atop covered with mold. We picked up Deacon and life returned to normal with all happy to be home.

Within days, I felt overwhelmed with calls and things to do. Karen called and after reporting on our trip, she shared her first big crisis at the new church. My guitar instructor, Howie, told me our minister friend Tom was facing a difficult "vote of confidence" at his church. A Wayside parent called to report his son tried to commit suicide by jumping out of their truck. He remained unconscious in serious condition at the hospital. Not sure if I was up to it, I went back to work.

Significantly, I began a daily yoga routine, inspired by a 10-cent book purchased from a small San Anselmo thrift shop. I practiced each morning before praying my routine prayers and affirmations. I began fasting a day each week and reconsidered resigning from the Peace Task Force. While visiting a church member in the Psychiatric Center, I met a well-known political activist with whom I had worked two previous summers. Overwhelmed and depressed with the "Reagan years," he had collapsed and consented the need for help. There had to be a better way.

Chapter 15

Radical Changes

> *"We are not at peace with others because we are not at peace with ourselves."*
>
> –Thomas Merton

I missed the San Francisco area with its sharp contrasts to Buffalo. I found it difficult to stay organized with a schedule being "on call" 24/7, yet I enjoyed the freedoms of a "self-employed" vocation. I continued to practice daily meditations and affirmations after relaxing yoga stretches.

Slowly, I began to feel more content, more in charge, even more conservative, at least less strident about social issues. Distrustful members commented on my softer attitude. I began seeing worship services as more contemplative centered rather than lectures on social issues. When mentioning social issues, I tried to explain more and be less certain, provoking thought rather than telling people what to think or do. I considered quitting the "Peace Task Force" which now seemed mostly a nuts and bolts process following denominational recommendations.

In early September, I apologized in a sermon for being so judgmental with my know-it-all attitude. Some of the more social action minded members expressed disappointment, a few walking past me afterwards in silence. Others shook my hand warmly and with smiles said, "Dave, that was one of your best sermons!"

I began doing exercises from Roy Oswald's workbook on clergy self-care. A staff member of the Alban Institute in Washington, D.C., an organization to encourage pastors, he urged constant attention to time management. It often seemed impossible. I took Oswald's "assertive test" and discovered I was high, if not aggressive, tending to hurt people when feeling trapped or over-extended. The image of Dad flashed back, seeing him rudely drive salesmen off the farm when they annoyed him on a busy day. I was often impatient with certain board members, even Naomi and my family. I remembered the angry anti-war chants suggesting we "Hate and damn those against peace."

As Advent approached in early December, I strained under the season's extra activities and parties. I deplored shopping. I committed to work no more than three consecutive days each week. With twelve hours per day, I would fulfill the hours or "segments" required by Presbytery and Wayside's contract.

My parents, who now traveled to Florida for winters, offered me their heated home in Sherman for a place to rest. I drove there for two days in Advent to prepare for the season. Exiting the Thruway at Westfield, I drove slowly up Oxbow Hill, coming to the more rural and forested areas of the 12 mile, 1000-foot ascent to Sherman. Arriving at their quiet, rural home, a flush of relaxation flooded over me. Like an Algonquin experience, I sensed home, not just with its familiarity, but also with peace and appreciation never experienced there. Tension draining out of my body like air from a balloon, I took quiet walks through the old familiar woods, stunned with joy and release. The house, with memories of family bustle and reunions, became a hermitage for simple eating, solitude, and reciting my affirmations.

I returned to Hamburg feeling ready for Christmas. As the guitarist Howie and Jo played accompaniment, we sang Sister Theresa Winter's song, "Bit by bit the river grows, until all at once it overflows!" My yoga, meditation and affirmation exercises seemed to be paying dividends.

I continued using my parents' rural home during winter months for the next few years. In the solitude and quiet, the first winter I read 15 required books along with writing three papers for San Francisco Seminary. One of my most memorable and life-changing authors was Thomas Merton. I read his *Seven Story Mountain* memoir with excitement and hope. "I am tortured by his words," I wrote, reading how he contrasted knowing about God versus knowing God. "But how?" I asked. Merton, like myself, had abundant energy and even wilder passions. He described the Roman Catholic Church as a safe refuge with its orders, first becoming a Franciscan monk, then moving into the more disciplined Cistercian or Trappist Order.

I even considered becoming a Roman Catholic, admiring their contemplative orders and discipline for daily prayers and meditation. I shared my ideas with Karen Lipinczyk, still with her new congregation in Buffalo. She mentioned the Roman Catholics had "Third Orders" for Protestants within the Benedictine Order. I decided to learn more, perhaps even join and keep their disciplines while remaining Presbyterian.

In sharing my enthusiasm with Naomi, the baffled lady expressed more questions as to who I really was. Afraid I might be preparing for another major change she asked, "When and where will you ever settle down? When and where will you ever find and be at home?" Unsure, I would keep searching. Meanwhile, I began feeling deeper hope and peace for longer periods of time.

In late February of 1985, after making hospital visitations, I stopped at the Catholic bookstore on Main Street in downtown Buffalo. Inspired by Merton's memoir, I purchased a Stations of the Cross prayer book along with a Rosary. That evening, I began practicing. Filled with excitement, I drove back the next day to the Sisters of St. Paul's book store, also on Main Street in Buffalo. I spotted the compact little book Merton used called, "Christian

Prayer: The Liturgy of the Hours." A small maroon vinyl covered book with 1700 pages of thinly bound India paper, it was like finding a diamond. I bought it and driving home, stopped to share my discovery with Fr. Alton LaRusch, my older priest friend who served at nearby St. Mary's. He briefly showed me how to use the prayer book, and on the first day of Lent, I began.

Feeling euphoric, I quit thinking about moving to a smaller parish or even making more money, hardly able to wait for the next prayer hour. I learned many of the hymns and responses as I read and prayed it. Following Merton's practice, I recited the readings and prayers while walking along the nearby abandoned train tracks. Rails and wood ties were long gone but snowmobiles and small recreational vehicles kept the dirt path open. Bordered by small trees and bushes, our loyal dog Deacon trailed along behind, sniffing the delightful whiffs with her tail wagging happily. Sometimes, we climbed up and over the four active tracks to walk through the worn paths of adjacent woods. A construction union owned the quiet woods, often used to train members to drive road graders. We walked various unplanned trails of the mini wilderness through quiet trees, with scampering squirrels and fluttering birds accompanying us. Feeling peace and closer to what I supposed a "spiritual leader" might be, Naomi held her breath!

Despite these changes, I still experienced frequent "demons" or sudden anger tantrums. One day I returned home to find our children arguing and quickly became angry and verbally abusive. Frustrated, I walked to our bedroom and heaved the new prayer book into a wall, nearly breaking its thick binding. More images of Dad flashed into my mind.

In late May, I returned to Christ the King Seminary in East Aurora to have another quiet day and night reading and praying. I stayed in an unused dormitory, never used for expected seminarians. A single spring mattress bed with a chair and desk were the only furniture in a gray painted room. A garish crucifix hung on the wall over the bed.

I took a break from reading to stroll through the nearby library. There, I stumbled upon a magazine article which described how to survive life as a parish priest. It claimed solitude must become an integral part of the priest's vocation. I wondered if the idea might become a dissertation topic.

Back On the Mountain

"Dave, you must go to India!"

– Sumio Koga

In mid-June, 1985, I packed my bicycle into a bike bag and flew west to San Anselmo. Many worries and concerns were left behind in my wake, but not my guilt. I would miss Lisa's high school graduation. Our oldest child, I wondered if I ever left much of a positive influence on her with my many absent hours attending meetings and my endless search for answers. Lisa, however, was smart, independent, a good student, and would leave for college in September.

Shortly after settling into my apartment, I put my bicycle together and pedaled in the lowest gear up narrow dirt paths to the top of nearby Mount Baldy. There, I sat, alone and free, able to view the surrounding peaks and communities stretching to San Francisco Bay. I prayed through my "offices" from the prayer book, and coasted back down to discover my roommate for the summer, Sumio Koga, a Japanese American and retired Presbyterian minister.

Sumio was an older, stocky man with a large round head and thinning dark black hair. He quickly detected my spiritual interests and began explaining to me, in his Japanese accent, Buddhism in a positive light. Sumio was also an excellent cook and, learning I now ate mostly vegetarian, prepared excellent meals in our small efficiency apartment. He was the perfect roommate!

The first weekend, with my van driving experience, I drove the blue seminary van with a load of graduate students to the Glide Memorial Church in San Francisco. The Sunday morning service was led by Cecil Williams, a well-known African American speaker with a deep, resonating voice. The church boasted a first-rate band in an old downtown Methodist church. With no organ or chancel cross, the full congregation consisted of around 50 percent gay and lesbian members. Uplifting praise songs filled the old sanctuary, nearly closed until Cecil arrived. Hugging and laughter prevailed throughout the hour-long service. Cecil delivered his sermon dressed in a brightly colored kimono vestment made by his Japanese wife. I felt uncertain and overwhelmed in such an entertainment type atmosphere, but it certainly fulfilled all of Pittsburgh Seminary's ideals of a worship event.

The seminary morning worship services were a variety of styles presented by students taking turns designing and offering their own events. The one I most remembered was led by a Lutheran candidate. He poured a bottle of olive oil into a large glass bowl and invited all forward for "healing." I later added a similar opportunity in Wayside's worship.

One Sunday I attended the nearby San Anselmo Roman Catholic Church hoping to feel a sense of order. However, it felt odd as people walked in and out at various points of the service, shortly before and right after the Eucharist.

In many ways, San Francisco Seminary was like Pittsburgh Seminary. Students, in contrast however, worked hard, seemingly twice as myself. I seemed to be the only one with regular hours for rest and my time became more like a vacation retreat. I felt pity for some candidates and began caring less about getting a degree or to be called "doctor." With Merton in mind, I decided to make the summer mostly a spiritual pilgrimage. I attended classes, which were less interesting than the previous summer, with mostly lectures and little discussion. I refused to take many notes thinking I would just read, learn what I could, return home and quit the program. I enjoyed daily 20-minute sunbaths after my noon prayers and light lunch, lying near our apartment on bare ground in the warm and healing sun.

On June 21, I awoke from a deep sleep for the second straight night. A dissertation topic burned in my mind. It had to be on solitude. In the dream, I felt excited and motivated by living and working with it for the next few years. I jotted down a few notes on a tablet and went back to sleep.

Five days later, a Roman Catholic sister named Doty Donald, came to the seminary to spend time as a speaker and consultant. Impressed in hearing her at chapel, I decided to ask my faculty advisor, Dr. Roy Fairchild, if I could set up an appointment with her. While walking to ask him, I suddenly heard my name called. "David! How are you doing?" It was Doty herself! I answered, "I'm fine. You are just the person I want to speak to!" She had been with Dr. Fairchild shortly before. She asked me to meet in 15 minutes at her office.

After exchanging greetings, wearing regular street clothes, she quickly asked, "So what is your dissertation topic?" I had a summary typed out from my dreams and handed it to her. She loved it and immediately recommended I contact Abbott Fr. John Eudes from the Genesee Abby to become my advisor. She gave me other resources to check out, including Quaker John Foster as the only Protestant she knew who wrote a chapter on solitude. She noticed the prayer book in my pack and said, "And good for you. You are right on!"

I returned to my apartment flying high, took another sunbath and resumed reading. The next morning, I got up at 4:30 and pedaled back up Mt. Baldy's narrow paths for morning prayers. As the sun rose over the eastern horizon, encasing the scene with a euphoric and heavenly presence, deep peace suddenly overwhelmed me. Before coasting back down the mountain I wrote:

Here I wait with the shining morning sun
So at peace and yet there lingers
The storm below,
A storm of things to do
With things left undone and people waiting.
Is this the path? I do find much joy.
Make me patient,
And may I take this holy rest each day.

I reported my progress to Dr. Fairchild. He liked my topic. He then looked over my recent Myers-Brigg's inventory and said, "Dave, with your extreme intuitive/feeling characteristics, you'd better have a highly organized person around you!" I assured him I did.

Later, while sitting through another boring lecture, with heads bobbing around me in sleepiness, the topic of form and freedom came to mind. Suddenly, it occurred to me I must find more individuals to take leadership roles in the church. I began seeing myself more as a "theologian in residence." I would encourage others in the congregation to frequently offer sermons and lead worship. I would become more of an overseer or coordinator along with my good secretary.

In the later part of the summer program, I took a class taught by Sandy Park, a beautiful blond haired middle-aged woman, native of Alabama, who spoke with a southern drawl. Sandy was a staff member in the Pacific School of Religion. Ordained a United Church of Christ minister, she kept pushing us male ministers to get more in touch with our feelings and sexuality. She asked us to do exercises in self-care and trust by wrapping each other in blankets and then hugging closely! She got us on the floor with mats doing yoga to help relax and feel our body sensations.

She asked us to create drawings and use crayons to manifest our deeper emotions and feelings. Some of the Anglican pastors from Australia scorned the class as degrading and demeaning for doctoral candidates!

When Sumio saw my color crayon art work he responded, "This is so Eastern with its colors and strokes!" Then he added; "Dave, you *must* go to India to study for your dissertation!" I sat in shock as he insisted I apply for an available scholarship to visit India for research. Unsure and a bit confused, I discarded the idea. A couple days before summer studies ended, Sumio pressed me to sit and write a proposal stating why I ought to be sent to India to study. He pulled up a chair before my typewriter on the table and stood behind me as I typed! Seeming quite far-fetched and a long shot, I typed a proposal.

I defended my dissertation on solitude to three faculty advisors. Surprisingly, they loved it and gave me more tips and advice. One, a Dominican monk, asked me to include how Protestants used solitude in their tradition. "It must be in there some place," he said, "You just need to look for it."

Preparing to return home, Roy Fairchild invited me to his office and gave high marks for my work and attitude during the six weeks. The Australian liturgical teacher, who at times seemed quite distraught and confused, came to see me. Facing me, he put his arms on my shoulders and began to weep, saying he wanted to find what I had! He hoped to soon visit me in New York. I flew home with exciting and nervous anticipation but deeply thankful for the summer experience. It had been life altering.

Arriving home, I discovered myself quickly tested. Perhaps concerned about my "liturgical drift," Wayside's Session had voted to recommend a young fundamentalist from the nearby Evangelical Tabernacle to become our youth director. Surprised and discouraged, I fought against anger. However, I had been the one who encouraged them to take more actions on their own.

In a few days, the San Francisco Seminary Australian instructor and his new girlfriend, whom he'd apparently found in San Francisco, arrived to spend a day and overnight. Both had left their spouses. Uncomfortable, we didn't know what to say. I gave them directions to Niagara Falls, expecting later he might wish to talk. Getting back late, the next morning they rose and left around 4:00 a.m. leaving us a short note, confessing how mixed up they both were. Back home in Hamburg, life continued on in its crazy and puzzling ways.

Sumio Koga

Chapter 17

Finding My True Home!

*"The Kingdom, the Presence of God is within you, the
True You. It's your home!"*
- Anthony de Mello

In mid-September San Francisco Seminary sent a letter saying I had been awarded the India grant. Excitement, with tinges of fear, rippled through my mind. Soon another letter arrived from instructor Sandy Park. Aware of my grant, she urged me to take a year off to study and write. Encouraged with growing confidence, I still asked myself, "How?"

Meanwhile Fr. John Eudes, Abbott of Genesee Abbey, refused to be my advisor. He explained in a handwritten letter his previous work in this area as too overwhelming. I contacted a Benedictine Monk from Elmira, whom Quaker Douglas Steere and Roy Fairchild recommended. He also said "No."

On a suggestion from my friend Chas' wife, Pat, I drove to Christ the King Seminary in East Aurora to meet Sister Joanne. Sister Joanne taught "Spiritual Formation" and was known as very knowledgeable of the contemplative life. A pleasant person looking about my age, but older by perhaps 10 years, I quickly felt comfortable. Accepting her offer to advise me, I sent her credentials to San Francisco Seminary who quickly approved her.

When I left, Sister Joanne encouraged me with a quote from Carl Jung: "Follow your inner world, this is always your first and most important priority."

Throughout the winter, I returned almost weekly to my parent's rural home. I began practicing the Ignatius 30-day retreat, as Sister Joanne suggested, using the exercises to help me decide whether to stay or leave Wayside before finishing my dissertation. The answer said, "Stay!"

As winter moved into spring, Sister Joanne urged me to attend a July conference at Le Moyne College in Syracuse, led by a Jesuit priest named Fr. Anthony de Mello. She wanted me to meet and hear him. A native of India, perhaps he could suggest a few worthwhile ashrams to visit. Sister Joanne also jolted me by suggesting I think more about becoming a Roman Catholic priest! Being married as an ordained Protestant minister, she claimed I could easily move into her tradition.

In early July, I packed a few clothes, sleeping bag, camping supplies, and bicycle into our van and drove to Syracuse. I made camp, using my van for a shelter in the wooded Green Lakes State Park. I then drove to nearby Le Moyne College for the first lecture. Fr. Anthony de Mello quickly grabbed my attention. A dark skinned Indian citizen from the state of Genoa, his family had emigrated from Portugal in the 1600's. The oldest of 11 children, Tony became a Jesuit priest, studying in Spain, and then earning a certificate in counseling from the University of Chicago.

Standing around and often leaning on a raised platform table, he talked in an informal conversational style as if we all were gathered around a dinner table. Dressed in dark slacks with a short-sleeved colorful summer shirt, his long thick black hair lay wrapped around his head somewhat like a turban. In his mid-50's, small patches of gray feathered over the tops of his ears. He wore large black-rimmed glasses and at first I thought he looked sort of nerdy. He wore no evidence of being a priest. The large Jesuit lecture hall auditorium was nearly full. I found a seat left on the front row. After the first lecture, being perhaps the only non-Roman Catholic present, I wrote, "Without exception, this is the most 'radical person' I have ever heard! I am so thankful and lucky to be here." It became a pivotal week in my life, after my many years of searching.

I spent four days listening to de Mello's talks and discussions. Over and over he repeated, you are one with God! Your Higher Self IS God!" "Repentance," he explained, using the Greek word *metanoia,* means to "change one's mind or thinking." Heaven and happiness are not outside of you. It is all within. It is your consciousness. It is your True Self, the I Self. It is God! It is our true Home! This, de Mello taught, was the essence of Jesus' teachings. The I Self is the observer present who sees our bodies and the world as the third person. It is never "I body, I head, or I heart," but always referred to as the observer: "my body, my head, etc." It is the Self we have lost consciousness of in our "sleep."

De Mello amplified his startling talks with simple stories, saying if we are normally unhappy or dominated by guilt, fear, and anger, we have lost our identities as one with Spirit. We are "sleepwalking," attached to mortal bodies, families, institutions, forms, and egos. "Ah!" I thought, "so *that, this* is where my Home is!" All my years I had scrambled and searched like a lost dog looking for food and shelter. "Home" had been with me all the time. It was so obviously simple, and involved only a change of perception in my thinking.

"Of course," de Mello continued, "it relates to our ideas of God, for God, being unseen, is an Idea." He ridiculed the church for portraying the idea of God from the Bible as a Judge, a cruel one, one who requires blood for appeasement and satisfaction. "That God," he explained, "is worse than an Adolf Hitler!" I sat mesmerized by his words.

"So this," I pondered more, "is what 'being born again means!" It is an awakening from our sleep walks, our continuous pursuits searching outside of ourselves for peace. De Mello repeatedly emphasized we are *not* our bodies. Being mortal and time bound, bodies perish but our Inner Self, the I observer, is eternal. We can know we are attached to our egos if a spouse, child, friend or institution controls us, causing us to hate, rage or cling in attachment.

"Attachment" was a commonly used word by de Mello. Unhappiness controls us because our ego-body-self-identity is a false programming of who we are. Asleep, we become caught in the illusions of mortal time and space, which is only a tiny speck or blink in timelessness, and thus is not reality. Our task is to reprogram our brain computers so we can awaken, become happy and free. At the time, computers were just becoming popular and de Mello alluded to them frequently for analogies. What we program into our mental computers is what comes out.

I hung onto every word, often holding back tears, realizing what a needy, foolish and ego-centered person I was, and always had been. I allowed my family, my location, my vocation, the church and its beliefs to determine my levels of peace and happiness. I too, as de Mello described, lived as a "sleep walker," totally unaware of Who I was. "I have never had so much all at once," I wrote. "How I can ever be the same!" I wanted to "wake up!"

Suddenly I realized my search for a universal love had been found. All my spiritual teachings, heretofore, claimed acceptance by God's presence was conditional on belief in a man named Jesus, who died on a cross for our sins. Believe that and Jesus will come in. Unless a person accepted this, he or she was doomed to eternal punishment, banishment from God, forever in flames of hell! The message had frightened me since the first time I heard it.

Although Presbyterians and mainline churches did not emphasize the punishment aspect, it remained, and continues, in weekly creeds and beliefs needed for membership. Our emphasis on social action and changing society replaced the creeds' emphases. Now I saw the teaching as narrow and brutal. Love or the idea of God, or whatever the name, is everywhere and in everyone! It is our Identity. I needed to awaken to It, understand, and remember my identity. I am not a physical body but part of the Great Spirit Oneness of the universe! It seemed like religious Christmas had finally arrived, and I had been given the greatest gift I could ever want, freedom!

Fr. de Mello continually chided the church for missing this critical teaching over the centuries. He referred to church denominations as "abominations!" The church deepened personal guilt with its rules and laws, forcing dependence rather than empowerment and freedom. The church had become a cruel institution by deepening people's guilt with its obsession on sex as a filthy aspect of human bodies.

Sex was an issue de Mello discussed frequently, accusing the church of loading it with guilt and fear. He said he once suggested to his mother in Bombay a possible decision to quit the priesthood and become married. His mother replied;

"Oh Tony, you know what the Church would do to you! Breaking your vows would carry serious consequences. You'd be shunned. They would despise you!"

"But mother, what about you? How would you respond?"

"Oh Tony, you know I would always love you regardless of what choices you make."

"Now there," de Mello summarized, "is unconditional love!"

De Mello stated the Bible was one of the most misused books in history. It was not to be taken literally but seen as a pointer toward metaphysical values. He explained, "When the wise man points his finger toward the moon, all the fool sees is the finger." We are like a person who goes to a restaurant and asks the waiter for the menu. When the menu is brought, the person begins to eat it! The waiter returns and asks, "What would you like to eat from the menu?" The patron replies, "Oh really nothing, I am just fine eating the menu! Please bring me the check."

I began to see my whole life as living in illusions. De Mello destroyed the God I had learned. He destroyed my Bible, how I used it as a crutch and weapon, missing its themes of love and forgiveness by focusing on its sin and judgment. He destroyed my relationships used to maintain illusions of control and attachment. He inspired me to see a new kind of freedom and awareness, a new way of living. But what would these ideas do to my family? My vocation?

I walked past priests and nuns sitting in the lobby weeping profusely, clutching to crosses and rosaries, claiming de Mello had attacked and destroyed everything they believed was important! Apparently, they too never experienced a teacher like this. Yet for the first time, I felt pointed toward my True Home.

During a break, I asked Fr. de Mello where and who I might visit in India. He quickly responded, "Bede Griffiths." He then opened a small address book and I copied the address. Bede Griffiths had been a Benedictine monk from England who moved to India around the age of 50 after 25 years in an English monastery.

I began reading Bede's writings, his recently published book, "The Marriage of East and West." Just celebrating his 80th birthday, Bede described his move to India as raising a curtain from his mind, opening him to a deeper spirituality. In India, he soon moved to an ashram where two other Roman Catholic priests were offering a broader option for spiritual growth. Bede, with the two priests, became a crossover or bridge to a deeper and universal spirituality. He claimed the early Christian universalism was lost in 4th Century creeds, its creation of a mostly exclusive Bible, and the emperor-enforced Roman Catholic dogma.

Bede became one of a few Christian monks who adopted and incorporated ancient Hindu/Buddhist concepts into their teachings. Both French priests had since died but Bede continued the ashram leadership.

The first day after hearing de Mello's presentation, I returned to Green Lakes State Park campsite where I was camping. Preparing supper, I was suddenly stung by a bee. Within seconds I began swelling in my mouth and feeling dizzy. Weakly I climbed into my van and drove to the ranger station. Stumbling inside, I told the ranger what happened and collapsed in a chair. Apparently, I was having an anaphylactic reaction to the sting. I woke up in an ambulance hearing people ask for my name as they took me to the Crouse Hospital in Syracuse. I remained for an hour, recovering with antidote shots. I missed supper but walked back to the Le Moyne campus arriving just before the evening's lecture. A participant volunteered to return me to the campsite. Later I thought how the bee sting symbolized what was happening to my thinking during de Mello's conference. I was dying to much of my former theological teachings and awaking to a new life.

A few nights after returning home, I experienced another vivid dream. Sliding rapidly down a steep hill of snow and ice, just as a few years earlier, I lost control. Suddenly I awoke in terror, wet with sweat. I drifted back into sleep. Shortly in another dream, I saw a man breaking through our bedroom wall and with a raised pencil as a knife, he was charging towards me! He was from Bob Jones University. I screamed so loud Naomi awoke and slapped me. What was happening? Since the de Mello conference, everything seemed nightmarish and new. The pencil seemed to represent my attempts to figure everything out, the creeds and beliefs I tried to understand. Now it was impossible. God was the Unknowable, an entity to be experienced, beyond dogmatic creeds and doctrines. It seemed like the 1960's with everything crashing the old into the new.

After a vacation break to Maine and my last group bicycle camp around Lake Erie, I began planning my India trip. I read two more of Bede Griffiths' books plus one by a Trappist Monk named Basil Pennington. As his book title stated, Fr. Basil recently returned from a "Pilgrimage to India." He described

Bede Griffiths as the best bridge to India and de Mello as one of the best teachers I could find. I wondered if after the trip I might begin my own ashram.

Naomi, with just cause, became more nervous and concerned. What was happening to me, again? Would this search ever end? I wondered myself. She expressed fear and worries about my drifting away from her. She said my "detached life" was becoming too distant and admitted discussing alternatives with friends. Stunned, I prayed, asking if I now needed to sacrifice my family to "follow my bliss." How far would detachment take me? She asked what I would think if she decided to leave me and take a two-month trip alone by herself? After pausing I wanted to say, "Yes! Yes! Please do. Find yourself apart from me." This new "awakening," like previous ones, left her in confusion with rolling eye balls.

In October, with Naomi accompanying me, thanks-be-to-God, we took a "vacation" to visit people who might help plan my India trip. Staying at a Bed and Breakfast in Corning, I discovered another Bed and Breakfast home in Newfoundland, Pennsylvania called "The White Cloud Inn." After traversing the rich autumn colored mountains of Pennsylvania, we arrived. Surprisingly, it was an old farm taken over by a former Episcopal Priest called George, and now used as a bed and breakfast Ashram. George, I discovered, had traveled to India a few years earlier, experienced his own "awakening," and now ran the inn. Large pictures of his Guru hung on walls in various rooms. Vegan meals were served and I ate my first delicious soy meals with tofu used as a meat substitute. A large collection of books on enlightenment and meditation filled a library located in the once used barn milk house. George, a tall older man with a full head of hair, seemed around 55 years old. Kind and gentle he spoke with a quiet voice. Discovering my job as a Presbyterian pastor, he warned me it would be difficult to practice a deeper spiritually while remaining as a busy church pastor. I left overwhelmed with his ideas, concerned about possible changes, yet thankful I met him.

We drove a few miles further east to Honesdale, where we spent two days at the Himalayan Institute. A former member of Wayside, who recently left her husband, now worked there on the staff. I attended her morning yoga classes. She explained she had to leave her confused and hurt husband to begin a new and deeper life, practicing simple living and teaching others. I discovered most of the residents also recently left Christian churches and in many cases, their spouses. I felt more stress. If I pursued and became more "spiritual," would I too be giving up my family? Didn't Jesus say, "Whoever comes to me and does not hate father and mother, wife and children, brothers and sisters, yes, even life itself, cannot be my disciple."? (Luke 14:26 RVSV) Fortunately, I no longer took the Bible literally.

We drove on through equally beautiful and colorful Massachusetts to Spencer. From there we drove carefully up a narrow pavement road, through lush Maple and Oak woods, to reach St. Joseph's Abbey at the top of a mountain. Fr. Basil Pennington, a large man, well over six feet tall, was expecting us. Wearing his long white monk's gown, he entered our meeting room ducking beneath the lintel of the door opening. With his white beard, he reminded me of Santa Claus. Having read his memoir book, *Pilgrimage to India*, he reviewed my plans, stopping often to commend me and make suggestions. Naomi's decision to not accompany me to India became final as he described the dearth of western conveniences in India ashrams. No chairs. No running water. No toilet paper. No western meals, but mostly spicy vegan food eaten with fingers.

On advice from my supporters at San Francisco Seminary and Sister Joanne, I also contacted Quaker teacher Parker Palmer. He lived on a Wisconsin "Quaker farm" where they grew and harvested food, seeking to live a simple and peaceful life. Some, like himself, studied, wrote and taught living the life of peace.

I told him about my study of meditation and silence with plans for an India visit. I asked for his ideas and suggestions. In our conversations, twice he urged me to think seriously of moving out of the busy parish. One evening, as we talked by phone I asked, "What about my family? I have four beautiful children and a very patient, faithful and longsuffering wife?" Confused, I chose to remain focused on finishing my dissertation study. Then I would decide the next steps. A few years later I read Parker and his wife had divorced.

On November 5, we voted at our local polling station. For the first time I felt a calmness remembering de Mello's words, "If you are detached from expectations, you *will* be social action." I threw out piles of mail on my desk requesting more social action responses. In reading more of William Sloan Coffin's indictments against our government, I began losing interest. I remembered Douglas Steere's words, "...good or great mystics always radiate a strong sense of leisure---they are never rushed."

In early December, I attended a Presbytery meeting and some colleagues chided me for going to India for a vacation. One warned that Presbytery would frown and disapprove of my using accumulated study leave to do such a thing. When I returned home I wrote, "I am feeling so out of step with Presbyterians."

I drove to Sherman for another overnight retreat where I read Bede Griffith's biography. In the deep quiet and remoteness, I again felt the monk within myself. I kept saying, "Don't argue, and don't push for anything! Just be there and let it happen. Enjoy God in all!" It would be much easier said than done.

Shortly before Christmas, San Francisco Seminary sent approval of my trip plans. They were delighted I included a visit to Iona in Scotland. Knowing it would take time from India, I sensed it would make them more comfortable in allowing me to make comparisons. They wished me well and sent a check for expenses. I ended the year giving thanks for Fr. de Mello, my "Teacher of the year!" Perhaps my life.

In mid-February I received vaccination shots for my trip and at the monthly Presbytery meeting, my departure was announced with several congratulating and wishing me well. I grew more restless in the remaining days. At times I fought a deep loneliness, fear, and sense of alienation from Naomi and my children. Lisa returned home from college to say good-bye, and I felt weepier and alone. On March 1, I called my parents to tell them good-bye. When Mom answered she expressed worry about my going, fearing for my safety. I called Naomi's mother to say farewell and she warned how far I had departed from the faith.

Chapter 18

India Pilgrimage

> *"Unless the church can discover its center mystical tradition, it might just as well close because it has nothing left to offer."*
>
> *-- Bede Griffiths*

After lunch on Shrove Tuesday, March 3, 1987, Naomi with Dorinda, Dawn, and Eric, left me standing alone at the Buffalo Airport. Another deep loneliness flooded over me as I fought back tears facing my first overseas trip.

After three hours, I still waited on the tarmac as people worked to properly shut the plane door! Finally, they moved us to another plane. Arriving at Kennedy airport, I rushed through the unfamiliar halls among daunting crowds to find the waiting Kuwait Airline flight. My large canvas shoulder pack had been left in Buffalo! Minus clothing and supplies, including the chloroquine pills to prevent malaria, I panicked but quickly took a deep breath and let it go. "Oh well," I thought, "if need be, I'll just repurchase supplies in England and somehow get the pills." A beautiful young Tanzania nurse, with perfectly styled hair and dark shadowed eyes, sat next to me. Sensing my anxiety, I shared a few nervous words. Responding in beautiful English, as if she had unknown powers, she assured me all would be okay. I finally drifted off to sleep, thankful I still had money, books, and my passport.

At Heathrow, the agent promised my bag would be delivered to me as soon as possible. They needed an address. Before leaving home, Wayside members George and Audrey Wilson gave me an address of their relatives in Glasgow, just in case. Now was the time. Riding and walking my way through the huge airport, like a kid at Disney World, I found a double decker Red Bus with a sign saying "Victoria Train Station." Bouncing along with eyes wide open and nose nearly pressed against the upper deck window, I arrived at the station. The station reminded me of an old castle with it stately brick walls and several white painted chimneys, once used to ventilate room heaters, now pointing to the skies like guardians. Purchasing my ticket, I boarded what appeared to be a new train, plopping down in a seat by the window. The train sped along at speeds I estimated to be nearly 100 mph, zipping past autos and trucks on adjacent roads.

Reaching Glasgow, I asked a man where I might find a telephone. He mumbled a few words in what I concluded were not English. A kind woman recognized my dilemma and came to my rescue, explaining he was a "commoner" with a strong Scottish brogue. She showed me a nearby pay phone, or "tele," and I called the Gorman's. Jim picked me up in 15 minutes to spend the night with him and Nessie.

The Gorman's lived in a pleasant upstairs apartment where they prepared me a delicious dinner. Both were around 60 years old, Jim a recently retired optometrist. They treated me as a relative, sensing we were friends for years. They offered me a guest room where after a hot shower, I crawled under the thick padded blanket called a duvet.

In the morning, Jim gave me warm clothes, as we were about the same size. Nessie drove me to a nearby store where I purchased a Wooly hat and Jim called his pharmacist and got another supply of chloroquine tablets. After lunch they drove me to the train station where I boarded a small, narrow gauge train to Oban. It was a beautiful ride between and around majestic mountains, alongside glistening lakes and abandoned castles.

At Oban, an owner of a small Bed and Breakfast "popped me into a room" for the night. I bathed, dressed in Jim's warmer clothes, and called Heathrow. My bag had arrived and would be sent to the Gorman's. Relaxed, I ate a delicious dinner in a small Indian restaurant before a long sound sleep.

In the morning, dressed in Jim's warm sweater, I boarded a large ferry for the Island of Mull. After crossing the island in a bus rumbling over narrow roads, I was helped aboard a small ferry, which cut through the windy and choppy channel waters to reach Iona Island. Jumping off, I grabbed my bags and in damp ocean air, walked the dirt path past an old church and a field of grazing sheep to reach the ancient Iona Abbey. Large 7th century Celtic stone crosses on the front lawn welcomed me.

The Abbey, now owned by The Church of Scotland, began restoring the old Benedictine ruins in 1938 with unemployed craftsmen. The buildings were presently heated through a hydro process that removed heat from the nearby Gulf Stream. After waiting two hours in the lobby, staff members finally greeted me after their long meeting.

The leader, with whom I had corresponded for weeks, responded to my India journey with mostly disinterest. Chapel services were conducted evenings in an old stone chapel. One night I was asked to share my reasons for travel to India. With nearby sea wind whistling through old chapel stained-glass windows, neither Ian nor his wife attended. I expected to become part of a volunteer workweek to help open the facility for the year. Fiona, a young spirited woman in charge of volunteers, seemed the most interested in my journey but said I could not participate in work efforts due to insurance issues. Disappointed that I had not been so informed, I spent most of my time praying the "Liturgy of the Hours" and walking the old monastery's acreage. One day I walked the dirt path around the island watching busy border collies herd sheep. I stood over remains of small hermitages where 7th century monks returned from "evangelizing" area pagan inhabitants on the mainland. Spending silent weeks in the hermitages, they were visited each day to receive food rations and have chamber pots cleaned.

I enjoyed evening gatherings around a warm fireplace led by staff member Fiona. Most of the 30 or so volunteers sat on the floor as I squatted down in the cross-legged lotus position. One evening I was asked me to lead the meditation and discussion time. The volunteers filled the cozy fireplace heated room, without the disinterested director, as I summarized de Mello's ideas followed by a meditation time. I assumed my experiences in India would be much different. I regretted the Iona side trip had removed a week from my India trip, but felt it had helped secure my travel grant.

Back in London, I called home before boarding my plane to India. I choked up again when Naomi answered but quickly gained control. Not receiving my post card, they were relieved I was still okay. Naomi seemed fine and Eric told me the Sabres had moved into 4th place. Waiting in the huge airport for departure, I wondered if I should have worn a clergy shirt. Maybe it would help when I reached India.

The plane lifted off making scheduled stops in Paris and Bahrain. In Bahrain, shortly after midnight, we were not allowed to walk beyond the well-guarded souvenir and snack shop. I purchased a small red alarm clock. Looking around, I noticed I was now a minority surrounded by Asians and Indians. They dressed well and moved with class and poise, their beauty and attractiveness inspiring. We departed with a full plane and adjusted our watches to 1:15 a.m. I reviewed my steps in landing at Bombay before reading 100 more pages from Shirley Maclaine's new book, "Out On A Limb." It seemed apropos. Her last words read were, "Remember, it's only your perception and not reality." It soon would become a very difficult test.

The jumbo jet landed in Bombay (renamed Mumbai in 1995) at 5:30 a.m. as the sun broke through the eastern horizon in bright orange rays. As we descended I stared out the window over Bombay, a city with around 8.5 million people, surrounded by a carroty pall of heat and pollution. Departing the plane, I strolled in line to the lobby where looking up, I saw hundreds of people jammed together! In thick humid heat, they stood shoulder-to-shoulder, double and triple deep outside the airport's ground level windows. They peered in as if looking for arriving relatives or foreigners.

I spotted a currency exchange booth and after registering my journey, traded 100 dollars into nearly 1200 rupees, equaling four months of average India income. After checking my bags and papers, I took a deep breath, hoisted on my packsack and shoulder bag, and uttering a short prayer of protection, stepped out into the sea of people. I spotted a small bus with a sign reading "Downtown Bombay." Moving slowly toward the bus, scores of beggars swarmed around me shouting with outstretched hands. Feeling rising anxiety over my Pied Piper status, stress flooded over me as I pushed through to the small bus. Thinking safety and relief, I grabbed the step rail and scampered up into bus. I sidestepped to the rear to sit down and looking back saw several had followed me. Some jostled to get in front, then beside and behind me, begging for rupees or dollars. Fearful of attack, I sat down in frozen alertness, like a surrounded scared dog. After what seemed like an hour, but much shorter, the driver finally appeared. A few other passengers boarded, the beggars chased off and we headed slowly toward downtown Bombay to another train station named Victoria.

Exiting the airport, I looked out the window in shock to see thousands of people living in open fields along the airport road, some spread out toward runways. Cloth-covered dwellings transformed the airport grounds into a giant camping area. Along the main road to the city, thousands more people lived sharing space with dogs, monkeys and birds, many in open or makeshift shelters. I stared in disbelief at people living in drainpipes, most looking sad, malnourished and pathetically lonely. I sensed nausea as emotions churned in my stomach.

Reaching a crowded city stop sign, the driver pointed to a taxi area where I could get a ride to the train station. Stepping out of the bus, another sea of shouting beggars surrounded me. I walked quickly and opened the rear taxi door of an old black English Ford, crawled in and slammed the door. Five others quickly followed me in through the other doors, still shouting with outstretched and open hands. More frightened and ready to strike if necessary, I repeated "no" and ordered the arriving driver to get me to the station!

At Victoria Station, today renamed Chatrapati Shivaji Terminus, things seemed little different with more mobs of people--travelers, transients, and beggars. I found the ticket booth and purchased one bound for Tiruchirappalli, site of Shantivanam Ashram in Tamil Nadu province. I would need to change trains in Madras, ignoring Fr. Bede's earlier suggestion to fly directly to Madras. I ordered a first class ticket, assured the food would be safe in an air-conditioned car, which included a bed cot. The ride would take about 2 ½ days, time I expected to enjoy the landscape, meet and chat with Indian folks.

Since my train wouldn't depart until 3:30 p.m. I had most of the day to wait. I earlier anticipated a little tour of the city. Not having eaten or slept much since Glasgow, I now felt uncertain about what would be safe to drink or eat or even how to get it. Feeling cultural shock, it began to seem more like a bad dream.

I decided not to wander outside as originally planned. I sat down on a bench and asked myself, "What the hell am I doing here?" as I angrily chased beggars away like pesky flies. I moved to another bench where a nice looking English lady quickly came and sat next to me. Angry and unable to read her map, she asked me, supposing I was a seasoned traveler, if I could help. I couldn't.

More beggars stopped, some looking gentle with pleading, sincere looking eyes. I tried to ignore them. Feeling a shadow, I looked up and one stood waiting quietly, with deep brown eyes with reddish glints. He patiently waited to make eye contact. With long uncut and unwashed hair, his abdomen was wrapped in what appeared to be a dirty brown cotton cloth. Simple, well-worn leather sandals were lightly strapped to his rugged and well-calloused feet. Making eye contact, he spoke in clear English asking if he might be able to help. I coldly responded, "I am just fine!" Irritated I stood up with my bags and realized I must somehow find lighter clothes and sandals and more fluid intake. Still wearing my clothing from England with hot jogging shoes, I was sweaty, weak, and hungry.

I decided to move outside and ignore the beggars. As I moved toward the door, the same beggar who gently asked if he could help, stood in front of me with his kind looking eyes. He gently asked in clear English, "May I help you?" I thought, "Well, maybe God sent him." I said I needed a few light clothes and sandals along with some food and drink. He replied, "The shops are not open, it's too early. But follow me." He motioned me to follow him back into the station. I trailed cautiously in hopeful desperation as he cleared the way. Shortly he pointed out a nice room with cages to lock up my luggage for a few hours! After storing my bag, he led me to a pop machine where I quickly purchased and drank two bottles of cold orange. Maybe this man *was* from God?

We walked outside, assuming he would find me a clothing store but instead he led me to a little eating shop. "It is clean," he assured me. As a beggar, he insisted he must wait outside but I asked him to please come in since I didn't know what to order. He consented. Inside slow moving ceiling fans swirled above and the gentle warm breeze felt refreshing. I drank another bottle of pop and got my new friend coffee. More relaxed I began asking questions. He said he was 34 years old with three small children. His father died before he could finish schooling so he became a "tour guide." Asking me to call him "George," I ate what he suggested after I saw a sample—a large bowl of dalia, cracked wheat cooked in milk, along with a fresh orange that I peeled. I washed it down with a cup of Chai, or tea. Refreshed with more confidence, George led me to an open clothing shop where I purchased a light cotton shirt and pair of sandals.

Getting out of the jogging shoes, we began strolling among the throngs of people bustling off to work or to meet friends for breakfast. Restaurants, made out of bamboo with open-air windows, seemed overflowing with laughing people and loud chatter. We nearly bumped into a lotus sitting flute player, enchanting a huge Cobra arching out of a jar. Suddenly George stopped and I noticed blood oozing from his lower left leg. A large scab had opened. I dug out my first aid kit and quickly sanitized the wound and bound it with clean gauze tape. I looked up and saw scores of people had gathered to watch us.

Arriving back at the station, George led me to a quiet, air-conditioned waiting room for foreign travelers. On the second level it had showers in a large concrete walled room! George then left, probably to guide someone else, saying he would return before 3:30 to make sure I boarded the right train. I took a long soothing shower and dressed in light clothing. I sat and wrote a few words in my journal, trying to remember this was not a bad dream. "Holy shit! So this is India." I laid down on the wide bench in a fetal position and fell into a deep hour's sleep.

George returned around 2:00 p.m. and led me to a post office to purchase airmail envelopes. He then took me to a nicer restaurant where I ate a large delicious grilled vegetable sandwich washed down with two large orange juices.

Back at the train station, George found the car I would be riding which matched my $18 ticket. Passenger names were written in chalk on small black boards outside each car. I shockingly discovered I was *not* in a first class car with air conditioning but a "sleeper." My compartment, about eight feet square, included two folded down boards opposite each other near the roof. Covered with reddish brown vinyl, they were the beds! Below, two other well-worn wooden vinyl covered benches were bolted opposite to each other. Broken cabin fans hung from the ceiling. As the train began to move slowly away, hundreds of other passengers suddenly jumped aboard! My sleeper room, booked for six of us, two of us with the "beds," suddenly became jammed with at least 10 or 15 commuters, smoking, playing cards and having a great time. In shock and disbelief, I quickly climbed up to my bed, laid back with my pack for a pillow, and began praying the "Liturgy of the Hours." I also prayed it would be a quick trip, I would not get sick, or worse, go insane.

Weak and soon feeling dehydrated, poorly dressed vendors scrambled aboard at each frequent stop to sell chai tea poured into plastic cups used by previous patrons. The cups were swished "clean" by the vender's dirty towel or shirtsleeve. I had not brought my own water on board. Tense, I wondered how I could endure until we reached Madras. The idea of feeling a higher or a serene detached Christ Self meant nothing!

The express train, lumbering slowly along and stopping frequently, reached Poona in about 4 hours, roughly 100 miles south of Bombay. An India army soldier, looking to be about my age and dressed in uniform, seemed to sense my confusion and disappointment. He said this would be a long stop and I ought to get something to eat and drink. He offered to guide me. He led me up to a food counter where I ordered a pop and small grain biscuit. Knowing I needed fluids, I quickly drank two more bottles with the tasty biscuits. Finished, I turned around to notice two more large brown eyes staring at me from a short and young, dark-skinned man.

"Are you a minister?" he asked.

"Yes, how can you tell?" I suspiciously asked.

"Because I can see it in your eyes and you were very kind to return empty bottles to the vender."

I asked his name. "Kennedy," he said, explaining he was born on the day of President Kennedy's assassination. His family liked JFK, so they nicknamed him Kennedy. He then asked,

"Is there anything I can do to help?"

"Where is the airport?" I asked, "I want to fly to Madras!"

"You'll need to take a train back to Bombay but must wait for the next one tomorrow."

I said I didn't think I could continue on the train. I felt very weak, hungry and exhausted. Kennedy then replied, "Come with me! You can stay at the Christa Prema Seva Ashram! It is near where I live. The Sisters there will feed and help you."

Seeking for more possible evidence of his credibility I asked, "Do you know Bede Griffiths?"

"Oh yes," Kennedy shockingly replied, "he's a very nice and gentle man and the Sisters know him well. They will help you. Please come!"

Maybe this *was* a miracle.

I thanked the soldier and returned to grab my bag, still on the upper bed bench, and joining Kennedy, we began negotiating the throngs to reach waiting rickshaws. Suddenly a large policeman abruptly stopped Kennedy. They began shouting to each other in Hindi. "Oh no!" I thought. "When will this nightmare *ever* end?"

"Go!" Kennedy shouted, "Go and tell a rickshaw driver to take you to Christa Prema Seva Ashram! Now go!"

Confused and frightened, I pushed my way through the crowd to reach outside the terminal where I saw several waiting motorized rickshaws. Every driver begged for my business. Stammering I said to one, "Take me to...Prema Seva Christa Ashram," or was it "Prema Christa?" Drivers shook their heads in confusion. As I watched the train begin to crawl away, I spotted a hand waving in the crowd and heard Kennedy's voice. Reaching the hopeful driver, Kennedy told him where we needed to go. Piling on my bags, we jumped aboard the open-air tricycle vehicle and sped off, bumping and jostling through hordes of people, leaving behind a trail of smoke.

After about a thirty-minute ride, we turned down a dark, unlit dirt path surrounded by shadowy trees. Passing Kennedy's dorm, we emerged into the site of the secluded Christa Prema Seva Ashram. Two Sisters, Sara and Brigitte, were preparing to retire for the night but warmly welcomed me. They served me me a huge bowl of tasty, hunger-quenching oatmeal left from the earlier dinner. I drank several glasses of purified water. Finishing and feeling totally exhausted after the nightmarish day, they led me to a small private room with a narrow mattress bed, slightly raised off the concrete floor and surrounded with mosquito netting. They showed me the shower, a cement stall with a small bucket hanging on a pipe. They gave me brief instructions--fill once to wash with soap, then again to rinse. Refreshed, I took a sleeping pill, crawled onto the net covered bed, noticed a gecko lizard crawling along the wall, and drifted off into a ten-hour sleep. My first day in India ended.

I awoke to beeping horns, accelerating engines and screeching brakes from nearby traffic. The ashram lay only a short distance from a busy street. Sleeping through meditations, I joined a small group of 7 or 8 residents for breakfast. Sitting lotus in a circle on a smooth cement floor, we ate with our right fingers in silence. The food was tasty and good, consisting of unleavened flatbread called chapatti, often covered with hot cereal and eaten with fruit, yogurt and hot chai.

After the quiet breakfast I spotted a strange looking resident about my size but dressed sort of odd. From England, Sister Sara told me he had been in India for around ten years. He had dark black hair, his matching eyebrows accentuating his deep-set eyes. With a deep clear voice, he described himself as a "Buddhist-Christian." He explained he was fulfilling a year's pledge to wander India as a Sanyasi. "A Sanyasi" he explained, "wanders as a traveling beggar who offers love, assistance and spiritual counsel to people." His possessions were stowed away, he explained, in contrast to a Sadhu. A Sadhu is a beggar who gives up all possessions but stays in one place meditating, reading, and helping people. Although he had been given a Buddhist name, he asked me to call him "Christopher," never just "Chris." He saw himself as a bearer of Christ, the Christian word, he explained, for the Inner Self. He hoped to earn and use his Buddhist name when the year ended. He seemed kind and helpful but also quite strange looking to a foreigner as myself. He covered his face with bright paints and smudges of red, yellow and black on the forehead. He wore simple hand-made sandals and minimal clothing, carrying a light orange cloth wrapped around his waist like a skirt with a light tan cotton shirt. Over his shoulder he carried a larger orange cloth wrap called a dhoti. As part of his vows, he slept outdoors but never explained why.

The two Sisters, from Roman Catholic and Anglican traditions, supervised the ashram. I learned the ashram was created in 1919 as a spiritual center by an Anglican mission worker named Jack Winslow. Experiencing what he described as a spiritual awakening, he sought to blend Hinduism with Christianity. He wanted to help make reparations for the British racism and exclusion of the rich Hindu spiritual traditions. Eastern religions, he explained, were very universal. As de Mello taught, each person has a Higher Self, His True Self. It must be awakened to, to become conscious of. Winslow, a friend of Mahatma Gandhi, also built a small hut for Gandhi when he visited for rest and meditation. The hut foundation remained as a memorial. The ashram, I learned, was the first one to be modeled as a "Christian Ashram."

As I was observing, the essence of Eastern religions was very close to Fr. de Mello's teachings. Liberation is awakening to one's Atman, Self or as the early Christians called it, "the Christ." Christopher explained Hinduism as a much older tradition than Buddhism. Buddhism became a reform movement much like the

161

16th century Christian reformation. This ashram seemed to be the perfect place to begin my India experience.

Christopher told me he also knew and had stayed with Bede Griffiths several times. He agreed Bede was a wise and wonderful person but remained too "holed up" in his beautiful ashram, saying, "He needs to get out more!" Christopher claimed he also knew the shortest and best way to get there, bypassing Madras. He offered to become my guide if desired. He would only need transportation with small amounts of food since he slept outside. I asked Sr. Brigitte about him and she recommended I accept his offer. She warned me, however, he had been seriously abused as a young man in England and still had frequent outbursts of anger and deep depression. He could become domineering and controlling. However, she said I would be good for him. She described him as dependable, smart, and very independent. As a newbie in India, I accepted his offer. It was a wise decision.

I remained at the CPS Ashram four days, recovering from lack of sleep and becoming better oriented. I took part in the daily prayers and the silent sittings taking about an hour each morning and evening. "Sittings" were on a smooth cement floor in lotus position with legs crossed. A few small stools were available for the occasional visitor who could not sit cross-legged. A sense of being confirmed in my spiritual path deepened. I had been following daily prayer routines for over four years, mostly reading the daily offices from the "Liturgy of the Hours." More silence was now added to my daily disciplines.

Sr. Brigitte also recommended two important books for me to read from non-Christian sources, "Patanjali's Aphorisms" and the "Bhagavad-Gita." I checked both out of their small library and began to read, purchasing copies before I left. They too, mesmerized me, further amplifying what de Mello taught. From the Bhagavad-Gita:

*"The untrue never is: the True never isn't. The knowers
of truth know this. And the Self that pervades all things
is imperishable. Nothing corrupts the imperishable
Self. ...The embodied Self is imperishable. You have
no reason to grieve for any creature. .... who dares
to see action in inaction, and inaction in action,
is wise, is the yogi, is the one who knows what is
work. ...He forsakes hope, restrains his mind, and
relinquishes rewards—he works yet he does not work.
He is satisfied with whatever comes, unaffected by
extremes, free from jealousy. ...Restlessness is the
product of sensual joys, joys that are impermanent,
joys that begin and end. The wise do not seek pleasure
in them. He is reposed, he is happy, who has no anger,
who has no desire."*

(*The Bhagavadgita*, Transcreated by P. Lal,
reprinted, 1983, Orient Paperbacks, Delhi, India)

Such words would become important to my future teachings
and work as minister, pastor, father and husband. It planted further
the idea that this world and the whole universe were not "real,"
only illusion. They were Fr. de Mello's teachings driven deeper
into my heart and mind. However, the ideas still frightened me.
At times I asked, "Who then am I, this man named 'David?'" My
body/ego self, as explained, is only an illusion in time. My true
identity is my inward divinity, the Atman, or the Christ-Self. The
"I" is Spirit. Losing my ego with its familiar cravings and hungers
frightened me. I still remained identified primarily as my body.

Sr. Brigitte also knew Fr. de Mello, whose ashram named
Sadhana, was nearby. Despite her British accent, she spoke much
like him. With a bit of scolding in her voice, she suggested I leave
behind many of my western obsessions with personal hygiene in
order to make the trip more enjoyable. Thus I learned to take
baths with two small pails of water and after squatting over a

hole in the floor, use a small quart can to wash up after bowel movements. I gave thanks Naomi had not come.

Brigitte also showed me an article from the Poona newspaper reporting a passenger train, bound from Bombay to Madras, had been blown off a bridge in Tamil Nadu Province by Tiger (Buddhist militant) rebels. Several passengers were killed. We wondered if it had been my earlier train. Many Buddhists lived in southern India. Their main homeland was Sri Lanka, an island about 20 miles off the southeastern coast of India. They accused the India government of wanting to make Hinduism the state religion and drive them out of the country. Thus I learned radical militants exist in every religion of "love."

The day before leaving, I spotted a tall bearded man from Ithaca, New York. In talking with him, I learned the young man had come to India to study Sanskrit and its possible links to the ancient Hebrew language. He suspected the Hebrew language had evolved from the ancient sacred Sanskrit of India. It would give, he claimed, further evidence the Hebrew language and faith had its roots in ancient Eastern ideas.

After chatting awhile, I mentioned my newness to India with my shock and reaction to its poverty. He responded, "The poverty you see here is mainly your perception of it. The people in those shacks and tents are for the most part accepting of it. They live in peace; it's we who cannot handle our guilt." His response stunned me. I could not understand how people without running water, electricity, cars, larger homes and longer lives could be happy. Were not social justice efforts needed to make sure all had equal access to standards of living I enjoyed, the answer to people's deepest longings? He also told me India's culture represented one of the few places not destroyed by Christianity, even though deeply harmed by 19th century political and missionary invasions from the west.

On my last day at CPS, Christopher showed me how to purchase train tickets without waiting in long lines, using special queues for foreigners with passports. After buying tickets for our next day's train, I purchased him a few yards of orange cotton material to make more coverings for himself. Since I was a minister, he claimed I needed some identification since I was not wearing a collar. So I purchased a burnt rectangular orange piece of cotton, 8 by 4 feet, for a dhoti, which I could use to meditate with or cover as needed. In meditation, it could be pulled over the head. I still use it today.

Before leaving, Christopher took me to a large Hindu Temple, located on top of a hill. We passed pilgrims crawling slowly up the rocky staircase. Beautiful idol figures adorned the inner temple before which people bowed to the floor. I tried to keep an open mind but it seemed wrong. I recalled the verse" "You shall not make for yourself a graven image…" (Deuteronomy 5:8,RSV)

A brilliant sunset appeared as we gazed over the wall where we stood. In amazement I noticed hundreds of small homes, which looked like temporary shacks, lining a river with people scurrying about. The contrast seemed so bizarre and I commented, "I feel sorry for those poor people living in such poverty." Christopher sharply replied, "Those people live with more peace than you!" I then remembered an earlier sentence from the Gita, "You have no reason to grieve for any creature." It still left me uncomfortable.

Before leaving, I walked to Kennedy's nearby room to say goodbye with a final thanks, the "angel" of my first day in India. He lived in a nearby hostel reserved for law students at the University of Poona. I found him with other law students mud wrestling in a large rain-filled ditch.

"What are you doing?" I asked.

"Well," he said, "after straining hard to learn our studies, we need a mind break so we just get crazy!"

Ah! I could use more of the same. I told him I would be moving on to Bede Griffith's ashram and thanked him again for his "rescue" a few nights earlier. He hugged and wished me well, thankful for his opportunity to help. He had been so kind and gracious but I was anxious to resume my trip. Christopher said I always seemed in too much of a hurry.

With Kennedy

Before leaving, Christopher handed me a pajama type suit of his to wear. "You still look too much like another tourist smuck!" he declared, "You need to give some sign you are on a spiritual pilgrimage." Reluctantly I put it on and as we headed to the train station, I even felt a bit like a Sannyasi.

We traveled three days and nights including changing trains in the middle of a night, before we arrived at Shantivanam in Tamil Nadu. It lay about a 20-minute walk from the small village of Kalutali. I felt much more secure with Christopher's companionship, even though he rode most the way on top of the train. No wonder, as he said, "Bede thinks I'm crazy!"

In Kalutali, we climbed aboard a human drawn rickshaw for the short ride to Shantivanam Ashram. The rickshaw, a two-wheeled wooden vehicle, looking like a harness racing cart, moved along over the dusty path as I was amazed at the strength of the young wiry man who pulled us. I generously tipped him before we strolled down a 100-yard tree lined dirt path into Shantivanam, the name meaning, "Forest of Peace."

When I identified myself, an Indian assisting Bede came quickly and said they had been expecting me. He led me through the ashram, perhaps encompassing 10 acres filled with trees and gardens. We came to one of the two guest huts. The huts were gifts from a Swiss woman engineer who, after a year's visit, built the huts as a thanksgiving. Most of the 30 or so guests slept in a nearby cement floor dorm. My hut actually had a small amount of piped water brought in from the nearby Cauvery River, which supplied a real sitting toilet and a shower which trickled out enough water for a quick washing. A mosquito net covered my small raised bed cot. Looking from the front porch I could watch the sun set over the beautiful river, on whose sandy banks we would sit for morning and evening meditations. Bede later told me I was in "The Ashram Hilton." An English woman occupied the hut next to me and a few times offered me "biscuits" or cookies. "Ah," I thought, "I could easily stay here another month and return home!" I felt deeply honored and relieved to finally be there.

My Ashram Hut

Fr. Bede came by the first evening to welcome me, go over the schedule and answer any questions. Sitting across from me in the hut, he spoke with a gentle voice, being about my height, a thin man who recently turned 80. His hair was wavy white with a reddish, narrow face and blue eyes. Some commented we could pass for father and son, or grandson. In the ashram, the Indians knew him as Swami Dayananda, named after a famous Hindu teacher of the 19th Century. Bede returned late each afternoon to check on me and answer questions, often staying nearly an hour. He never seemed rushed. The first day he walked me to the library with its outside walls covered with gorgeous flowers. Having a wonderful collection of spiritual books, he introduced me to one explaining the Upanishads, some of the earliest records of ancient Hindu ideas.

I rose each morning at 5:30 with the sun breaking over the horizon, crawling from under the mosquito net before a quick trickle shower. I then joined the silent line walking the dusty path to meditate along the Cauvery River. We sat about an hour as the sun rose higher into the sky. I then rejoined the line in moving back to the open-air temple where Bede arrived with his assistant at 7:00. Sitting on a slightly raised platform, Bede led morning prayers before offering the sacrament. Most of the residents seemed to be native Indians interspersed with five or six foreign visitors from around the world. On my first day in the temple, I removed my sandals and sat quietly on the right side. After about 10 minutes of quiet meditation, I glanced up to notice that only women were surrounding me while men sat on the left. I quietly moved over noticing a grin on a couple faces.

After morning prayers, we walked to the open-air dining room where visitors sat around the edge of the clean cement floor painted maroon. Fr. Bede sat at one end under a picture of his mother, and during meals, eaten with our right hands, a person next to Bede read from a book on spirituality. Presently the readings were from Fr. John Main's book on meditation, which discussed the use of a mantra. A mantra is a single word or short phrase one silently repeats with the breath flow while meditating. Mantras help keep the mind anchored from wandering thoughts. John Main, a contemporary of Bede, was born in England and studied for the priesthood, but soon quit and became an attorney. Working for the British in Malaya, he met a swami named Satyananda who taught him meditation using a mantra. Deeply moved, Main returned to England, became a Benedictine monk and spent the rest of his career studying and teaching Eastern meditation and thought.

The food was not nearly as tasty or filling as I experienced in Poona. At Shantivanam, it was very spicy and hot. Ashrams were vegetarian, including milk products from one of the Indian cows, which roamed freely in villages. Yoghurt seemed a natural way to cool the hot-spiced foods, many overcooked. Lentil and other beans with rice were among the staples cooked in water and various plant oils. Chili peppers, black mustard seeds, cumin, and turmeric with garlic were common flavors. One of my favorite items was chapatti flatbread. I ate several pieces to help cool my "stomach fires."

Among books Bede suggested, I found Patanjali's Aphorism Sutras in the library and took it to my hut to finish reading, having begun in Poona. The essence of yoga seemed to be discipline, the discipline of remembering, as de Mello taught, our inner Spirit Self, our True Self. In meditation, quieted through silence and repeating a mantra, one can more likely experience the higher Self. Hatha yoga, I learned, can also help relax the body and mind as a method into higher awareness. Patanjali also taught mastery of the physical world by concentrating on objects to the point of controlling them. Ultimately, however, one yearns to move more into a deeper inner consciousness and away from outward appearances. Such methods can also be used for evil or dangerous goals unless the goal of love is remembered. What one thinks about and gives dominance toward, consciously or not, becomes manifested in one's physical life. Remembering one's Spirit Identity, one lives more in the present moment moving naturally and patiently in accepting one's destiny. It seemed so simple and reasonable yet so very difficult to remember. Could the mind ever be trained or mastered? Especially mine?

Bede talked to me about the older Upanishads, composed between the 8th and 6th centuries B.C. and translated by one of his favorite authors, Swami Prabhavananda.

> *"The Self is not to be known through study of the scriptures, nor through subtlety of the intellect, nor through much learning. By him who longs for It is It known. Verily unto him does the Self reveal its true being."*
> (*How to Know God* by Swami Prabhavananda and Christopher Isherwood, Vedanta Press, 1981)

Again, the emphasis was universal, applicable to all. The Atman, Self, or Christ is within all people by whatever name given. Awareness, or awakening, moves one in the same direction:

detachment from mortality toward the experience of Oneness, or love in its deepest expression.

On the third or fourth day, I found myself considering a move from Shantivanam. Christopher felt seeing a few other ashrams would be good for me. What I had been learning was basically the same as de Mello taught me but reinforced. During the 3:30 p.m. tea break, a Swedish man named Ulf, a retired school principal, loaned me his ashram directory. It warned some of the ashrams were mean and intolerant. It rated Shantivanam very high as a gentle place. Maybe I ought to just stay here and finish my final week with flights to see Madras, Calcutta, and then back to Bombay.

Hungry after another spicy supper, I yearned for a more filling meal, remembering Sister Brigitte's warning about the awful food at Shantivanam. My throat became sore as my eyes and sinuses began flowing freely. I was suffering reactions to the thousands of flowers surrounding the nearby library. Before going to bed I took a Thailand antihistamine Christopher left me. Around 4:30 a.m. something banged loudly on top of my hut and I quickly sat up. I discovered a coconut fell off the tree hovering over the hut.

Sleepy, I attended morning's prayers and after breakfast, walked into nearby Kalutali with small children following me. The exercise felt good and my head quickly cleared. Large cows wandered freely or lay on and along roadways. Main Street featured cotton sheets stretched over tall poles to create a 200 feet long village mall.

After purchasing fresh fruit and vegetables, I stopped at a tailor's shop while walking back to the ashram. Two small wooden tables with an old Singer foot treadle sewing machine, sat under a porch. Various colored cotton rolls lay across a table. The tailor and his wife, Joseph and Mary, invited me into their small one room home. Smooth and odorless, hardened cow dung shined as floor covering where they lived with two children. Joseph surprisingly asked if I could sponsor him to come to America and get a better job. "Where would you work?" I asked. He replied, "On the streets of a big city like New York!" Joseph measured me and made two cotton suits. He brought them the next day to the ashram. Much lighter than Christopher's, they seemed to fit in better with the Indian landscape, identifying me as more than just a tourist or westerner on business.

When Fr. Bede stopped at my hut that day, I shared my ambivalence about staying longer with the increasing allergy issues. He agreed and said a broader experience of India would be helpful for my journey, especially if this might be my only trip. Appreciating my work with de Mello, he said I would benefit by visiting Sri Ramana Maharishi's ashram in Tiruvanamalai. We discussed Patanjali's book, which he knew very well.

I asked Bede about the "Liturgy of the Hours" prayer book or breviary, which years earlier he declared very helpful in his book, "The Golden String." He confessed giving it up after coming to India and suggested I seemed ready to do likewise. He said it easily becomes too mechanical. He encouraged continuing what I was doing: yoga to help quiet the mind and body followed by meditation using a mantra or verse. But he reiterated, "Keep your body with you, center in it, especially the sex organs. The sex organs give power and energy to your desire for Oneness." For an extended solo retreat, he suggested seven to ten days. He recommended I take along one spiritual book to use as the need arose. "Remember," he said, "you must allow renewal to take place gently for it cannot be forced."

We also discussed Bede's renewed interest in the Trinity and how he had been rethinking the idea. He suggested thinking of the "Son" as our "True Self" and not just Jesus, a radical shift from traditional Christianity. God the Father, Jesus the Son, and Spirit are all one yet each is within us. Jesus can be a name for the True Self, the universal Presence in all.

I asked Bede about the use of the 4th century's Apostle and Nicene Creeds. He replied, "The Apostle and Nicene Creeds were written to basically shut down the earlier centuries' 'creative thinking.'" It would take me a few more years before I could absorb, understand and have the courage to accept his response. The creeds had strengthened the 4th century formation of the Roman Catholic Church as the exclusive dispenser of holiness and salvation.

I told Bede of my earlier visit to the large temple in Poona, feeling uncomfortable seeing people bow down to idols. He responded, "Well, what do you call yours?" It stunned me as I recalled our forms, creeds, beliefs, dogmas, traditions and practices. "At least," Bede responded, "they call theirs 'idols.'"

I loved and deeply respected Bede for his brave and courageous journey. I knew I would enjoy talking more to him but felt the continual desire to move on. God bless him, I prayed, in this "Forest of Peace." We would exchange letters for several months.

After prayers and breakfast, on March 25 we said good-bye to Fr. Bede. Christopher took a blurry picture of Bede and me, and leaving Shantivanam, we headed east toward Madras and the city of Tiruvanamalai in Tamil Nadu. I wore my new light cotton clothes but Christopher declared, "You still look like a smuck!" He thought I should dress more like a western priest.

We walked back into the little village of Kalutali and boarded a bus to Trichy, or Tiruchirappalli, the center of Tamil Nadu. I noticed women working in fields as we road by, one wearing the extra shirt I had left in Kalutali a few days earlier.

Calling ourselves Swamis (my new white suit helped) we climbed the city's "Rock Fort" and toured the magnificent temple while waiting for our bus. Covering our foreheads with red ashes, we entered the high temple where the view was spectacular alongside ornate paintings and idols. An old Swami showed us around until he began asking for money. Christopher then rudely told him to "bug off!"

After eating supper on fresh banana leaves, I waited for Christopher who went shopping for oranges. I now felt secure watching the passing buses, bicycles, rickshaws, oxen and elephants – similar to a crowded fairground or mob outside the Bill's Football Stadium. Reaching the station, a bus prepared to leave with two empty seats. We jumped aboard.

We bumped and rattled along for hours with thousands of buses, lorry trucks and cars roaring past on a narrow two-way paved road toward Madras. Service stations along the way seemed non-existent. At one stop I needed to relieve myself. Christopher said to go behind the bus where I found others relieving themselves alongside the road. "Crazy place," I thought. We changed buses and turned onto a narrower country road bouncing north to Tiruvanamalai. We arrived at 4:00 a.m., walked two miles to the Sri Ramana Maharishi Ashram and plopped down to sleep on the front cement porch.

At 6:30 we were awakened and fed a delicious breakfast of fresh fruit and chapatti bread. Warmly welcomed, we registered and were led to a nice room, which featured a private bath and toilet with window screens and fan. I quickly went back to sleep while Christopher went hermit hunting.

The Ramana ashram existed as a memorial to the famous spiritual teacher. A large sign, given by the India government, gave honor to his life. While a teenager, Ramana experienced an unusual spiritual awakening, and in a few years, an ashram was literally built around him. There he wrote and taught until age 65 when he died of cancer in 1950. My guidebook described the ashram as now mostly a waste of time for spiritual teaching but each day, one of the teachers came by to ask how I was doing and if I had any questions. Overshadowing the ashram and city towered nearby Mount Arunachala. Mount Arunachala contained many caves where seekers and hermits spent time meditating. Some still lived in them and I hoped to gain a few interviews.

The food in the ashram was excellent as we sat on the cement floor using our right hands as spoons and forks. I watched a man across from me sweep a whole bowl of soup into his mouth with fingers. In contrast to Bede's ashram, few foreigners were present, most recognizing the ashram guru as a nationally respected teacher. Meals were eaten in silence but no readings were shared. The higher elevation with drier air quickly cleared my sinus congestion and I sensed an improved rhythm and comfort with Christopher.

We attended morning meditations in the large roomy temple, easily able to seat 200 on the shiny cement floor. A life-sized statue of Sri Ramana sat in lotus meditation at the front on a raised platform. I assumed Sri Ramana sat there years ago answering questions from those who came. Concluding the 40-minute meditations, a few robed priests quietly carried in rice and coconut milk and placed them on a small stand. After chanting prayers and waving incense, all were invited to walk forward, bow and consume. I noticed the comparison to the Christian Eucharist— we imagined eating and drinking in the spirit of a person who incarnated love by his life and teachings.

We climbed Mt. Arunachala to interview a man Christopher had found, a middle aged Australian who moved there to become a spiritual teacher. A constant talker, I found him hard to follow. When we left, Christopher said he was "cracked!" I returned alone the next day to ask more specific questions about solitude. He suggested I purchase a book of Sri Ramana's teachings in the ashram bookstore. Ramana wrote little in his later years but an English journalist named Paul Brunton, visited him in the 1930's. Brunton recorded copious notes of Ramana's discussions during daily sittings or satsungs. I purchased the large book, "Talks with Sri Ramana Maharshi" and began reading. Today it can be downloaded in a few moments from the ashram website.

I immediately noticed similarities between Sri Ramana and de Mello's teachings. What especially struck me was Sri Ramana's strong emphasis on this world, the material physical plane, as being illusion, even death. He likewise emphasized our identities not as bodies but as spirit. "Find out who the observer is, the one who asks the questions, and you will find your Self." Bodies are ephemeral and passing, locked into time and space. The I-Self is immortal, timeless, and One with eternity.

The fear of leaving my body identification, my ego, and living with less guilt frightened me and would remain a slow lesson to learn. My Christian teachings strongly emphasized our identities as bodies. Bodies were real and would be raised from the dead as the 4th century creeds stated. Theologically and personally, I sensed myself moving deeper into dangerous territory, into what I remembered being called heretical "Gnosticism."

Sri Ramana taught solitude not be thought of as being alone in a forest or wilderness. Different methods work for different temperaments. Solitude is a place of the heart, an understanding of reality by which one lives. Christopher also told me that for extroverts, more like myself, frequent solitude experiences are more essential than for introverts.

On Mount Arunachala, we also visited the cave where a 70-year-old spiritual teacher, a personal assistant to Sri Ramana, remained 11 years after Sri Ramana's death. I found the cave's darkness overwhelming. It was okay as long as I could see the entrance light, but moving in deeper felt like a curtain dropping over my whole life, blocking out everything! I didn't stay long enough to see the "light" as people reportedly experienced.

Still living, Christopher introduced me to Ramana's assistant, Swami Satyananda, in his small hut near the ashram. He answered a few of my questions but nothing new was learned. He said I had a good understanding of Ramana's teachings. We also corresponded a few months after my return to Hamburg, his replies coming to me on stationary still bearing Sri Ramana's photo. Leaving his hut, I noticed a large anthill, which stood over six feet high. Crowds thronged around it and when I asked "Why?" a person who spoke English replied, "A large Cobra snake is inside which usually crawls out about this time of day. If you see it, you will be blessed!" After waiting five minutes, I moved along.

Eating supper that evening in the ashram, Christopher surprised me saying he considered me a "rare buddy" with whom he felt quite comfortable. It moved me, feeling the loneliness in his life, yet I desired more time without his constant presence. I felt thankful for his guidance but I longed to be more on my own, without his frequent edgy flashes of anger.

After supper, we stopped to see a German musician named Tapasvini, whom Christopher discovered and recommended. Tapasvini, her adopted name for a year, was an accomplished musician who had studied music at The Julliard Music School. After working a few years in Germany, she moved here to live as a monk for a year and discover more her "Inner Self." I envied her but realized I could not do such with my family. While talking on the roof at sunset, we suddenly looked up to see Mount Arunachala glowing with bright flames streaming out the summit! A rare event, this phenomenon occurred often from which the mountain received its name meaning, "Mountain of Fire." Christopher said I was blessed to see it.

With Tapasvini

The next evening, as darkness came around 6:30, we boarded another bus for the next ashram in the state of Kerala. Christianity came to Kerala in the 1ˢᵗ century, purportedly by one of Jesus' disciples, Thomas. The Kerala Christians, still comprising 20% of the population, assimilated with the Hindu faith and taught a universal presence of Divinity. The Roman Catholic Church took control during the 19ᵗʰ century missionary movement and destroyed most similarities with Hinduism. Today Kerala still remains the most democratic state in India including a socialist party in its congress. Christopher wanted me to see the state and a woman guru he knew I would appreciate.

We traveled nearly 125 miles northwest that night on a rattling bumpy bus, winding up and over mountains on more narrow, low-grade paved roads. Passengers, including myself, curled up in coats and blankets to keep warm before we arrived in Bangalore around 3:00 a.m. One of the most modern cities of India, we exited the bus, hoisted our packs and walked three miles to the train station.

We passed through streets with families sleeping, noticing rats scampering among them looking for food. At the station, we lay down and slept with scores of others stretched out along the rim of the large circular cement floor. At 6:30, covered with my orange dhoti, police guards walked along poking people with sticks to awaken and move them out. Christopher whispered, "Keep still." Seeing our orange dhotis, the policeman moved quietly by after which we got up, my shoulder numb from the concrete. Crowds of people stood huddled around small TV screens, a recent new phenomenon. Entering the large bathroom, several men leaned over a long trench sink irrigating their noses, reminding me of a huge neti bowl.

Christopher immediately began checking for the location of the Kerala woman guru from his contacts in Bangalore. He discovered she had gone on a six-month retreat into the Himalaya Mountains. I thought, "What a great job; work six months, then retreat another six!" I was disappointed but Christopher suggested we visit a newer ashram in Mysore, not far south from Bangalore. He said it would be another good example of assimilating Christianity with inclusive Hinduism.

Grabbing my bags, we walked to the bus station, purchased tickets and boarded the bus for Mysore. Bouncing along another narrow highway, we realized the young driver was playing "chicken" with oncoming traffic, especially buses and lorry trucks! Christopher became furious as I sat praying. Reaching Mysore, Christopher jumped off and walked quickly into the terminal office. I waited outside while he shouted, swore and ranted in Hindi demanding the staff fire the bus driver before several were killed. He emerged still red with anger. Walking past me he uttered, "You just saw a very pissed off Sannyasi!"

We climbed on a motorized three-wheel rickshaw to bounce and rock our way to the Anjali Ashram. Anjali Ashram was a new complex spread over a few acres of wooded land on the edge of the city. We arrived in time to hear the last hour of Guru Amalorpavadas' lecture to several residents who sat in lotus on a cement floor before him. He spoke clearly and powerfully, reminding me of Fr. de Mello. The presentation ended a weeklong series, the next one to begin in three weeks.

Amalor, his common title, was a 50ish year old Roman Catholic priest from the Bangalore diocese. He also sought to blend and assimilate 4th century Christianity with Hindu/Buddhist traditions. Having influence in the diocese, I noticed some residents were young priests nearing the end of their seminary training. Amalor cynically told me, "After three or four years of indoctrination in creeds and dogmas, they send them here for two weeks of spirituality. It ought to be the other way around!" Amalor claimed many Catholics saw entering the priesthood or a sister order as a quick way out of poverty, since the church existed among the richest institutions in India.

I was given a private hut and slept 10 hours the first night. In the morning Christopher came by and as we chatted, I told him I was thinking about finishing my time in India alone. Time was running out and I felt I could now trust my own "inner guru" to guide me, confident in navigating myself. He became surprisingly defensive saying he still had important things to teach me. If I continued alone, he warned, I would be "torn apart" by India. Angry, he abruptly turned away in disgust and left. I was shocked. I felt controlled and uncomfortable.

Still amazed at Christopher's response, I began reading Vandana Shiva's book on spirituality, which Christopher himself had recommended. Almost as if on cue, she warned of a common misconception among many self-appointed India spiritual teachers: they assume most western visitors are totally ignorant spiritually. The seekers, she wrote, are often beyond the self-appointed gurus. It gave me more encouragement to move on alone.

On invitation, I enjoyed a private and lengthy discussion with Fr. Amalor. I learned he was President over many newer south India ashrams. His mission was to blend the East and West around a common idea of spirituality in which we all have access to the Divine within. We talked about meditation and the church's present hunger for a deeper spirituality.

Soon after I returned to my hut Christopher stopped by. He coldly said he would leave tomorrow and I would never see him again. I felt relief amid disappointment in his attitude.

I remained at Anjali five days, meditating an hour and a half each morning with residents around a fig tree. As the sun rose I repeated a mantra suggested by Fr. Bede. On the in breath I repeated, "Who am I?" Holding the breath, I thought, "I am not my body or my feelings," and then exhaling with "I am the light of the world."

I outlined and updated my intended trip to the Himalayan Mountains, deciding to leave Monday evening. Suddenly Christopher appeared again and said how sorry I will be for not keeping his company. I wanted to curtly tell him, "Just leave!" but kept still.

In late afternoon I took another little self-inventory. The trip was revealing I am not to become a sanyasi or an ascetic person but to continue on as husband and father. Perhaps my role might become similar to Frs. Bede or Amalor: make a blend of Christianity and ancient Eastern faiths, and as Bede suggested, include our Native Americans. Earlier on my ride into Mysore with Christopher, a passenger had asked me, "Would you like to remain here in India?" Before I could even answer, Christopher said, "No, his mission is in America." The comment felt very appropriate and comforting.

The evening before departing, Christopher surprisingly entered the circle of silence, a room where many of us were sitting in meditation with Amalor. Suddenly I heard someone weeping and glanced up to notice it was Christopher. He seemed so lonely, so much in need of wanting a friend, perhaps hoping I would remain one of his rare buddies. I prayed he would find peace.

The next morning Christopher surprisingly came to my hut to say goodbye. He gave me a warm blessing, saying with tears how nice it was being together. I felt happy we could part as friends. We exchanged addresses and after I returned to the United States, we shared several letters. In one he proudly wrote he finished his sanyasi experience and had been anointed as a Lama teacher and given his official Buddhist name. The following year, however, Sr. Brigitte from Poona, wrote me and said Christopher had been deported from the country.

Christopher

I left Anjali Ashram the next day but not before enjoying a friendly and moving farewell from the residents. Most gathered at the entrance to wish me well, including around 20 young Catholic Sisters. I found my way back to the bus station and after another hazardous ride, reached Bangalore around noon. I met a Hindu priest who helped me find a rickshaw to the United Theological Seminary. As part of my grant, I also promised to compare ashrams with this traditional theological seminary in

India. One of my Pittsburgh Seminary teachers had taught there one semester.

The contrast became very apparent with modern desks, chairs and plenty of flush toilets. It seemed more like a traditional Christian college campus. I met one woman among the mostly male class. As I talked with students about their motivation to study, I remembered Amalor's words, "To escape poverty." I asked one group of students what changed in their thinking while at the seminary. One said, "Before we saw ourselves as 'spiritual teachers' but now we are 'social justice prophets!'" As far as theological beliefs, they followed the 4th century creeds.

A woman faculty teacher, who overhead my recent visits to south India ashrams, strongly suggested I visit an ashram in the Himalayas started by E. Stanley Jones. She gave me the address and then warned me to avoid all Hindu ashrams which were filled with crooks and corruption. The comment felt very inappropriate. Another seminarian spoke despairingly of Fr. Amalor, accusing him of stealing land from peasants and then becoming controversial in his teachings, which opposed church traditions.

I attended graduation ceremonies in their western funded auditorium where we sweltered in 100-degree temperatures. Traditionally robed staff gave long boring talks. Afterwards I joined a lawn festival where the hot spicy food included, unlike ashrams, chicken meat chopped into rice. We sat on chairs at tables eating with fingers, dropping our leftovers on the ground for a few roaming dogs.

The next morning, I climbed onto a motorized rickshaw and stopped at the large Bangalore postal station. There I could finally call home. When Naomi answered, I became overcome with emotion, hardly able to speak. The connection was quite clear and I felt relieved they all were okay. During my weeks away, they had been wondering about me. Saying good-bye, I felt a lifetime had been lived in a month, and felt anxious to return home.

I got another rickshaw ride to the train station. I planned to head north and hopefully spend time in the Himalayan Mountains. At the train station, I purchased a ticket to New Delhi and found a veggie sandwich to eat with orange juice. Waiting, I walked to the roof to watch the evening sunset and meditate. Suddenly I noticed one of the graduated seminary students moving toward me. Recognizing my earlier presence, he began expressing his frustration. "I now have a seminary degree but will remain in poverty if I stay here. Would you please help sponsor me to come to the United States?" I recalled Fr. Amalor's statements.

The train ride to Delhi moved along slowly in the growing seasonal heat. Many stops were made, some lasting over an hour. I seemed to be the only one anxious to reach Delhi. One passenger told me trains in India only leave on time from the departing city. Yet I slept quite well and enjoyed good conversations with people in my car. One was a medical doctor from Bangalore traveling to Delhi for a conference. "Why are you not wearing Levi jeans?" he asked, sitting in his new pair with cowboy boots as if he owned a ranch. I replied, "Because I am in India now and need cooler clothes!"

The doctor had studied medicine in London and said the most beautiful site there was watching classy British women walk down the street. Once I asked him, "What do you think of the English invasion and colonization of India? Will India ever recover?"

"Well," he replied, "the British invasion left in its wake a confused and uncertain society. But overall, the impact was about 50-50. It was time for India to change. We needed to join the modern world. We are slowly gaining." It seemed to be the typical long range India view.

At one train stop, I stood with the doctor looking out over hundreds of apparently poor people. I asked, "What can we do to help?"

"Really nothing," he answered, exuding the attitude of karma and repetition of history. Yet he worked in a Bangalore medical clinic helping young families plan and care for their children, including use of modern birth control methods.

Reaching Delhi, I pushed slowly through more crowds, careful not to be pickpocketed. Using Christopher's example, I negotiated the cheapest cost for a rickshaw ride to the Brothers Place in Old Delhi. Weaving our way through six lanes of traffic, I safely arrived to a welcoming but small group of Episcopal monks and brothers. Recommended by Fr. Basil Pennington, they gave me a comfortable small room. I showered, washed my clothes, and rested with needed quiet after the long train trip. The Brothers were all older with few visitors. They remained Western in structure and prayers. Their chapel contained beautiful hardwood furniture, a rarity in India. Yet I was warmly received and remained a couple days eating with them, reading, resting, and joining their prayers.

I made my way back on another rickshaw into New Delhi where I purchased a plane ticket for my return to Bombay. Riding the narrow rickshaw in four lanes of traffic, we nearly tipped over when he ran into a stopped bus! The Indian Air office was air conditioned with plenty of computers. I then stopped at the overhead fan cooled bus station where I purchased a ticket to Bhovali, a city in the Himalayan foothills.

A well-dressed businessman offered to show me the city and its interesting sites. Kind and trusting, we walked around an hour or so around looking and chatting. When I asked if he practiced meditation or ever visited ashrams, he said it was his very lifestyle. I asked what effect the Christian missionary movement had on India. "Very little," he said, "although they did help with the 'untouchables'." He explained the caste system as a misunderstanding and misuse of the ancient teachings. However, when it came to metaphysics and spirituality, he continued, "western religions were far behind in providing answers for liberation and freedom."

On Friday, April 10, I rode another rickshaw to the nearest bus station, a short distance from the Brother's, and began riding north toward the mountains. Another well-worn older bus, we wound our way over narrow roads and jammed streets out of crowded Delhi. We passed a huge city dump covering acres, where flocks of large black vultures dug and scavenged alongside the poor. We rumbled across flat terrain in surprisingly open country, stopping often to move slowly around the remains of gruesome accidents. At one stop, I relieved myself along the road behind the bus, only to look up and see the queue of riders waiting outside two nearby covered toilets.

We came upon a wreck where twisted remains of two lorry trucks lay tipped over, one with a broken off cab. Large camels labored to pull the pieces apart. Later the driver stopped before slowly negotiating around a peasant woman drying her grain on the hot pavement.

After riding most of the day we arrived at Nanital where I stayed overnight. At the edge of the towering Himalayan Mountains, I gazed up in awe and felt a sense of arriving home. In the morning I boarded a shorter mountain bus to navigate narrow mountain roads and passes as we headed upward toward Sattal Ashram in Uttarkhand province. I decided to visit the ashram recommended by the woman staff member from Bangalore. I had doubts about what I would find. After riding hours up and through mountain passes with no guardrails, the bus stopped. A Buddhist priest stepped aboard, chanted a few prayers and offered blessings with the "Eucharist" to all needing help to settle fears. We continued slowly on, gazing down hundreds of feet into adjacent valleys.

The bus finally stopped and I stepped off. Nearly 8000 feet high, I had eight kilometers left to walk. Hoisting on my bags I began, only this time with euphoric, breath taking views of surrounding snow-capped mountains. Many rose above 20,000 feet near the border of Nepal. I inhaled deep gulps of crystal clear thin air, the first in weeks. Along the narrow dirt path, I met two or three people who paused, bowed and with folded hands, gave me the Namaste sign. After being among crowds of thousands, I experienced an Algonquin Park kind of euphoria among the rural, majestic and powerful beauty.

Reaching Sattal Ashram, I quickly became disappointed. E. Stanley Jones founded the ashram in the 1930's but it still remained under jurisdiction of the United Methodist headquarters in Washington D.C. Each year a representative came to make sure they continued as "Christian." So this was the ashram the teacher from Bangalore Seminary said I needed to visit! I should have known.

After checking in, the teacher named Titus, soon began expounding to me his "Christ only theories" and asked me to attend a 10-minute silent time after supper. During the ten minutes of silence, he talked for seven. An older man, Titus seemed delighted to have another rare visitor, perhaps suspecting I might be a Methodist spy from Washington, making sure he taught the traditional faith.

Two other people were at the ashram, a young man and woman from England. Arriving earlier, they had been wandering India for nearly five months. We quickly became friends and shared hours of conversation. Our impression of Sattal Ashram was similar. We were overwhelmed by the beauty and surrounding silence but disappointed in the atmosphere and thinking of the teacher. Titus used his talks to condemn Hindus but became defensive when the English couple asked about reincarnation, a topic I had never considered. The English couple found it helpful.

My large room was located on the mountainside a short walk from the office. One of several empty rooms in a large wooden structure with cement floors, it felt more like a church camp facility. Being the only resident, the front porch gave me a fantastic view of the adjacent valley and mountain. Mornings I watched a long line of women climb the mountain in single file to get spring water. I could hear them chatting, singing and laughing while making the trek across the valley, seeming at peace with their lives. After filling the jars, they placed them on their heads and with perfect balance, returned downward with their families' daily supply, singing and chatting along the way.

I used my time at Sattal to rest and reflect over my past weeks of travel, meditating and making notes for my thesis. I felt more confident to take life less seriously, especially the endless search for right methods or forms to pray and live. I wanted to keep listening for the "guru within" and follow my own pace toward a deeper sense of freedom and love. Evenings I sat on my balcony in silence watching the sunset behind the 15,000 feet high mountains, thankful I had first traveled to South India.

On my fourth day I announced I would leave the next morning. Titus responded, "Oh, you don't like it here? Is the food okay? What can we do?" I summarized my trip and earlier time at Bede Griffiths' ashram. I shared my week with Fr. Anthony de Mello. Pausing, Titus responded, as if feeling relief, "Oh!" he exclaimed, "we cannot compare with those two--they are the best!" I began to understand Titus as more knowledgeable than presumed, but perhaps concerned in keeping his job by pleasing the Methodists. I would soon discover a similar conflict.

The next morning, I packed my bags and stopped to make a financial donation. Titus handed me a printed statement and I discovered I was charged more than all previous ashrams combined! I walked the eight kilometers back to the main highway on another gorgeous, bright, breath-taking morning. Greeted by a few more residents with the traditional Namaste, I reached the main road and waited thirty minutes for the bus to Bhowali.

The only passing bus of the day arrived with people jammed inside and out on the roof. It stopped and friendly arms and hands waved and helped pulled me in. Somehow they all packed in more closely as I squeezed in standing by the door for the ride. When we reached the nearest small village, the bus stopped and it seemed to explode with people jumping down and out including a couple goats and a few chickens.

After purchasing fresh fruit and vegetables I boarded another dilapidated bus with only four passengers and departed for Ramikhet. The bus had no side mirrors and the driver turned frequently to look behind while weaving through narrow mountain roads. He played loud Indian pop music over cheap speakers placed around the bus. The old seats were poorly bolted to the floor and one snapped off when we bounced over a rut. After three hours winding up and down narrow mountain roads with gorgeous views amid mind-numbing music, we reached Ramikhet.

An enterprising and clean little town, I walked another hour to reach a tourist bungalow owned and run by the government. Children often followed me asking for pencils, a possession required to attend school.

The bungalow was clean and quiet with full bath, washrooms, and a front reading porch where I could view the majestic Himalayas. Not bad for 50 rupees, or about four dollars. I ordered an Indian supper from a full menu, one I now better understood. It was delivered hot to my room and tasted delicious with chai tea!

In the morning I took more pictures of the Himalayan Mountains, many over 20,000 feet high with snow covered caps. I then walked back to board another bus for Ramnagar. After five more hours winding and descending along narrow roads without guardrails, we reached the hot dry plains. At the Ramnagar bus station, a tourist guide gave me a map. I found another government bungalow and booked a bed in a men's dormitory room. The bungalow set almost directly across from the John Corbett National Park entrance. I discovered park reservations were full for the next day. Disappointed I decided to stay overnight and return to New Delhi in the morning, perhaps visit the nearby Taj Mahal before flying back to Bombay.

In late afternoon, four young men arrived on motorcycles and reserved beds near me. Civil engineers, they recently graduated from the University of New Delhi and spoke good English. One planned to marry in a few days so they had taken a four-day bachelor's party trip into the Himalayas. After brief introductions, they invited me to supper as their guest. It was my best vegetarian meal of the trip and I enjoyed good conversation. They also were fascinated to hear so many westerners come to India to learn meditation.

In the morning the engineers asked if I wanted to tour John Corbett Park with them, perhaps spot a tiger. I told them the park was full. They laughed and asked if I would go if they got a tour bus, driver, and rifle guard. "Well, yes!" I said. In about 30 minutes they returned in a small tour bus with driver guide and rifle guard! Looking at the small vehicle, I imagined it was the first Land Rover ever produced by the British company. We jumped in and road to the park's entrance. The agent repeated the park was booked for the day. One engineer then quickly jumped off and pulling out his wallet, paid the guard extra rupees, hopped back on and away we went. At noon, after driving all morning on jungle paths with no Bengal tiger sightings, we stopped at the beautiful park lodge. We sat under a large rosewood shade tree chatting and eating shared orange sandwiches. Finishing, they asked if I would like to ride an elephant through the park to find tigers.

"Sure," I answered, "but I think they are probably all reserved."

"No problem," one responded as he headed to the elephant barn, paid some extra rupees and returned saying we could board in 20 minutes. When the elephant and Nepalese driver arrived, all five of us climbed aboard, sitting on an attached platform. Several French photographers looked up in obvious disgust, suspecting what had happened. The engineers then politely asked them to please take our photos, with our cameras, of course! As we lumbered off into the jungle, one of the engineers explained, "After bribing the elephant manager, he told the French their elephant came up lame but we had reserved the 'good one.'" Then he added, "I think the French are very pissed!"

Elephant ride

Unseasonably hot, they said the tigers apparently retreated to higher elevations for cooler shade. We lumbered along atop the elephant which plowed through small trees like a bulldozer. After three hours and no sightings, we re-boarded our small bus and drove around more narrow dirt paths looking for a tiger.

Suddenly the vehicle stopped, unable to move. The well-worn shifting linkage had broken! Unfazed, the small driver crawled under the bus with a toolbox while the guard watched over us. We walked a few yards to rest in the shade of another large Sheesham or Rosewood tree. Suddenly a huge elephant appeared. My heart beat rapidly as I stepped closer to snap a few pictures. Returning the men said, "You were very lucky the elephant didn't charge and kill you! That animal was wild, not circus trained!" Soon the worn linkage was relinked and we jostled back to the bungalow, no tiger spotted.

At the bungalow, the young manager asked if he could purchase my portable Sony tape player/radio and 35 mm camera. He kept pleading, "How much?" Hoping to discourage him, I said, "3000 rupees, cash!" feeling like my father bargaining with a car salesman. It was an amount I estimated would cover about one fourth of my trip's expenses. I expected him to laugh or bargain for less. "Okay!" he replied on the late Saturday afternoon. In less than an hour he returned with the cash! I took a picture of him and he reciprocated before I unloaded the film and handed him the items.

In the morning I was awakened in the large dorm room, filled with 15 or 20 men, by a uniformed soldier chanting prayers while standing before his mandala placed on the wall. After breakfast, the engineers insisted I put my bags on their motorcycles and ride free back to Delhi. I kindly refused and found a bus.

I enjoyed another quiet ride across the flat arid plains on narrow roads, interrupted occasionally to creep slowly around more accident ruins. We stopped to circle another woman drying grain on the warm pavement. No one complained or shouted obscenities. It was if she too owned rights to the pavement.

The Brothers welcomed me back with generous food and curiosity about my pilgrimage to Sattal Ashram. Later I played with some children who tried to teach me cricket before taking one last trip to downtown Delhi to purchase a few more gifts.

The next day, Easter Sunday, I attended the Brother's service with their rigid and formal liturgical style. It finalized my decision to stop using the "Liturgy of the Hours" prayer book. Bede was right—it was time. For dinner we ate a simple English meal of steamed vegetables and fresh fruit, concluding with a pound cake made by a visiting English woman. An English professor from the University of Delhi joined us and invited me to come to his home for more conversation and refreshments. I went but against better judgment, drank mango juice made with unfiltered water. I had left my purification tablets at the Brothers.

That night I slept fitfully and became sick! During my trip I had remained very careful. In the morning I sat nauseated bumping along in a taxi to the crowded Delhi airport. I climbed aboard a large aircraft bus with stadium seats bolted in rows looking like a large classroom. Thick air pollution surrounded us, the end of the runway barely seen through thick smog.

We landed a short time later in Bombay where earlier memories flashed back. While exchanging my rupees into dollars, the officer asked why I had so many left. At the same exchange a few weeks ago, I suddenly remembered my sale of the camera and Walkman. Chills flushed over me. I realized I should have made the exchange elsewhere, not in the same office where I arrived and filled out my itinerary. Fearful of being caught selling on the black market, I reminded them of my ashram itinerary. Checking my earlier record while waiting anxiously, they finally stopped scolding and shouting at me. Still nauseated and weak, they frisked me several times before telling me it was now doubtful my plane would have an extra seat left! Panic began to set in with anger. Remembering Kennedy's earlier experience in Poona, I realized they wanted bribes. I remained stubbornly quiet. Time for the plane's departure arrived but they would not allow me to board. I would not give in. They frisked me and checked my bags again, then coldly ordered me, "Go!" I walked into the waiting plane. A jumbo jet, there were scores of empty seats. Dropping into a seat, I swallowed more antacid tablets before drifting into blissful sleep as roaring engines lifted us toward London.

I felt so relieved to reach London and Heathrow Airport! The crowds seemed so much smaller than before. Everything was so clean and polished. I had a deep sense of appreciation for my normal ordered and hygienic surroundings. Needing to wait a few hours in London and feeling better, I took another red bus to tour a nearby shopping area. Compared to India, the streets seemed barren and devoid of people. Everything seemed so easy to navigate, so ordered. I shopped for a small gift for Naomi, without the constant pleading and urgings to "buy this" or that. Arriving at JFK, the airport and city streets also appeared empty as if people were hiding during an air raid alert.

Approaching Buffalo's airport, I became excited and nervous about meeting Naomi. How could I ever summarize my trip, my quest? Landing, I wearily walked in anticipation to get my bag. When Naomi appeared, I suddenly broke down and cried in relief as I held her tight and we embraced. Arriving home, I hugged Dawn, Dorinda, Eric, and our dog Deacon. I had survived the odyssey of my life into a very new and different world. Now adjustments would begin in a world I knew so well but would never be the same.

Chapter 19

Putting it Together

> "So, we start with an inquiry to find out what is true,
> what the significance is of this misery, this struggle,
> this pain; and we are soon caught up in beliefs, in
> ritual and in theories."
>
> — Jiddu Krishnamurti

My first day home seemed as unreal as India with our contrasting luxury and wealth. I became easily irritated and confused over complaints about home, food, and school. Wasted water annoyed me.

Quickly, the sense of being overwhelmed with my pastoral roles returned with little time, it seemed, for inner peace. I vowed anew to bring more simplicity into my life, but the walls seemed higher and more difficult to climb. I attended a Presbytery meeting and felt out of place, like a child walking into the wrong home. So much anger remained over social injustices. It seemed trivial compared to India. I wanted to resign from the "Peace and Justice Committee" remembering de Mello's words, "Become detached and you are social action."

The Presbytery Executive's husband, very active in Presbyterian social justice issues, drove to my office. A tall man with years of working hard on social reforms, we greeted each other and sat down. He scolded me for becoming like all "new agers" who discover meditation—cool to social justice actions. A few days later a minister friend asked me to join the new "AIDS Task Force." With conflict and guilt, I reluctantly accepted but quit two years later.

I visited my advisor, Sister Joanne Wagner at Christ the King Seminary, and found welcomed support. She seemed deeply interested in my India experience and evolvement. She encouraged me saying the frequent angry social action/justice movements in the Roman Catholic Church had caused divisions and discord.

I remained in conflict. I supported most liberal movements toward social change including liberation of women, racial minorities, people with different sexual orientations, and anti-war movements. But the frequent anger with apparent lack of inward peace bothered me. If lasting change would ever come, would not it come from loving and peaceful minds? "Peace is the path to peace," I often heard, yet I could not forget the words from de Mello, Sri Ramana and others who said, "The ego centered world *is* insane, it *is* death."

Stubbornly I continued my daily prayers with meditation and journaling. I used the "upper room" over the garage until Lisa returned from college and moved into it. I resumed 40 to 45 minute daily walks with our dog Deacon, repeating readings, affirmations and prayers, often sitting on rocks and logs in the nearby woods. I began to see the area around our home as a gifted retreat. Sister Joanne also reminded me again of a hermitage in the woods on seminary property in East Aurora. It soon became a regular place for refuge on selected days and nights.

In mid-June, I attended the General Assembly of the United Presbyterian Church in Biloxi, Mississippi as a voting delegate. Housed in a five-star hotel along the shores of the Gulf of Mexico, I met my roommate, a teacher from Grove City College in Pennsylvania. He arrived with his Greek New Testament and latest Book of Order. It was a difficult week. There seemed to be little contemplative awareness during the long and often cantankerous, confusing sessions. "Leading brains" argued to modify and update rules, practices and positions on various social and church issues.

Exhausted after the first day, I rose early for quiet prayers. I walked across the street and sat in meditation on warm beach sands along the Gulf of Mexico, waves crashing onto the beach relaxing my mind. I returned almost daily. Later I overheard an assembly participant refer to the "peaceful looking person" sitting on the beach each morning, wondering if he was "one of us."

I met a respected minister friend named Dave Lewis, who had lived and worked in Western New York during my first years at Wayside. Wearing a beard as myself, he left the traditional church to lead a committee of the General Assembly. I wondered how it could have been an improvement. Like myself he questioned many forms and attitudes in the church. When I told him of my studies and travels to India, he shook my hand with congratulations and best wishes. He reminded me the "house church" would be the movement of the future.

In July I began a 10-day solitude retreat in the Allegany State Forest near Bradford, Pennsylvania. As part of my dissertation plans, I carried a loaded backpack with hiking stick about an hour into the woods amid 80-degree temperatures. With deepening peace and relief, I set up camp near a small trickling creek. I expected to enjoy and record insights found in being alone in the woods with the Great Spirit. Maybe I would even be favored with a vision or clear voice telling me exacting what to do.

By the second day I became doubtful. My head felt dizzy as heat and humidity soared into the mid 90's. It seemed more strenuous than India as swarms of mosquitos buzzed and sucked into my open body areas like miniature vampires. On the fifth day, covered with mosquito bites after another restless, scratchy night, I moved camp upstream to a flatter area, hoping the bug population might decrease. But headaches and dizziness continued as weariness settled in deeper. Prayers, walks, and sittings became more difficult. That night, curled in my small tent a short distance from the creek, loud grunts and rustling noises awakened me. Forgetting black bears were common here, I remembered leaving food packs on the ground. I slowly pulled back the tent flap and starred into the darkness. Nothing moved. Only the trickle of the creek could be heard. I turned on my light––maybe a raccoon. Suddenly I spotted a huge black bear standing on two hind legs near the creek a few yards away! Perhaps a bit freaked out, the large bear dropped down and lumbered off into the dark woods. My sleep ended and the headache deepened.

As the sun rose after little sleep, I pondered quitting. With red itchy bites on arms, neck and face, a fever chill encompassed me. I tried to divert attention by gathering small branches to start a fire for breakfast. I splashed creek water over my body, ate and felt better, but soon realized I must give in. With arms looking like measles, I conceded defeat, packed in my camp and plodded the narrow worn path back to the van. Tossing in my gear, I sat in the luxurious bucket seat and drove north to Hamburg, surprising Naomi and family with my "surrender."

I remembered Christopher's warning in India when I considered joining a 10-day intensive solitude retreat— "You likely would return home in a strait jacket!" Maybe he was right. I thought of St. Anthony's words, Desert Father of the 4th century, who warned that desert solitude often vomits up novices like bad food.

Another dissertation requirement included leading two weekend retreats separated by 3 months. The purpose was to test solitude and meditation with a group of volunteers. On the second weekend of September, 20 participants gathered at Presbytery's Duffield Camp. 35 miles south of Buffalo in remote woods of maple, pine and oak trees, with a relaxing creek bubbling through the acreage, it seemed like the perfect location. Participants agreed to participate for two weekends. Most were Presbyterians but a few came from Roman Catholic backgrounds, some with none. Meeting Friday evening, we planned to conclude late Sunday afternoon. I asked participants to remain silent except for morning and evening prayers, including time for feedback and questions. I tried to model the experience of an ashram, especially Shantivanam. I would be available if a participant needed to talk or had serious questions about the experience, or even wanted to leave.

With Naomi planning and preparing meals, silence quickly became the most difficult issue. At first, most conversation centered on deserved praise and appreciation for Naomi's culinary skills: fresh baked breads including her irresistible banana bread, steamed oat meal, scrambled eggs with onion and tomatoes with fresh coffee. On Saturday it rained most of the day making silent walks throughout the camp trails more difficult. Confined by rain, some refused or were actually *unable* to keep silent.

The worst participants were a retired Presbyterian minister and his wife who talked incessantly in open defiance. They soon even gathered various participants into the lodge basement and outside for conversation. I repeated the silence agreement and posted hand written signs around the pine-paneled lodge. The minister and his wife, however, continued to ignore keeping silent. I decided not to invite them back.

When the retreat ended, discouragement and doubts filled my mind. Maybe such silence would not work among extroverted Americans. Maybe silence would never find a home in their spirituality. I would describe the failure in my dissertation.

In a few weeks I received a letter from the Presbyterian minister, chastising me for departing from Reformed understandings of spirituality. The letter shocked and dazed me but gave relief when promised he and his wife would not return in January.

In mid-January 15 of the 20 returned for the second weekend. It was cold and snowy, but bright winter sun flooded over hiking trails creating bright crystals of glistening snow. On the first day, however, Naomi received a call reporting her grandfather, Pappy Stouffer, had died in Maryland. She returned home to attend the funeral. "Would this weekend be another flop?" I wondered.

Amazingly the group took over the food preparations, even *preparing them in silence!* Soon the weekend reminded me more of what an ashram experience might be. Late Sunday afternoon we conducted our closing time including prayers and the Eucharist, modeled again from Bede Griffiths' Shantivanam Ashram. I invited people to share discoveries or comparisons from their two weekends. I suggested using an object found on a silent walk to help illustrate. Tears often flowed, and a surprising sense of community poured over all. People shared how major releases had come into their lives. One woman told of meeting a deer along a wooded path, which brought a deep sense of healing to her past abusive life. Another brought in a ball of snow and watching it melt before us, described how her resistance to silence had melted. Most wrote their evaluations for me to use in my dissertation. I drove home thinking anew about becoming a spiritual director. Maybe this would be my place, my home to teach others about our Self Home.

In late April, 1988, after a busy week, Naomi and I drove to Boston, Pennsylvania where I had begun my pastoral career. I spoke at the Sunday installation service for a friend I met a few years before in Buffalo. I was tired but enjoyed meeting our former friends and assisting in his installation.

We returned to Hamburg on Monday and early Tuesday I began another busy week's routine. I drank more coffee than usual at breakfast. I returned home for lunch and a quick nap before leaving to join the long afternoon and evening meeting of Presbytery. After another cup of coffee, I laid down on the sofa for a short nap. Suddenly sharp pains and tightness rose in my chest. Realizing how busy I'd been since Easter, I wondered if I might be experiencing a heart attack. I called Naomi who immediately phoned the doctor. He suggested she get me to the hospital as soon as possible. I could not believe it. Refusing the ambulance, Naomi drove me to the emergency room. I arrived in a slumped, exhausted posture before they wheeled me inside for tests and observations.

I remained hospitalized three days during which doctors decided I had not suffered a heart attack, but experienced exhaustion and indigestion. Reflux from excess coffee acid backed up into my esophagus. Relieved, I decided I must let go of more responsibilities.

While waiting to be released, my recent new friend, Chas Griffin, came to visit. We chatted briefly and before leaving, he left me a thick blue covered book called *A Course in Miracles*. I left the hospital feeling more resolute to not be such a busy pastor, but a more contemplative leader/director in the community.

A few weeks later I went on a two-day retreat at the nearby Roman Catholic Columban Retreat Center. Once a mansion of a Buffalo family, it was located along the shores of Lake Erie in Derby. I slept, took walks, and began reading my new book, *A Course in Miracles*. Immediately I became excited. It seemed to include the same universal spiritual ideas I had discovered with de Mello, and the Eastern religions of Hindu and Buddhism. It also was written in the similar Shakespearean King James Bible language. It began by summarizing its message:

> *Nothing real can be threatened.*
> *Nothing unreal exists.*
> *Herein lies the peace of God.*

It seemed so Eastern. I discovered it was written, or scribed, by an atheist psychoanalytical researcher named Helen Schucman, from Columbia University's College of Physicians and Surgeons in New York City. She claimed it came to her through a voice heard for over seven years. The voice identified itself as Jesus, and in 1975 the recordings were published in three books. Assisted by her co-worker, Bill Thetford, the voice quoted and explained over 800 Bible verses, giving correction to the many errors and false teachings of the 4th century church creeds and their literal interpretations of the Bible. It seemed incredible, but became another important resource to enhance my learning and practice of the idea of a universal salvation for all. It was just what I needed, or didn't!

In September I learned one of my former pastor friends committed suicide. He and I had established the "Reverse the Nuclear Arms Race" task force in 1978, but in subsequent years we drifted apart. We met often at Presbytery meetings where we still shared some of our cynicism. He expressed surprise as I kept moving more into spirituality, what he called my "contemplative life." After the India trip, he once asked,

"So what does Hinduism and Buddhism teach about your body?

"Well," I responded, "It isn't real! Bodies are part of the illusionary material world." Rolling his eyes in disbelief, he replied,

"Well, I am now *into* my body!" as he showed me his growing pectorals and biceps from working out.

A few weeks later he was discovered laying naked in a public park giving his body an apparent sunbath. Police spotted him and arrested him for "Indecent Exposure." His name quickly spread into local media. Overcome with stress, he evidently drove to the nearby Niagara Gorge and in deep despair, jumped into the rapids, never to be seen again. Shocked and saddened, I wept hearing the news. His death pushed me further in pursuing my new directions.

I continued reading older and current spiritual teachers such as Francis DeSales, Vivekananda, Matthew Fox, Parker Palmer and others. Increasingly I became attracted to books written by Ken Wapnick as he taught and explained the *A Course in Miracles*. His book on Gnosticism clarified further its contrast to the 4th century church that I was within. Ken often frightened me, however, with his radical new ideas and interpretations, planting deeper the ideas I heard earlier from de Mello and repeated in India.

"This world, including your body, is only a dream. It is nothing but your imagination. God made none of it. The world is our dream of separation, a separation which in reality never occurred."

Ken Wapnick seemed so Eastern and brilliant in providing me with another source of spiritual teachings that featured even the channeled "Voice" of Jesus. I began to further understand the Bible and story of Jesus in complete reversal from what I had learned. The story is really about an experience of love, obtained by understanding and living with forgiveness, first for oneself, then others.

Soon *A Course in Miracles* became like a new Bible for me. I integrated parts of it into my dissertation. I could sense future conflicts but completing the dissertation became my major goal. After finishing the doctoral work, I might be able to discern new options for a work place. For now, I would not leave or move my family. Our daughters were in college and Eric soon would be finishing high school.

In March, upon invitation, I led a "Spirituality Workshop" at a "Presbytery Day" in East Aurora. Surprised, the packed room of Presbyterians seemed fascinated with my recent evolution, as I tried to share deeper meanings for meditation, the getting in touch with our Higher Selves. I felt encouraged to continue my path, perhaps even become a catalyst for a new direction in the Presbytery. Naively, I began seeing myself as a bridge, sort of a minor league Bede Griffiths or Anthony de Mello, combining Eastern and Western Christianity with other mystical traditions to teach a universal Divinity within all. Maybe I could even remain in the parish to model my new direction.

Buoyed by optimism, hope and naiveté, I started sharing passages from the *Course* for various Gospel readings during Sunday services. Chas expressed surprise and urged caution. Soon, however, I realized a fire had been lit, perhaps with my father's "go-wide-open, put the pedal to the metal" attitude. Discussions began to emerge about my use of the *Course*.

At the September, 1989 Session meeting, a few members came to request *A Course in Miracles* be banned from all church worship readings. They had even consulted the Presbytery Executive and she recommended the action. Surprised, I felt fear and puzzlement. "Well," I thought, "this might be the time to *seriously* leave and begin a farm/prayer center, become my own ashram teacher!" I left the meeting strangely renewed in excitement, hope, and freedom.

A few days later, I met with the Executive who sternly charged I had moved outside the Reformed boundaries of its basic and traditional beliefs. An older woman with thick glasses, who reminded me of Grandma Dean, I tried to summarize my spiritual evolution. Shaking her head, she stopped me and said, "I do not want or need to hear about your 'India experience!'" I later was told her own daughter had stayed the previous summer with Bede Griffiths in India. She also informed me that the Presbytery Christian Education Committee would soon examine my teachings, and then report what actions might be taken in response.

In September, two concerned members of Wayside came for another specially called board meeting. One was a large man raised in strong Lutheran traditions and taught science in a nearby high school. A long time member, he carried respect and authority. The other was a fairly new member, dark and handsome, and apparently a very successful businessman. They both opposed my use of the *Course* and some of my ideas shared during Sunday services. The science teacher properly outlined the *Course's* contradictions to the Apostles' Creed. The session listened and wanted to hear my reply. I tried to explain my attraction to the *Course* but quickly realized its futility. My new friend, Chas, who also attended, was charged with being my devious mentor.

After the meeting, Chas suggested I no longer use the *Course* for Sunday Gospel readings. Discouraged, I felt my time with the

Presbyterian Church might be limited. The members of session, however, voiced their wish I would remain, but be less impulsive about introducing new ideas! They hardly had gotten over my recent "Stop the Bomb" emphasis. I prayed, "God, I place the future in your hands."

In early November, after receiving a call, I met with an older Buffalo Diocesan priest named Fr. Jon. A stocky, energetic man with soft and clear voice, Fr. Jon served as chaplain in Viet Nam during the American invasion. He escaped by clinging to one of the last evacuating helicopters. Fr. Jon heard I had spent time with Bede Griffiths and said he planned to visit him that winter. I described Shantivanam to him, mentioning the hot spicy food and the wonderful hut I used. I mentioned the ashram had no chairs. Noticing my small wooden prayer stool, he asked where I got it. I explained a Wayside member's Uncle, who traveled often to India on business, made it for me. Fr. Jon asked if he could borrow it, since he felt uncomfortable sitting in a lotus position on the floor. I loaned it to him. He also told me of similar ashrams, called "Prayer Centers," being developed in America. One of these might be an opportunity for me. Hopeful, I considered looking into such options after finishing my dissertation.

Another kind Wayside member heard I was writing a dissertation and stopped by one day to ask if I used a computer. He said I exuded the idea of riding around on my bicycle with a laptop to write in a secluded place. Newly married, the young man with bright eyes and a keen mind, taught computer science at the University of Buffalo. Discovering I had no computer, the next day he brought me a large IBM left by a company at the University of Buffalo laboratory. It wouldn't fit on my bicycle! Excited, he helped me set it up in my office where I began typing Sunday bulletins and newsletters, and then my dissertation. Before Christmas, he brought me an upgrade, a small IBM computer with hard drive, clear screen, and taking up but a fraction of the space.

Meanwhile Presbytery investigations continued. A week before Christmas I met with two more Presbytery representatives to hear my explanations and teachings of the Reformed faith. Feeling increasingly annoyed and worried, I tried to be honest as we sat in my office. They had met earlier with two angry Deacons and bluntly told me what I did not want to hear. The older man declared, "Dave, unless you keep the *Course* very quiet and remove the discussion group from the church building, you will become dynamite in controversy!" Ouch! I began to wonder if my dissertation would even be accepted. I had included many quotes from the *Course*.

In early January I finished my first dissertation draft. Relieved, I mailed it on the way to Christ the King Seminary. I planned to rest a few days in the forest surrounded Poustinia, and meditate on my options and feelings. My workbook lesson of the day from the *Course* was, "Let all things be exactly as they are."

I began rereading the sayings of Ramana Maharishi. I noticed many connections with the *Course in Miracles*. Ramana also saw the world and observable universe as "made by the Ego." It is death, an illusion of reality. No wonder I was being charged with being a "Gnostic." So where did I belong? Where was my earthly home?

A few days later, I met again with members of the Presbytery in another specially called meeting of Session. Feeling anxious, enduring more restless and sleepless nights, I again wondered if I could sustain myself by moving into another career. The minister Chair of the Committee on Ministry, a well-respected pastor from Buffalo, conducted the meeting. Accompanying him was another respected member who taught at Canisius College with a Ph.D. in Eastern Studies. On the cold January Sunday evening, I walked to the meeting sensing only a matter of time would likely conclude my career at Wayside. And as a Presbyterian.

Naomi, concerned and worried, prepared a few refreshments including tea and coffee with a few thawed out Christmas cookies.

We met in the attractive church parlor, recently redecorated with comfortable furniture resting in appropriate places along the walls and beneath curtained windows. After a short prayer, the Moderator, the city pastor, asked session members for their questions. After a few silent moments one, who chaired the committee that recommended me to candidate as pastor, broke the awkward silence by asking, "Would you please tell us what a 'gnostic' is?" pronouncing it with a long "o." The professor answered with a good summary in his skilled professorial manner, describing it as an early description of many Christians before the 4th century. More questions? Another member meekly asked if I was being forced to leave. After 20 minutes, the Moderator surprisingly said, "I feel very uncomfortable about being here. Since we have refreshments, we will end this meeting and enjoy them!" He closed with a prayer and we ate.

After the board members left, the two representatives took me aside. The professor had not only read the *Course* but saw it as a spiritual book for our time. The pastor chair added, "Dave, I believe you represent the future of the church!" Neither wanted me to quit, and instead, encouraged me to remain as pastor in the Presbytery. They did warn, however, I needed to heed more closely the parable of being "wise as a serpent and harmless as a dove." I nodded in dazed agreement. A part of me, however, still wondered if I ought to feel vindicated or disappointed. I dreamed of being out of the parish vocation with a less busy life. So what now?

In subsequent weeks, the two visiting ministers, along with the Clerk of Presbytery, called frequently to make sure I was okay. They kept repeating, "If you have any more trouble, let us know!" Sadly, the two Wayside Deacons never returned.

A few days later I returned to the wooded Poustinia at Christ the King Seminary, but stopped at the library before heading into the woods. I checked out recommended books suggested by the two Presbyterian representatives at Wayside, one by Elaine

Pagels titled, *The Gnostic Gospels*. Reaching the quiet Poustinia, I unpacked and began reading. Pagels' book introduced me to the important Nag Hammadi documents discovered in 1945. Like eating more "idea candy," I discovered the Nag Hammadi documents were letters from the early church that escaped the fires of the 4th century Christian church. The Roman Emperor Constantine, supported by current leaders in the church at Rome, voted to exclude all earlier writings except their "canon." Excited, I had found another source, a body of literature from ancient times *before* the 4th century creeds and dogmas! I felt more included. I began to realize there were many others from ancient times in my own tradition who lived by inner experience, who also saw the physical body as part of the illusion.

I also read the second recommended book by Kurt Rudolf, *The Nature and History of Gnosticism*. Fascinated, I was finding a stronger bridge, it seemed, connecting me to an important part of the faith I missed and had been denied. But how would Wayside survive with my new kind of leadership, a person who never again would take the structure and 4th century doctrines so seriously? I also was confident I would someday find a more mystical and experiential setting. But where? How? With whom? Meanwhile, I would try to remember Fr. de Mello's teachings, "It's all within you." There I would always find my true and timeless Home! I would also try to remember the *Course* lesson, "Let all things be exactly as they are." It was and would be a hard lesson for me to learn.

On February 17 I received a letter from San Francisco Theological Seminary declaring my dissertation had been approved pending minor revisions. Of the five committee readers who had reviewed it, four overwhelmingly gave approval. Elated and relieved, I relaxed in seeing this chapter of life ending. A few days later I received the one reader's criticisms. He charged me with being unchristian, non-reformed and with absolutely no place in the Presbyterian Church as a "Teaching Elder." The committee requested me to write responses to him in anticipation of probable future animosity from the church.

Sister Joanne, my advisor, expressed her own shock at my approval. Having read my dissertation before submission, she confessed she never would have given me endorsement but respected my honesty. Our meetings ended and soon she moved from the Seminary to a Retreat Center.

In early April the Presbytery Executive called to congratulate me and surprisingly apologized for not calling earlier during my *Course* conflict. She even asked me to review for her two books on ashrams! I felt more support, healing and peace. The Presbyterian Church seemed to be the place where I could remain indefinitely. Several days later, San Francisco Theological Seminary notified me my dissertation was accepted and invited me to attend commencement ceremonies in May. The Wayside congregation voted to give us extra funding toward the trip, including four more weeks for vacation.

A few days later a young schoolteacher, having grown up in Wayside and now teaching school nearly 50 miles south of us, called. After congratulations, he offered a few acres of land near wooded areas on a farm he had recently purchased. There I could begin an ashram! My cup seemed to be running over.

Naomi and I drove our new Camry to California, stopping to officiate a wedding in Grand Rapids for a young man from Hamburg. He had completed several bicycle trips with me. He took me to visit a nearby monastery. Located in Fennville, I immediately felt at home as I entered Vivekananda Monastery, wishing one like it was located near Hamburg.

Graduation ceremonies in San Anselmo seemed somewhat surreal with few people there I knew. Most candidates, who began with me, either finished earlier or were still working on dissertations. Sumio Koga, my link to India, had not finished and was absent. I felt disappointed. The Associate President asked, however, if I would be interested in relocating to become part of the future direction of the Doctor of Ministry program. I could not conceive of moving unless we had more financial help than they were offering. Our children and my heart remained in Western New York. The Seminary Director and President, whom I helped purchase quality bicycles, told me, "Dave, in Western New York, you will become a missionary among fields 'white unto harvest!'" Again, I felt confirmed.

Driving around mansion-filled Marin County to visit remembered sites, I pulled out in front of a Mercedes Benz at a traffic circle. Screeching to stop, the driver in the shiny new car shouted, "Watch out! You Dumb Fucker!" Shocked, I responded, but not quite as loud, with a similar line from "Short Round" in an "Indiana Jones'" movie; "Well, now you must call me, 'Doctor Dumb Fucker!'"

After memorable stays in Zion National Park and along the North Rim of Grand Canyon, Naomi and I crossed the long and often boring Great Plains to reach home in Hamburg. Emotionally and physically fulfilled, I saw myself happy. Hamburg and Wayside seemed to be my temporary earthly home. Why search for it somewhere else? I quickly got back into my pastoral routine, including reading more from my beloved Eastern books: *Upanishads, Bhagavad-Gita, Pantanjali's Aphorisms*, Lao Tzu's *Tao De Ching*, and of course, my recently acquired, *A Course in Miracles*. Like Frs. Bede and Amalorpavadas, I too might become a bridge to a more inclusive and universal spirituality.

Chapter 20

What Next?

> "Free your brother here, as I freed you. Give the
> selfsame gift, nor look upon him with condemnation
> of any kind. See him as guiltless as I look on you, and
> overlook the sins he thinks he sees within himself."
>
> A Course in Miracles, chapter 19.

Soon after returning to work, I attended a Presbytery clergy retreat at Christ the King Seminary in East Aurora. Renting one of the empty dorms, 12 to 15 of us sat in a circle in the social area. After introductions, the counselor leader asked how we experience fulfillment and peace in the church. When my turn arrived I said, "Give up expectations and goals! Be content and let things happen without attachment or judgment." I had not arrived at such a place but they *were* part of my goals. One colleague responded, "Dave, you have certainly changed!"

In late June my 16-year-old son Eric accompanied me on a canoe trip to the Adirondack Mountains. By invitation we joined a youth group led by a minister friend named John. John, a very bright and well-read colleague, recently left his church pastoral position to become a college librarian. He asked for my assistance, knowing my canoeing background, and that I might share ideas with the group from recent studies and time in India.

After the five-hour ride into an area north of Tupper Lake, we unloaded canoes and equipment and launched our expedition with 12 high school boys. Eric and I, fairly seasoned canoe campers, quickly became a bit weary as we helped carry poorly packed bags and canoes for youth with little or no wilderness experience. Mosquitos, often thick as fog, and pesky black flies, left few body parts untouched as we carried equipment through woods over uneven dirt trails. We paddled down Spider Creek, which lived up to its name as spider webs dangled from tree branches sweeping faces clean for more bites. Evenings, around crackling campfires, I read various passages from mostly eastern writings, especially the *Bhavagad Gita*. After comments and discussions, I led short meditations, enhanced by the wilderness settings with loon calls and lapping shoreline waters. I thought, "Maybe this will help me in my contributions to Presbyterians and 'liberal' churches."

As Naomi and I celebrated our 25th wedding anniversary in July, it appeared increasingly apparent she would not be resuming a teaching career. For years I assumed, as the kids grew older and left home, she would again teach. She was good at it, and received many accolades from colleagues and friends. Not only would it alleviate more of my financial pressure, it would create a more secure retirement, especially for her. I was surprised and disappointed at her refusal but unwilling to do anything to destroy our relationship. It was too important to me, even though I would continue to worry about financial independence, something inherited from my father.

Two weeks later, during my annual physical, the doctor surprisingly suggested I might be in a "low-grade depression." I asked, "How could I?" I meditated daily but admitted I often felt loneliness. At times, I felt out of place and lonely with my career in a denomination where I seemed to be an enigma. I admitted frequent outbursts of anger, finding myself cursing and swearing over simple annoyances. I craved daily peace but still squeezed by the surrounding structure, the myriad of pastoral and family duties. I knew some of my new attitudes and actions, or non-actions, still concerned a few in the parish.

My favorite secretary, Betty, retired and our new one, a staunch, orthodox Lutheran, began criticizing my reading choices and lack of "normal pastoral activities." I once shared with her readings from the classical spiritual book, *A Cloud of Unknowing*. Amazed, she could not believe I read such things.

> "A contemplative is one who just
> sits. Or, he may get up and fly.
> An active one seems to always
> fly, even when sitting.
> A contemplative is at peace in whatever,
> But usually when things are quiet."
>
> (*A Cloud of Unknowing*, translated by
> John Watkins, London, 1922, Kindle Version)

In late summer, an older member came into my office for a visit. She questioned my faith and fitness to remain Presbyterian. With a hardened face, she scolded my recent moves, blaming it partly on summers in San Francisco, the hotbed of hippies and pot-smoking dreamers. She said her concerns included other Wayside members.

Amid such criticisms and with my doctor's warnings, I decided to look elsewhere for possible employment. I wrote the Unity Church and the Unitarian Universalists. Naomi and I had visited the Unity Church in Buffalo on a previous summer Sunday. We returned again to hear Ken Wapnick speak on *A Course in Miracles*. Both of us enjoyed a deeper sense of freedom and openness. I wrote, "If I ever get kicked out of the Presbyterian Church, this might be a good option!"

To worsen things, my attraction to *A Course in Miracles* would not stop. The more I read and understood, the more I agreed

Presbyterians would ban it. I listened regularly to tapes by Ken Wapnick while driving or on retreats.

December brought more stress. Eric escaped serious injury in an accident when his car was nearly crushed by a semi-truck. I shuddered for weeks at the thought of what might have happened. Fr. Jon also called to tell me Guru Amalor from Mysore, India, was killed in a car accident. On Christmas Eve, my good discussion friend, Dr. Bill McLimans, a science researcher at Roswell Hospital, died suddenly at his home. He had been almost a weekly supporter for over four years, meeting at one of his favorite restaurants for lunches. After surviving the last week of Christmas services and Bill's funeral, I drove exhausted to my parent's home in Sherman for a retreat.

I stayed in the quiet, rural house a few days to rest and ponder. I cooked simple meals of mostly vegetables in mom's small kitchen, where I looked out the window to see an apple orchard and open fields, across which lay the beckoning woods. For desserts, I ate some of Mom's canned Bartlett pears from her storage closet. I plodded through deep snow across meadows into the thick maple woods, spooking deer sleeping under a pine tree grove on seasoned beds of ripened needles. I stopped often to catch my breath and inhale the crystal clear 20-degree air, feeling surrounded by the mysterious Presence saying, "relax and enjoy." I arrived back in Hamburg with another renewed attitude, determined to let more things go.

Replies from the Unity and Unitarian Universalist Churches arrived. Sitting in my office alone, anxious for suggestions and possible new directions, the Unity Church required me to move to "Unity Village" in Missouri to study for an indefinite period of time. A Unitarian Universalist Church leader in Boston, Massachusetts called me. Sounding annoyed and disgusted, she voiced contempt for my journey and charged me with belonging to a "homophobic" denomination. She doubted I could accept their pluralism. Discouraged, I sat in confusion, feeling more like an outsider, a threat to already table set church parties.

On Easter Sunday, with some trepidation, I offered my first sermon on the resurrection of Jesus as a mythical event. Standing before two large congregations, robed in my new white gown with red doctoral stripes purchased by Wayside, I declared the resurrection represented a spiritual awakening. I pointed out the root of the Biblical Greek word for resurrection, *anastasia,* meant "awakening." It was also the meaning of resurrection from the *Course in Miracles.* The idea related to de Mello's emphasis on "waking up" and coincided with the Nag Hammadi documents, which I continued to read. It seemed so simple: Christ or Divine Wisdom lies within all.

In retrospect, this period may have been time to leave traditional Christianity. Dogmas and creeds still reigned in most of my colleagues' minds and churches. I was deleting more often in services the "Prayers of Confession," or revising them to say, "Yes, we all make mistakes but so what?" Yet events seemed to say, "Don't be in a hurry." Perhaps SFTS director Walter Davis was accurate: I was in the right place at the right time. I waited.

In early September I led another Camp Duffield retreat. Only six people came. Gathering amid the wooded camp, now with leaves turning from green to orange, brown and yellow, one man came who was about my age named Malcolm Muir. Malcolm drove from South Florida in a van loaded with his computer, printer and booklets he had written and printed. An electrical engineer graduate from Rensselaer Polytechnic Institute, Malcolm worked for General Electric in Utica and conducted research at Princeton before settling in Florida as a private contractor. Reared in Hamburg and confirmed at Wayside, I had conducted his mother's funeral in 1989. Shortly after the retreat Malcolm began calling me. His appearance and manners coincided with my ideas of the "Absent Minded Professor." He smoked a large pipe, had a thick head of disheveled hair, and a left glass eyeball replacing the original following a high school explosion experiment. The left glass eye frequently was turned inward or outward out of alignment.

Malcolm displayed a deep interest in Eastern religions, and from my conducting his mother's funeral, he detected I did as well. We remained friends and spent hours over the next years sharing ideas through phone conversations. His recommended books and frequent talks further strengthened my direction. He claimed science, with discovered theories of quantum relativity from Einstein, Nils Bohr and others, helped displace the traditional reliance on Newtonian theories of order and predictability. Science had also driven Malcolm to study eastern mysticism, especially from his favorite book, the *Tao Te Ching*. Through our frequent phone conversations, he confessed I was one of his few trusted friends.

Surprisingly, Fr. Jon called and invited me to help lead a retreat at the Roman Catholic Stella Niagara center near Niagara Falls. Having returned from India and his time with Bede Griffiths, he advertised the event for "burned out clergy." Around a dozen priests came. Most looked exhausted from working in large but often declining parishes with fewer priests. Some conducted 70 or more funerals a year. One 40-year-old priest looked like an 80-year old, shuffling along the halls hunched over with tiredness.

Fr. Jon offered his clear presentation on the "Light Within." For my turn, I sat cross-legged on the tile floor and summarized Fr. de Mello. I suggested they replace crucifixes in private rooms, halls and eating areas with a risen Jesus figure! I offered a period of silent meditation with focusing on the breath. Most priests seemed surprised, perhaps wondering how I even got there!

Early the next year, I accepted another invitation to attend a Presbyterian Synod meeting in Syracuse. A new committee called, "Spirituality and Discipleship," had just formed. People suggested I might help, or maybe it could help me. Riding an Amtrak train to Syracuse, we spent the first morning planning a future workshop on spirituality. I felt hopeful until most of the time focused on who might be invited as a "great preacher." After selecting a name, they discussed how to ensure his water contained enough electrolytes to keep him preaching and listeners listening! The second day's meetings droned on through more long and laborious hours. I tried to use the time to practice forgiveness and patience.

One staff member, with Asian roots, shared with me her hopes to soon leave the church for something more liberating for women and minorities. I shared my interest for a more inclusive group beyond the endless gender and sexual orientation debates.

In November 1992, I walked home for lunch and arriving, Naomi showed me how the entrance porch was falling off into the driveway! More income or not, we had to take action. We borrowed $45,000 from the bank and another $15,000 from the church. Deeper than ever in debt, I found myself simply resigning. It looked like we'd be staying in Hamburg a few more years. Integrating my new "spiritual awareness" into life's realities was not always easy.

In the spring we drove to Atlanta, Georgia where I officiated a wedding for my nephew and his fiancé. Returning home, despite Naomi's worries, I stopped at Bob Jones University in Greenville. 10 years earlier they had sent me a printed order stating that due to my beliefs and practices, I would never be permitted to visit the campus. We stopped at the gate guarded by young, well-muscled armed guards. I identified Naomi and myself as alumni, wanting to show our kids the campus. Waved on without showing ID's, we took a memorable tour around campus, pointing out our dorms and known buildings. I felt little animosity, hatred, or even regret. I was thankful for how I had grown and awakened there. "They are where they are on their own journeys," I thought, hoping I would grow deeper in my own love and forgiveness.

In June I returned to Roscoe, NY for another week with Ken Wapnick. One afternoon I met an older woman from Vancouver, sitting on the wooden dock stretching out into Lake Tannanah behind the main building. Tall and thin with grayish hair, she might have been reflecting on one of Ken's intense lectures. She nodded and said, "Hi, how are you? What did you think about Ken's lecture?" speaking with a familiar Canadian accent which pronounced "about" as "aboot." She expressed surprise when I mentioned I was a Presbyterian minister. I admitted I often felt like an anomaly and wondered what I should do. "Maybe I'm in the wrong place," I mentioned, "some of my colleagues think I'm a bit outside the *parameters*," a common word used to describe Presbyterian boundaries. The kind woman responded, "Well, none of us actually knows why we are here, where we are going or what we are even doing. She said the purpose of it all is to let it go and stay where we are working to forgive—our self and others, while growing in love." It became my most remembered conversation of the week. "What next?" would take care of itself.

Shortly before Christmas, I attended another Presbytery meeting, intending to love and show kindness to people who strained hard to save the world from its many injustices. Surprised, a few people approached me and suggested I represented a new way of thinking and modeling the future. A bit befuddled by such positive remarks, I drove home feeling freer, encouraged to again remain and keep moving in the current direction: listening, forgiving and enjoying as much as possible each moment. Maybe I could be a model for the future.

Still, I decided to consider other options. I drove to the Jewish vocational center near downtown Buffalo on Delaware Avenue. The center had given helpful guidance to our children. After registering, the secretary sent me to a quiet room to answer questions by checking boxes and writing answers. After reviewing my inventory and asking questions about my background, the beautiful and confident counselor claimed I could quickly find a college to teach classes or become its chaplain. She also suggested I could work on counseling certification.

Suddenly, the sense of vocational entrapment lifted higher. Yet after a few days and weeks of reflection, I never pursued the alternatives. The personal freedoms I enjoyed to read, grow and teach, according to my own schedule, seemed quite satisfying. My pay increasingly seemed more adequate, as our children, all pursuing college degrees, were able to secure financial aid and loans. It seemed the worse storms about my ideas had passed. "Why change anything?" Although I still preferred Naomi to teach regularly, I felt more confident with the outlet options available. I brought the *Course in Miracles* group back into the church after meeting a few years in a member's home. The group continued to be led by my friend Chas, who remained my supportive and important friend.

One day Chas' wife suggested I get him more outside, away from so much reading. Dad also had asked me that year, since I turned 50 years old, to golf with him Monday mornings in a Chautauqua "AARP League." I was an awful golfer but quickly became hooked on the game. I had pretty much stopped bicycling. I loved the slow walk among trees, flowers and chirping birds. I asked Chas if he would like to golf with me. "No," he said, "but I'll think about it." The next day he asked when we could begin— he had purchased a set of golf clubs! We made it a regular date: 9 holes Wednesday afternoon, 18 on Friday mornings. At his suggestion, I also joined a local health club where he belonged, and in winter months, we played Wednesday afternoon racket ball games to keep our golf legs limber. Chas became a closer friend, like a "paid perk" to remain in Hamburg.

On the first Sunday of December 1993, inspired by the writings of Eknath Easawaran, whose book I used in a confirmation class, I shared some of his illustrative stories in a sermon. I talked about overcoming our "monkey minds," a struggle I continuously worked on. When I finished the sermon, I received a standing ovation! Why *would* I want to move elsewhere?

In January, urged by clergy friends, I attended a Presbyterian "Spiritual Directors" retreat in a place called Montreat near Ashville, NC. One of the first persons I met was my earlier executive who had found my ideas controversial. She warmly greeted me and said, "I sort of felt you would be here!" It was a wonderful and hopeful time, and I thought a place might always remain for me among Presbyterians. Sequestered in a beautiful wood paneled lodge surrounded by mountains, Presbyterians practiced yoga and tai chi each morning as I climbed up and down surrounding mountain trails. During meals some asked about my India trip and sharing summaries, I found myself even more confirmed and at home.

My sense of acceptance was shaken somewhat, when I shared my appreciation for *A Course in Miracles*. Few were aware of the book but my interest spread to a teacher of "Spirituality" from Dubuque Seminary in Iowa. She approached me in the food line and asked to eat together. After we sat and exchanged greetings, her tone quickly changed. A relative once gave her a copy of *A Course in Miracles*. "I found the book very dangerous!" she said. It begins beautifully and then, skillfully, begins to destroy one's Christian faith!" She declared it blatant Gnosticism, very Hindu, with absolutely nothing to give traditional Christianity. Agreeing with her but not her conclusions, she grew increasingly impatient and irritated. Starring into my eyes, she gave me a threatening and hopeless look. How could I explain to a seminary teacher, a recognized published scholar in church beliefs, that she is blind to a deeper universal spirituality? It would be like telling George Patton that war is not the answer.

As the conference ended, however, I left feeling encouraged. A woman asked if she might share a personal visionary experience with me, knowing I would not criticize her. Another man asked me for the most effective book I used since returning from India. I told him "*A Course in Miracles*." Meeting my former executive as we prepared to leave, she confided the conference would most likely backfire with all sorts of negative publicity. It did. Again, I was naïvely surprised and wondered why we just couldn't keep going on and ignore it. Change would come regardless of the walls that beliefs, creeds and traditions had built against it.

Despite usual seasonal stress, Advent and Christmas went well. The first snows seemed exciting and welcomed. Naomi did most of the shopping, and on Christmas we opened up baby bibs from Dawn and Jeff, with surprising news she was pregnant, and we soon would become grandparents! The church also gave us a record monetary Christmas gift, which paid off most of our bills. The year ended with hope and renewed peace.

Some opposition continued, however. In early January 1995, a former Presbytery Moderator sent me a scathing letter with "lessons" in how to be Reformed. She expressed anger about recent services I helped planned for Presbytery, where I still had a leading role. A few members, one a Session member, began visiting other congregations, which were more "evangelical." For a little extra insurance and encouraged by Chas, I sent a letter to the state Certification Board for counseling requirements.

In spring of 1995, a bright young man, who grew up in Wayside, became our secretary. I always liked him, having ridden his bicycle on a couple of my camping trips. A former member of the US Secret Service, he was in good physical condition, despite a recent back injury. Impressed with his administrative abilities, he exhibited good humor. Paul became interested in upgrading our bookkeeping procedures and fundraising. I suggested a fundraising program called "Consecration Sunday." Paul skillfully led it and we experienced the most successful financial boost with pledges pushing our income over $200,000 dollars for the first time.

Entering 1996 my sense of release and abundance grew. Now with two beautiful grandchildren, our third arrived on January 11. Expressions such as "I am so happy, fulfilled, complete, my cup overflows" became more common in my journals. I had longer periods of hope, relaxation and peace amid my busy life and expanding family. Given a coupon by my family, I began getting regular massages, monthly respites continuing for years.

Becoming much more computer literate, I found online discussion groups. One was called the "Jesus Seminar." Made up of progressive scholars, they published materials to help churches move out of the literalism, which still bound many to actual miracles with bodies rising from the dead. I decided to use some of their teaching suggestions during Lenten season. The "Seminar" scholars sought to integrate the Nag Hammadi gnostic writings into traditional Christian teachings.

Excited, I included gnostic readings in our Lenten discussion along with a series of videos explaining the documents. Some members were surprised and puzzled. One night, after a video of Markus Borg's mythological interpretation of Jesus and his death, a couple became angry. Others declared the materials were too new for them. One charged I ruined her lifelong idea of Easter. Shortly after Easter, however, some of the most critical participants came to me and apologized, saying the stories of Jesus actually made more sense to them, and they enriched their season with appreciation of new possibilities. I felt emboldened as if I were coming "out of the closet."

"Patience," as the Course teaches, "produces immediate results!" New people soon began to attend, people who appreciated my new direction. We added classes with yoga and meditation. Like the farmer, I loved the rhythm of planting new seeds and watching them grow. Wayside's finances became more stable. I sensed I would most likely finish my career as their pastor. Despite the negatives, I enjoyed my new sense of freedom as staff leader of a mid-size congregation. I began seeing Wayside as a large "ashram." One of my clergy friends even called us, "The Ashram by the Lake!"

Chapter 21

Grow the Church

"Even though you going backwards, you're making progress."

- Alison Levine,
1st woman to climb Mt. Everest in 2012,
coming 200 feet short in 2002.

In the summer of 2000, I met Tom Bandy in an online discussion group. Tom was a church-renewal consultant who lived near Toronto. A wiry, thin man, Tom wore glasses, which he often peered over the rims as if to ask, "Don't you get it?" Blunt and direct, he indicted the church for becoming mostly a social club, with power figures making sure nothing happens that might enhance spiritual growth. Tom graduated from the Presbyterian Princeton Seminary, and later became Director of the United Church of Canada's Education program. Until he was fired. When he spoke, he seemed to care little if people disagreed or thought him crazy. Many did.

I read some of Tom's books: *Killing Habits, Coming Clean, Moving off the Map,* and *Christian Chaos.* In the later, Tom claimed the dying church played the game of croquet whereas a thriving church played "jai alai!" In today's world, he explained, the information people learn changes as fast as computers. We can't wait for the ball to roll slowly or stop—we must catch it on the fly and keep running! Tom felt committees, representative government, democracy and consensus decisions destroyed most personal initiative. Thriving churches had strong leaders who were grounded in a deep spirituality with clear visions and decisiveness.

The ideas reminded me somewhat of ashrams, established by a spiritual teacher or Guru. The ashram succeeded or failed dependent upon the teacher's credibility. As a leader, I considered myself fairly well grounded in spirituality, and with a desire to deepen the vision of an inclusive and growing church. I thus joined Tom's online discussion group. Most participants were pastors from North America but surprisingly, most were evangelical, or based on 4th century church creeds and beliefs. Yet the idea of encouraging people to find and use a deeper spiritual understanding intrigued me.

Tom encouraged new music, which we were already using, with functioning prayer cells, which meant to me meditation groups, to give birth to new ideas and expressions. Tom portrayed outdated leadership as working with the croquet model, using mallets and hoops to reach the already clear goal. Tom saw our world more like a jai alai game in which goals constantly change. "Goals," Tom once said, "should be written in pencil and revised every three months!" Tom saw life as more chaotic, which better fit my practice of mysticism and reading *A Course of Miracles.* Perhaps his ideas might help me encourage people to find and use their gifts through a deeper spiritual awakening.

Tom also predicted the future church would become more "eastern in thinking with more use of western technology." He encouraged using guitars, drums and instruments other than organ to attract people. Organ and traditional hymns were associated with older doctrines and order, the croquet era. Tom also urged study of the lifestyle and teachings of the pre-4th century church. He had my ear, at least part of it. I had encouraged the use of guitars and more contemporary music, helping to create the band

and orchestra at Wayside. Tom saw my role as mostly a spiritual leader, the visionary idea caster.

I showed a movie of one of Tom's talks to the Presbytery's Educational committee. I was then a member and trusted their feedback. The movie impressed them and realizing Tom lived nearby, it was suggested we invite him to come and share his ideas. After all, our churches were losing members much faster than gaining them.

I contacted Tom and found myself helping to set up a workshop to be held in Buffalo. Presbyterians were part of an Ecumenical Joint Christian Education Committee that included several other protestant groups. We quickly gained their support to help plan and advertise the event, set for May 2001. Having a friend on the faculty of Canisius College, he suggested we use their large auditorium space, complete with a drop down screen and the latest PowerPoint plug-in technology requested by Tom. The Committee did most of the detail work, which included box lunches for each participant and needed advertisement. We would need 150 participants to break even with a $1000 stipend for Tom.

We were overwhelmed the day of the event, running out of room to comfortably seat 250 jammed into a room for 150. Tom did a superb job, however, using his state of the art technology, explaining and motivating people to return home and adapt. Many Presbyterians attended along with a Wayside group including George, Wayside's newly elected Administrator. Mary Mohlke, the respected Christian Education Director of Presbytery, claimed Tom did a wonderful job making his points crystal clear. However, some found them quite shocking.

Wayside had hired George to help with some of the administrative work needed at Wayside. A retired school administrator, the Session felt George could help relieve some of the administrative work I did not enjoy. George, in his late 60's, was a short stocky man and several pounds overweight. A second generation person with Scottish roots, George often spoke with a wonderful Scottish brogue. He had a sharp wit and often used it to subtlety criticize people or events.

George met me in my office Tuesday morning after the Saturday "Bandy Event." Sitting across from my desk he said, "Well, I would summarize Mr. Bandy as saying we need to throw out everything we now believe and start over!" George was not ready to play jai alai or give up croquet! I realized his support would be tepid.

Later with the staff present, sipping on some coffee, I thanked those who attended the workshop and we discussed ways to incorporate some of its ideas in Wayside. The organist and music leader, Jo, attended the workshop and was ready to jump in. However, she confessed being tired and worried. A few months earlier she had been diagnosed with cancer, endured surgery and now continued treatments. She admitted a lack of energy, wanting to sleep more often. Deeply loved, we felt concern for Jo, and ourselves.

I put together suggested "Spiritual Gifts Awareness" groups, giving inventories to the Session and Deacon boards along with our committees. I tried to help people discern their gifts that might be used for Wayside's future. I urged formation of "Interest Groups" with the provision each include time for readings, meditation and discussions. Over 30 groups were soon identified. I felt hopeful.

On Sunday, September 1, 2001, just before I left to conduct services at Wayside, I received a call that our organist, Jo, died during the night. Sorrow and hurt sunk deep into my heart. I slowly walked the five-minute distance to the church, my head swirling with sadness and memories. The congregation gasped in disbelief when I shared the news. We all loved, respected and appreciated Jo. Her energy, talent, and adaptability had enhanced my work for many years.

Exhausted, the following week became dreamlike. Three days later, with the sanctuary packed with mourners, I worked to lead Jo's memorial service before grieving family and friends. The band, which she also helped create and nurture, offered their best with heavy hearts. The week ended with a longing and need for extended retreat. I slept most of Monday.

On Tuesday morning, eating breakfast together, Naomi and I sat in shock as breaking news reported, with live videos, terrorist attacks on the World Trade Centers. Wayside had a member in the building who escaped. Another member's friend, who lived nearby, was killed. Stunned, I walked to the church. Reaching my office, pre-school nursery teachers ran into the hall to tell me another plane just crashed into the Pentagon! Hugging each other, I walked into the office to see the secretary sitting in shock. Then another news bulletin announced yet another passenger jet crashed into a rural farm field in Pennsylvania. We became worried about our son, who at the time, worked near downtown Washington. Many gathered that evening in the church to share emotions, read scriptures, offer prayers, and feel the pain.

The following weekend I drove to Washington, D.C. to attend a scheduled workshop with Tom Bandy and his friend Bill. I stayed with our son Eric, who lived near the National Cathedral, and on Sunday morning, he led me quietly along the sidewalk to attend the service. We entered the huge cathedral where days before, a service of mourning was conducted for hundreds of government workers. Sitting in the huge stone cathedral with pipe organ sounds echoing through the walls, I felt disappointed. Ordinary lection readings for the day were strictly followed without a word mentioned about the recent attacks. It seemed inhuman and callused to those like me who needed more time to mourn. Afterwards Eric and I wandered the surrounding gardens in bright warm sun as carrion bells tolled for more than an hour, often filling my eyes with tears.

The next day I attended the Bandy conference in a large Methodist church a few miles north of Washington. The 9-11 attacks still lingered in minds like a heavy dark cloud. Bob, Tom's older partner whom I had never met, stunned me when told the 1000 plus audience in the mega church auditorium, that his greatest concern in the attacks was the fate of lost souls without Christ when the towers fell! During the PowerPoint talks, I began losing confidence and interest. One of the major speakers called *A Course in Miracles* a foolish and crazy book. I drove home late that night in a sober, melancholy attitude, dazed and confused.

In April 2002, I received a surprising call from a Presbytery Nominating Committee member. The kind lady asked me to consider having my name placed in nomination for Moderator of the Presbytery. Astonished, I pondered the offer a few days with family and friends, and accepted. Perhaps with my leadership in the Tom's workshops, people expected I could nurture needed growth in fading Presbyterian Churches. My duties would be to moderate Presbytery Council meetings, and help plan and conduct quarterly Presbytery meetings throughout the year.

It seemed somewhat absurd: an intuitive, mystical, gnostic, India ashram minded minister, was to be voted on for the next Moderator of the Presbytery of Western New York! A few weeks later, on a warm May Tuesday afternoon, in the historic Westfield Presbyterian Church, a mile from my birthplace, my name was placed into nomination and time offered for discussion.

Immediately one of the evangelical ministers rose to plead and declare I was the wrong person for this role. "Dave Persons is not the person we need. He is not a Reformed Presbyterian, and his election will certainly cause more harm than growth!" Meeting at the Biloxi Assembly and earlier in a New Jersey meeting, he knew my questions and observations. My ideas did not fit his very reformed, evangelical mind. A couple others stood to agree.

Two ministers from the area sat in front of me, one a colleague at Pittsburgh Seminary. A strong social activist, he twisted around and looking at me said, "Dave, in all my years in these mostly boring Presbytery meetings, I have never seen or heard such opposition to a Moderator appointment. This must be a first!"

The Moderator, a pleasant lady who seemed to admire me, asked me to respond. Nervously, I slowly rose and said, "I will do my best if elected. However, if people did not wish me to be their representative, I will be fine and continue my work at Wayside."

The vote was taken and I passed with a wide margin. For the next three years, extra meetings dominated my life. Meanwhile, I gave less time with lesser interest to "Growing the Church."

My experience as Moderator went well. My goal was to stay calm and offer everyone love during the often fractious meetings. I tried to remain non-defensive when challenged, often finding humor in proceedings that went on too long and accomplished so little. I desired the best for the group, best in the sense of seeing and experiencing our Oneness with each other, and all humanity. I viewed the experience as another opportunity to grow in my self-awareness and detachment. Realizing many Presbyterians would rather feel "right" than be happy or peaceful, I completed my term undeterred.

My chosen Moderator successor was a Native American friend from one of the small 19th century mission churches. I had been trying to encourage them over the past several years. A gentle and kind older man named "Calvin," most inappropriately I thought, Calvin was a long time recognized leader of the Seneca Nation or reservation, as called by non-natives. He had chaired over 50 Nation Committees in his 70 plus years. He quickly found the role of Presbytery Moderator confusing, troublesome and a difficult experience for both himself and the attendees. I felt sadness as he struggled to adapt his mind from its mostly intuitive base, to a group working from a fixed set of codes, creeds, and pedantic history.

Chapter 22

Letting Go

"...Seek not to change the world but choose to change your mind about the world. Perception is a result and not a cause."

--ACIM, Ch. 21

My hopes to "grow Wayside" soon faded with dwindling funds, energy, and three years involved as a Presbytery Moderator. I moved further away from trying to change anything but to become more, as the *Course* said, "Let all things be exactly as they are." (Lesson 268) I worked more consciously to change my own mind toward the outside world, including the church. I longed to be more forgiving: of the world, the church, my family and myself. Retirement thoughts became more part of my thinking. I anticipated moving past the weight of pastoral leadership years, being on call 24/7. I longed to get more back "home." I began rereading *A Course in Miracles*.

To help hold my intentions, I initiated monthly meetings with a counselor whom my friend Chas suggested. It was time to do more work on myself rather than working so much on others. The counselor, Neva, gave me personal support but encouraged my hunger to keep turning inward. She prodded me to follow what

"I needed to do," realizing how easily clergy types are driven by other people's needs.

Neva also introduced me to holographic breath exercises. Such exercises involved deep breathing techniques with background sounds of shamanic drumming and chants. The intuitive exercises would place me into an "altered state." The work helped release much of the tension and guilt I so often carried, most unconsciously.

In 2006, at Neva's suggestion, I attended a 10-day retreat at the Omega Institute in Rhinebeck, New York. Led by Dr. Stanislav Groff, a pioneer in holographic breath work, and Buddhist teacher Jack Kornfield, they helped me go deeper into my subconscious mind. Through more breath work and shamanic drumming, I encountered what appeared to be former lives in which I was a warrior, killed in the midst of battles. When I shared the experiences with my support group, they asked for my profession. After telling them, they pushed further, "Have you ever had or caused conflicts over your religious beliefs?" I grinned.

Returning home, a new woman minister in Presbytery told me of a Benedictine Monastery in Erie, Pennsylvania, operated by Benedictine Sisters. They maintained several hermitages in nearby woods. I called and reserved one for a Lenten retreat. In a late winter snow blizzard, I drove stressfully slow along the 90 miles of Thruway to Erie. The storm seemed somewhat symbolic of my life over the past years of "growing the church."

Sister Carla, a short, stout and very strong woman, graciously welcomed me. I then hoisted on my pack and plodded through knee-deep snow, trying to keep up with Sister, to reach an isolated, well maintained, and heated hermitage. Left alone, I put down my bags and took a deep breath, feeling stress run off my mind like standing in a hot shower. I cried in relief to be in such a place, a winter ashram! I was home, home with Spirit where we could again renew our love and Oneness. It seemed like having an affair, which I never experienced! I read from *A Course in Miracles*:

> "There is a place in you where the whole world has been forgotten; where no memory of sin and of illusion linger still. There is a place in which time has left, and echoes of eternity are heard. There is a resting place so still no sound except a hymn to Heaven rises up to gladden God the Father and the Son." (ACIM, Chapter 29. V.1)

I returned to Hamburg encouraged to create more community workshops with meditation and exploration of spiritual practices. Assisted by our talented Christian Education Director, Mary Lou, we invited people to come and conduct seminars in Native American traditions. We offered more yoga classes with meditation times. Invited by my daughters, I attended my first "reading" in the old East Aurora "First Spiritualist Church." My reader was a beautiful African/Cuban/American woman named Marsha. I loved her at first sight and as she "read me," she stopped and asked what I did! When I told her, she said I had been sent to her as a friend. Soon she not only offered me support and counsel, but led workshops and seminars at Wayside. She gave readings, taught "Belly Dancing," and helped people find their own psychic Inner Selves. It seemed so refreshing, so "un-Presbyterian."

Giving up concerns about fund-raising or church building, my last few years became the most enjoyable. My deepest loss was the retirement and move to North Carolina of my good friend Chas. For nearly 20 years he offered professional counseling at Wayside. He introduced the church and me to *A Course in Miracles* and created a weekly reading and discussion group. His departure left a vacuum in my life. I struggled weeks feeling loneliness without his companionship: sharing ideas, racket ball games and golfing.

He had given me constant encouragement about my role as a spiritual leader, placing scores of new books and ideas on my desk.

I grew to see many of my pastoral years as mostly an outside-in process. I sought to attract people by socializing them into a friendly atmosphere with relevant and life-giving services. I hoped they would become active, accept our beliefs and creeds, and of course, give financial help. I now saw it more as a backward process, motivated more by organizational business necessities. Buildings and programs left by predecessors needed to be continued and expanded. The subtle but busy process tended to ignore the central focus of the spiritual life. No wonder ashrams were so small! With larger religious "businesses," it is so easy to practice a substitute religious life, what G. I. Gurdjieff once described as, "imitational."

Of course, my busy farm boy background, often riding and driving wide open, became perfect preparation for such a life. Meditation and centering prayer were unknown worlds and practices, and for many years criticized as wasteful and even dangerous. Being part of a religious culture, which placed a high importance on social justice responsibilities, can also quickly displace one's understanding of "seeking first the Kingdom of God...."

For most of my professional life this dichotomy and tension remained. "Keep busy! Idle hands make a devil's workshop!" We burnout our minds and bodies trying to change forms and people toward a more just place for all. Mission work focuses on race relations, sexual freedoms, the ubiquitous poor, and learning how to speak for the exploited. The "harvest was always plenty but the laborers so few," an image borne from my days on the farm, and then with the church. The harvest aims more toward activities and socialization, the constant "show and tell" reports I often thought of as "Mission Envy" times.

The pastoral role in such a structure becomes more encompassing and busy than even a farmer's life. As pastors, we set aside few hours and days to roam the woods. We miss long winter seasons for rest and renewal on holy vacations. We constantly see work left to change the world rather than in simply seeing it differently. The world thus becomes a projection of our own fear, guilt, and anger.

The constant strain became more conscious for me in the later years, like a farmer with too many fields and animals. My idea of ministry evolved more toward the ashram model. I saw myself more as spiritual leader, one with an endless appetite for prayer who offers what he experiences to comfort those around him. In my final years as pastor, my daily meditations began pulling me back toward the discoveries found during in the early 80's. I mostly replaced the Benedictine Office Hours with *A Course in Miracles* and other spiritual readings: authors like Sri Ramana and Fr. Anthony de Mello, the Bhavagad Gita and early Gnostic writings translated from the Nag Hammadi discoveries.

Like Bede Griffiths and Amalorpavadas of India, I found collections of interreligious readings, which I used to prepare sermon talks or "Reflections." "Reflection" seemed less final or absolute in my journey alongside others. "Word of God" meant "soul food" that nurtures our awareness of love, freedom, and peace. I saw the 4th century Bible, which included earlier Jewish writings called "The Old Testament," as containing disturbing writings of violence. Both leaders in both church and state had used these writings for centuries to expand and destroy indigenous cultures. I saw the teaching of hell, as de Mello described, as one "making God worse than even people like Adolf Hitler!" Forgiveness, as often presented in the Bible and taught by the church, becomes conditional–either change by accepting the teachings of the church or be destroyed with eternal punishment!

My last years at Wayside thus became more like the naïve vision I had as a seminary student in Boston, Pennsylvania: prayer and study first, action second. Nearly 40 years later, I finally led with more confidence and peace, meeting weekly with groups for prayers and review of particulars in need of attention. Each meeting with a family or a task working committee became more as a "holy encounter," a time to listen, share forgiveness and give peace.

Chapter 23

Leaving Wayside

> "*Results are what you expect; consequences are what you get.*"
>
> – *Anonymous*

In early June 2008, two well-respected ministers of Presbytery called and asked to meet with me. We met a few days later in the library of the large church where one of the pastors served. The other minister was from another one of the wealthier congregations. Exuding auras of success in their own professions, they commended my career at Wayside. I had served with a record "clear and clean" of conflicts, leaving behind a congregation regarded as "thriving and growing." They recalled no record of desperate or worried parishioners phoning the head office for relief from a runaway minister! Obviously, they had not been around during some of my earlier years when anger often spilled over about my political and social justice actions, or later when I had become "awakened" to spirituality.

Sitting in the small, quiet library, they inquired about my retirement plans. I explained my intentions to retire the end of July 2009, hoping to prepare the congregation for my departure. I shared my idea of announcing retirement one year in advance to help people adjust. Both ministers agreed. They spoke of several long-term pastors who retired quickly and the congregations nosedived into major collapse. Not wanting this to occur at Wayside, they suggested I have a more proactive role in retiring. Surprisingly, they even suggested I partake in the process of choosing an interim pastor.

Surprised and relieved, I asked for suggestions about needing to quickly relocate. I explained we owned our home, which was a short walk from the church. Unexpectedly, they said remaining in our home would pose no problem. One shared how the former pastor of his present congregation retired a few years ago, but continued to attend services and even make frequent calls in the parish. The other pastor shared that in the large congregation he previously served, the senior minister retired and even purchased the nearby church-owned manse. It would be no problem, they assured, expressing confidence things would go well.

The two pastors also supported my idea to write a congregational letter one year in advance, helping people prepare for my retirement. Both also promised to report our visit to their Committee so representatives would be able to meet with Wayside's board in September. Help would then begin the process of leadership change. I left deeply encouraged and relieved by their kindness and support.

With naïve confidence, a few days later I shared with Wayside's board our meeting and my intention of writing a retirement letter in early August, a year before retirement. The board concurred and felt it would be a healthy beginning to my final year. The process would prepare for my departure while giving ample time to secure an interim replacement. With mixed emotions, I wrote and mailed my letter of intent in early August. I outlined steps for the coming year with arrival of the Committee on Ministry representatives at September's Session meeting. I sent copies to both minister members of the Committee who met with me.

Parishioners responded favorably with many early expressions of appreciation. People began thanking me not only for the long tenure but also for my supportive and very successful family. Confidence, anticipation and relief, mixed with sadness, surrounded us as I began my final year.

In early September, I called one of the ministers who met with me in early May. I asked if he received my earlier congregational letter wherein I reviewed the transition steps we had discussed. His reply stunned me--both ministers left the committee in June! Their terms had expired, so I would need to call the Presbytery office and talk with the next chair about my retirement plans. I felt like a fool. Apparently, they never reported back to the committee their meeting with me. I immediately called the new committee Chair for guidance. Her first comment was, "Dave, why in the world did you ever announce retirement one year in advance?" I sat in shock and amazement! She stated the earliest any one would be able to visit Wayside's board would be in December. "Call me back in November with a reminder."

I met the Session and embarrassingly related the change of plans to their and my dismay. Thus began the disappointing and sad process of my departure with consequences to extend years beyond my last Sunday.

I called the Presbytery Office in November to remind the new chair of the upcoming December meeting. "Dave," she replied, "you must know it is a very busy time for committee members as Advent begins with all the preparations for Christmas. Call me back in January!" More clouds of doubt rolled in, darkened by confusion, chagrin and distrust.

In February, a minister representative appeared at the Session meeting, six months past the expected date. He assured the board members they still had plenty of time to secure one of the many qualified Interim Ministers. He outlined the plan for Session to elect a few elders and members to become a "Search Committee." The Committee Minister assured everyone he would direct and counsel the process as he had many times before. He also stated I would have absolutely no involvement in the process. Closing, he repeated, "There will be plenty of time!"

In subsequent months, I had no part in the process except to give what hope and comfort I could to frustrated committee and session members. With no candidate names after several weeks, one Search Committee member contacted his brother who was on the staff of Princeton Theological Seminary. He promptly sent a list of possible names from General Assembly. Weeks passed by with no reports from interested candidates. In May the committee began interviewing possibilities. It seemed more probable I would be leaving without an interim successor in place.

In May, Wayside's many musical talents, led by Director Susan Gervase, presented a memorable night as a tribute to my ministry at Wayside. With choral and instrumental presentations, the program delighted all amid the discouragement of the search committee process. Our friends Mike and Judy Campsey drove up from Claysville to enjoy the evening. Our son Eric and his partner Petra came over from Syracuse. Stirring emotions of love and appreciation for Naomi, our family and myself were shared. Our grandchildren sang a tribute, making us cry in appreciation, wonder and nostalgia. A percussion solo by drummer Joe, one of the best in the area, rattled and drummed us all into a shamanic trance!

In June, over 250 people attended a farewell party for our family at the nearby Wanakah Country Club. Crowded together in the old respected clubhouse, no Presbyterian ministers attended, but several Roman Catholic priests came including retired Fr. Jeri Sullivan and my old friend Fr. Jon Mergenhagen. Fr. Jeri, a kind and supportive colleague, spoke graciously of our wonderful years of sharing ideas and interchurch programs. We even took up golf together for a few years. He surprised some when he shared hope I might once convert to the Roman Catholic Church, which was true. Fr. Bob, his successor at St. Mary's, claimed Wayside had an unfair advantage with its church sign located in front with a red light. The light forced people to stop and read my provocative signs such as "Salvation is a Collaborative Venture, Rest comes Not by Sleeping but Awakening," and "Meditation is Not What You Think." He said he wanted rebuttals with a stop light in front of St. Mary's forcing cars to stop and read his sign: "Salvation is by Jesus Christ alone!" We all laughed. Our son Eric, a graduate student at Syracuse University, an excellent speaker with a commanding tall presence and thick dark hair, gave a moving tribute not only for me, but especially deserved for Naomi, the mother who had kept the children clean, dressed and well fed, while dad was off "finding himself" on bike trips, India or wherever else. I sat in wonder at the program, and how my years were honored with so many people, in one of the exclusive country clubs near our home and church.

In mid-June, the weary search committee chair reported they had contacted around 10 candidates. Most said they were unavailable or too old for such an active church. After I left, Wayside would likely need to resort to a short list of Pulpit Supplies kept by Presbytery for weekend speakers.

In mid-July, two weeks before my final Sunday, they finally found an interim candidate they felt would be qualified. Having been her classmate at Princeton Seminary, the Presbytery Clerk enthusiastically recommended him as "just what Wayside needed!" However, he would not be available until September. Realizing chances for a smooth transition might be rougher than expected, I resigned myself, knowing I must move on and let it go.

Nobody, however, endured more emotional turmoil over my retirement than Naomi. During the last days of July, she often remained silent for hours. When she replied to my inquiries, she said I would be retiring but she would be losing her home and her close friends. The Presbytery Clerk called her and declared that she and all our children with our eight grandchildren, must immediately leave the church and not return for at least two years. It further shocked and hurt Naomi. One day, the church secretary came into my office to express her concerns, asking what she might do to help. I could not find any way to seemingly bring comfort or solace.

The mangled expectations of a smooth pastoral transition, Naomi's disappointment, sorrow and pain, a large wedding and sudden deaths of two beloved members in July, left me exhausted by month's end. I spent my final week cleaning out books and papers; most I gave away to members.

The final Sunday arrived and the session asked Rev. Mary Lyons, my pastor friend from Buffalo, to assist in my departure in case I "lost it!" Mary planned to soon retire from the 1st Presbyterian Church in downtown Buffalo. My last sermon, or reflection, described how much I appreciated the people of Wayside. I thanked them for allowing me to grow and expand my thinking over the 33 years as their pastor. I confessed I'd often challenged and disagreed with Presbyterians with their actions-first, 4th century based theology. It drew laughs and applause! With Mary's motherly assistance, we concluded with Holy Communion and anointings, the later appropriately using up all the oil I had left in my bowl.

I walked slowly home exhausted but deeply content and satisfied, leaving with a feeling of completion, of "finishing the race." I completed the course without an embarrassing mistake in deportment or morality as some of my colleagues. When I later dropped exhausted in bed, I found myself weeping, sensing how deeply blessed I had been with my life at Wayside, somehow escaping the frequent serious challenges to my thinking and spiritual path. I regretted knowing I would never see or hear again my grandchildren participate in services I conducted. I also sensed my inclusive, gnostic, Jesus Seminar influenced, Hindu/Buddhist enhanced, and *Course in Miracles* affected teachings, would likely end. My "race was over with Wayside." Bumpy laps would be circled in the coming years for the congregation, and myself. I wept hard.

Chapter 24

After Shocks

> *"Theology. . . demands free people. As a young theologian, I belonged to a school. It was not a bad school. I still think of my teachers of that time with gratitude. But later I had to free myself from their school, not because much in their thinking was wrong, but simply because it was a school."*
>
> - Karl Barth, Quoted from Douglas Hall

"How tired I am!" became my mantra for a few weeks. I took longer and more frequent naps, but after a few months, became more adjusted to my freedom. I had no weekly services and sermons to prepare, hospitals to visit, funerals to conduct, weddings to plan, or meetings to convene, moderate and attend. There were no administrative conflicts to mediate or grief to share with families jolted by losses of love or life. If I wanted to visit family, I left without calling for coverage or making sure staff knew of my whereabouts. I enjoyed monthly pension and Social Security checks earned by doing nothing! I joined the South Shore Golf Club and golfed when desired, but still missed my partner Chas. By Thanksgiving, I also discovered I weighed nearly 220 pounds. At 5 feet, 10 inches, I went on a diet. Later, after reading T. Colin Campbell's *China Study*, I became mostly vegan.

After a year, I missed occasional speaking, even a little pastoral work. I placed my name on the Presbytery speaking list. A few months later, I received a phone call from a Presbyterian Church in nearby West Seneca. A member of the board invited me to visit them and share ideas on how they might regain their ministry. They had heard positive things about my Wayside years. I accepted their offer.

Greeted at the door of the familiar church, I followed the older man downstairs into a nicely decorated room with comfortable furniture. I remembered years when the church was a strong presence. Now they were left with 15 or so families in a large building with two paid staff, a part time secretary and a music director. Sunday attendance might draw 30 or 35 people.

The five or six friendly session members welcomed me with compliments on my years at Wayside. They asked if I might be willing to come for a few months to speak and give suggestions for possible growth. Surprised, it seemed like a perfect situation. Part time, with no contract, I offered to work for weekend stipends up to six months when I would then make my recommendations and leave. They accepted and keys to the church and the old, once busy office, were handed to me. Sitting in the chair behind the well-worn desk, the room smelling musty from years of books and meetings, it brought back pleasant memories of my years at Wayside.

I soon introduced the West Seneca Church to some of the progressive ideas I had brought to Wayside. With an agreement I could conduct a discussion group each Sunday, I introduced the Nag Hammadi documents, depicting a more mystical and universal early church. I shared some Tom Bandy ideas about church growth, encouraging a more eclectic worship style, incorporating some Eastern and Native American traditions with contemporary music.

Shortly before meeting the West Seneca board, my retired science friend, Malcolm Muir, now living in Troy, New York, introduced me to a book he thought I might enjoy. Calling one night, as he did weekly, he said, "Hi Dave. I think I have found a book and YouTube interview you might find interesting." I did.

I watched the YouTube interview and ordered the book. Written by Timothy Freke and Peter Gandy, it was titled, *The Jesus Mysteries: Was the 'Original Jesus' a Pagan God?* I quickly devoured its contents. Being retired, it seemed to come just at the right time into my life. I planned to go slowly and maybe even introduce the idea to the West Seneca Church.

Freke and Gandy's thesis argued Jesus was a continuation of previous centuries of stories of avatars, or "God teachers," who came to various Eastern Mediterranean countries. All the stories coincided with ancient Zodiac signs developed by astronomers in ancient Egypt and surrounding countries. Over a 10,000-year plus period, at least six different countries developed similar stories. Freke and Gandy concluded the story of Jesus was a continuation of these earlier pagan or folk stories from surrounding cultures. It made surprising sense to me. Their ideas erased the exclusionary factor of Christianity, which had dammed so many "unbelievers." Jesus was not unique as the "only savior of the world" but one of a series of teachers, mythical or real, who taught a universal divine presence within each person. One need to only awaken to it. It was so Tony de Mello, Eastern, related to *A Course in Miracles*, the early Gnostics, and myself.

The West Seneca Church seemed to enjoy the services I conducted, enhanced by one of my guitar friends from Wayside's band. The discussion group was well attended and people seemed hungry to discuss and question ideas pertaining to faith and the future church. One older man had read several books on faith and Christianity. He brought me some books and tapes by scholars such as Bart Ehrman, who questioned the traditional teachings of the church. He seemed surprised when I agreed, supported, and encouraged him.

After a few weeks, I actually suggested the group read Freke and Gandy's book. Most were surprisingly receptive, claiming also it made sense, or seemed possible. A few said a former minister even shared similar non-traditional teachings in a small evening group.

In February, around Valentine's Day, I conducted their Annual Meeting followed by a luncheon. A woman stood and declared I was a special minister--"No wonder Wayside thrived!" She asked if I might stay longer. She also had not attended the discussion group. Upon recommendation, the members voted to have me stay for a full year, perhaps two, if desired. Love was in the air! I felt comfortable and *naively* confident.

In a few weeks, Lenten season began. About the second week, a Sunday edition of the Buffalo News featured a front-page story titled, "Why Are Masses Leaving Masses?" Showing a mostly empty church, the article suggested reasons for the empty pews: unfriendly people, not having welcome centers with food, and lack of contemporary music using electronics in sound and lighting.

I responded, drafting a few paragraphs using ideas from my recent readings including Freke and Gandy's book. I suggested the stories of people walking on water, changing water into wine, and raising people from the dead, were not to be understood literally but symbolically. They were religious myths. I summarized other ancient stories having similarities to Jesus: virgin births at winter solstices, 12 disciples based on Zodiac signs, miracles of healing including raising the dead, execution by angry religious leaders but arising in three days.

I sent the article to the *Buffalo News* and quickly received a call from the editor asking if I would shorten the article to 270 words. He wanted to publish my thoughts in the News' "Another Viewpoint" column. Feeling a bit stunned, and realizing the writing would incur some opposition, I edited the article and returned it. Maybe it might prompt some lively discussions. My editorial appeared a few Sundays later, the Sunday after Easter, on May 1, 2011. As I entered the West Seneca Church to lead the service, a member of the board grabbed my hand and exclaimed, "Great article Dave! It was great! I just loved it!"

Everything remained quiet a few days. The Buffalo News printed a few reactions, all in opposition. Our son-in-law, a medical doctor in one of the large Buffalo hospitals, congratulated me. He said the article made a "hit" with a few colleagues. Someone even pinned it on the lounge's bulletin board with words, "This makes sense!" Hopeful, I envisioned a lively discussion among a wider audience including my clergy colleagues.

A few days later I drove to the May Presbytery meeting in North Tonawanda. Presbytery, the area's governing body, included several Presbyterian Churches, with around 60 churches in Western New York. As I entered the vestibule, a newer minister I did not know extended his hand and said, "Great article! Thanks so much." Hopeful, I sat near the rear of the large old wooden theater-styled sanctuary. I anticipated dinner hour when I expected some friendly discussion. Perhaps I could even set up a reading and discussion group.

The controversy of the day was again homosexuality, debating whether or not a minister could officiate such marriages. Many of my colleagues had written previous articles on the topic, for and against, which were published in the newspaper. The lively debate took up most of the morning with the usual pleas argued from both sides. Approval finally won by a narrow margin. Ministers could now officiate "civil unions" but not marriages. Members took deep breaths and waited for dinner dismissal.

As usual, several short announcements were shared before dismissal. Finally, the last speaker stepped forward. A respected voice of the Presbytery, we had been colleagues at Pittsburgh Seminary. With a loud and clear voice, he looked straight at the Moderator, and shouted, "One of our Teaching Elders has publicly attacked our basic beliefs by recently publishing an article in the *Buffalo News*. With it, he has betrayed his colleagues of this Presbytery. His beliefs clearly lie far beyond the tenets of our faith. I urge an immediate investigation of his theology with consideration he never again be allowed to speak or teach in our Presbytery!" Homosexuality suddenly seemed forgotten.

Thus began another year of turmoil, possibly the most traumatic of my life. In shock, a few days later I called the Pension Board and explained my situation. "Could my pension be stopped?"

"Mr. Persons," the voice replied, "know you are not the first to call with such a question. Your pension cannot be stopped until you die. It has been independently invested." Naomi and I were somewhat relieved.

In a few days, as requested, I met with members of the Committee on Ministry. After two hours of quiet questions and answers, the meeting ended. One member said I represented the future, urging me to become more involved in his ecumenical, interreligious organization. Another asked how I could repeat my vows of ordination. I answered saying I had no problem as long as the understanding of the "Jesus Story" could be seen as one to help people to awaken to their Inner Christ, their True Selves.

A few weeks later, I met with the 24 members of the Committee on Ministry. Two supportive Presbyterian ministers accompanied me. The meeting took place across the street from the West Seneca Church where I still tried to serve. The church sign from Christmas still read, "One Candle, Many Lights." We discussed their questions for nearly two hours. It mostly entailed my answering, "How did you *ever* get to where you are?" At one point, I broke down in emotion. I naively did not anticipate this result. No decisions were made. Afterwards, one clergy privately complimented me for giving an "aura of peace."

Conflict over my beliefs rapidly spread and increased. Some members from the West Seneca Church began leading efforts to have me removed. In autumn, the Presbytery replaced me as moderator with a minister who might return peace to the church.

I announced my resignation and conducted my last service on Christmas Eve with only a few attending, mostly from my family. One granddaughter told me afterwards, "Papa, that was the best service I have ever attended!"

Two weeks before Christmas, two Presbytery pastors invited me to breakfast. One pastored the supposedly most liberal church, which always led the charge, as I supported, to accept the gay and lesbian community. The other pastor led of one of the more conservative congregations. Whether both were sent or even known to be "taking me to breakfast," I do not know. We met in a little restaurant in North Buffalo.

"Dave," they began, "You are no longer one of us. You do not fit within the Presbyterian boundaries of belief. We strongly suggest you demit from the ministry and move on to other places." They even offered to help write my resignation. I could read it at the next Presbytery meeting, which just happened to be at Wayside. Before leaving, they leaned in toward me and concluded with quiet voices, "We also want to warn you that if you do not resign from all jurisdiction of the Presbyterian Church, things are going to become nasty for you. Very nasty!"

I did not write a resignation letter nor attend the Presbytery meeting. I called one of my supportive colleagues in the Presbytery who was shocked. He said he would do whatever he could to help defend me. I decided I had enough. I would continue on with my life, without public speaking or discussion groups. Things remained quiet until late April when I received another letter from the Presbytery Clerk. Another minister, known for his expertise in Reformed dogma, had filed official charges to prohibit me from ever speaking or teaching in a Presbyterian Church. A special commission of three ministers would be appointed and I was asked to meet them for examination. I expected this would finally be the end.

A few days later I met the three ministers in another Presbytery office room, again directly across the street from the West Seneca

Church. From the window I could see the now closed church but still left with the front sign, "One Light but many Candles!" The commission of three, two women and a man, one a certified educator and two ordained ministers, summarized the charges and asked for my response. I briefly repeated my journey, which many had heard, summarizing why I felt evidence of Jesus being a mythological figure could be credible. The moderating minister mostly listened in silence, but the women often shook or held their heads in amazement with sighs of disbelief. The moderator asked me to return the following month. He asked I bring suggestions on how this controversy might be resolved.

Before leaving, I handed each a book written by Tom Harpur titled, "The Pagan Christ." Tom Harpur was a well-known Anglican Priest scholar from Toronto who wrote a lucid book supporting the idea of Jesus being part of a long myth. I asked if they would take time to read at least parts of the fairly short and lucid book. The moderator agreed, mentioning it was a good idea toward resolution.

Driving home, again I saw my response to the conflict: seek to engage people in readings and dialogue. If opponents would simply take time to read people like Tom Harpur, Tim Freke and Peter Gandy, we might come to a satisfying compromise, giving more freedom for others in our Presbytery. But I realized, as Karl Barth had said, it is a hard to leave one's "school." Perhaps, somewhat like Barth, I could feel the growing loneliness.

I met the commission again in mid-June. The two women said they had been too busy to read any of the book and the moderating Chair said he had begun but not finished it. The meeting seemed to be mostly a waste of time. They claimed my ideas were too radical and would cause even more upheaval and anger in an already decimated denomination. I sensed again my time was concluding as a Presbyterian. I advised them to do "what they needed to do" and not worry about me. Driving home, I continued to feel mixed emotions. Sadness and disappointment enveloped me with more loneliness, but also with appreciation for my many years exploring in the Presbyterian Church. I sensed a new freedom beginning to dawn on my life. Meanwhile, I would simply wait for the next move to "expunge me" from the Presbytery and the Presbyterian Church, USA.

The following week I drove to Troy, New York to meet my friend Malcolm. We planned to attend a weekend retreat at the Pumpkin Hollow Center of the Theosophical Society. Before driving to Pumpkin Hollow, Mac took me to a meeting of the "Secular and Humanist Society of Albany" which met in a room at SUNY, Albany. I thoroughly enjoyed the 90 minutes as they discussed the book, "The Righteous Mind" by Jonathan Haidt. The day's chapter was titled, "The Place of Religion in the Society." Introduced as a Presbyterian minister, they spent over 30 minutes questioning and quizzing me, a time I thoroughly enjoyed. Later they invited me back to lead a discussion on "The Mythology of the Jesus Story," another wonderful experience in my emerging life.

The Pumpkin Hollow Retreat Center, not far south of Albany near the Hudson River, was deliciously inviting with its rustic cabins and buildings with a nearby running stream with a swimming pond, roaring waterfalls, and groomed trails. I loved the vegan food choices and lush gardens. However, we were warned to remain alert for Lyme ticks when hiking.

Dr. Stephen Hoeller, the guest speaker, discussed Carl Jung's "Red Book." An older man near his 80's, Hoeller was also a recognized expert on the early Gnostic church. I had read his book, "Gnosticism," and he still served as founding pastor of the "Ecclesiastic Gnostica Church" in Los Angeles. His lectures, however, were somewhat laborious to me, sitting in a 90 degree restored barn with fans humming overhead, and many participants falling asleep.

Malcolm and I said our good-byes at the closing, and I began the drive home refreshed and hopeful. A short distance from

Pumpkin Hollow, amid the winding roads and welcoming Catskill Mountains, my cell phone rang. I pulled off on the roadside to chat. It was the clerk of the Presbytery of Western New York.

"Dave, how are you doing?" she asked.

"Great!" I replied, "What's up?"

"Well, Dave, all charges against you have been dropped! Please have a wonderful summer!"

"Dropped?" I asked.

"Yes, all charges are dropped. It is over. Enjoy your summer and your life as it continues in retirement. God bless you!"

Chapter 25

Closer to Home

"Clearly going home is both a powerful urge and a dangerous trek. But it's not something you can even contemplate until you have stepped apart from the clan and stood in our own right."
- Former Episcopal Clergyman,
David Robert Anderson in his memoir,
Losing Your Faith, Finding Your Soul

Unlike a pardoned criminal, mixed feelings surrounded my exoneration. I did not feel criminal in destroying people's faith but rather had hoped to deepen it. I remembered sharing new ideas at Wayside when surprise and even anger often emerged from some members. Yet, it seemed, with reason, dialogue and patience, new outlooks could be appreciated or at least considered. However, I'm sure it was relief to Naomi and my family that public discussions of my ideas would finally cease.

Fewer invitations came to speak or conduct services in Presbytery Churches. I learned my name had been quietly removed from the Presbytery's approved speaker list. One day I met an officer from one of the churches where I had spoken. Standing in front of the Walmart store, he was surprised to see me, hearing rumors I had "gotten quite ill," as if I had lost my mind in old age. His church is now closed.

From once enjoying respect as a minister, I now felt more like a pariah. I began experiencing sleepless nights. My family sensed my mental strain as I often repeated disbelief of what had happened. Naomi accompanied me to see my doctor who prescribed an anti-depressant. I returned for a year of counseling with Neva.

Soon, however, I began to be asked to speak at non-Presbyterian churches. I accepted an invitation to speak at the nearby Unitarian Universalist Church where my first talk was titled, "The Jesus Story As a Myth." I discovered one UU member had even attended the *Course in Miracles* discussion group at Wayside. I accepted another invitation to speak at the Unity Church of Buffalo during Advent on the same topic. Afterwards, a retired minister thanked me for discussing an idea he had frequently considered.

I accepted another invitation to speak at the Albany Humanist Society on the "Mythology of Jesus." I spoke at the Hallwalls Contemporary Art Center on the "Jesus Myth" and later on the importance of doubt and disbelief in religion.

As the years passed, a new sense of freedom from previous fears has come over me. My Bible or Guide has become mostly within, renewed by meditation and readings. My favorite book, perhaps because of its style and "voice," remains *A Course in Miracles*. I continue to reread Fr. de Mello's writings, especially *Awareness*, along with Sri Ramana Maharishi's talks, the *Bhagavad Gita*, and other spiritual books and writers. Thanks to digital book libraries, I can carry them with me on mobile computers and phones.

Thanks to my friend Malcolm, readings and discussions in quantum science also deepened my understanding of mystery and the abstract, timeless spirit world. I still use the word "God" but not in a denominational or traditional Christian sense. God is love, kindness, patience and forgiveness. God can be a good "idea" if separated from the idea of sacrifice and slaughter of "heathens."

To define God or divinity with specifics, loses God, or as Bede Griffiths pointed out, moves into idolatry. God, as an abstract, is everywhere and always. God just is. God is Who I am in my core, the Observer. My body is only a temporary part of the material world of change and impermanence, part of the "vast illusion" or "tiny mad of idea" of separation from Endless Love, other lines from the "*Course.*" I am *not* my body, but free in Spirit.

Such understandings can often be found in the Bible. "Be still and know I am God." "Be in this world, but not of it." "Unless one is born again, he or she cannot see the Kingdom of God." "Behold, all things are new! The old is past and gone." I still find such verses and readings comforting and helpful. The Bible "contains" God's word as a pointer, despite the many distortions and contradictions within it. Its miracles are seen as mythological lessons. Jesus remains important as a "rabble rouser," even turning religious leaders against him. Jesus, I noticed anew, conducted most of his ministry on streets with only a few people. Jesus never began a "religious business." The idea of Jesus still gives me strength and peace.

My major relationship for growth remains with my spouse, Naomi, and our large and diverse family, who along with many others, including myself, I try to treat patiently. I still have "ego flair-ups." Accepting what is without trying to force change is difficult. It is easy to become caught in form and structure. "Let all things be as they are!" is my perennial place to begin. "Infinite patience brings immediate effects!" (ACIM, T-5.VI.6)

I thus feel closer to home, not only in this mortal journey's end, but to the home of Divine awareness, my Spirit Self. It is as close as my breath. With few financial concerns, I feel the freest ever in my life. I also remain deeply grateful for my parents and family, for all my education experiences, the people of Wayside and the Presbyterian Church for my past freedoms and opportunities to search and follow my chosen path. My life experiences were and continue to be the anvils on which the hammers of life mold me into what I yearn to become, more free and forgiving.

A professional golfer named Phil Mickelson once said in a commercial, "The best part of every journey is arriving back home!" And so it is. Whether I remain in our old house a few more years or wherever in my remaining time, I will always be Home, at Home in the Heart. Finding It, and remembering, remain the best parts of life's journey. It continues on. Forever.

About the Author

David is a retired minister with over 40 years of experience as pastor of three churches, his last for 33 years in Hamburg, NY. He and his wife of 51 years, Naomi, presently remain in Hamburg near their four children with their families of 10 grandchildren. He enjoys the woods and wilderness along with closeness to Lake Erie. He has camped and hiked, and along with his wife, has traveled to Europe, the Caribbean, Hawaiian Islands and Alaska. For years he was an avid bicyclist and during the past 23, enjoys golfing with friends. He speaks frequently in various settings, and hopes to do future publishing of his ideas in religious interests. He shares writings and talks on his blog and YouTube sites, accessible through his web page, davepersonspirit.com.